Empty Pulpits

Ireland's Retreat from Religion

Empty Pulpits

Ireland's Retreat from Religion

Malachi O'Doherty

Gill & Macmillan

Gill & Macmillan Ltd
Hume Avenue, Park West, Dublin 12
with associated companies throughout the world
www.gillmacmillan.ie
© Malachi O'Doherty 2008
978 07171 4236 1

Index compiled by Helen Litton
Typography based on design by Make Communication
Print origination by Carrigboy Typesetting Services
Printed by ColourBooks Limited, Dublin

This book is typeset in Minion 11.5pt on 13.5pt.

The paper used in this book comes from the wood pulp of
managed forests. For every tree felled, at least one tree is
planted, thereby renewing natural resources.

A CIP catalogue record for this book is available from the
British Library.

5 4 3 2 1

In memory of my father in law,
Pat Boyle, 1930–2008

Contents

Acknowledgments

This book would not have been possible without the support of many people.

Of particular value has been my working relationship with colleagues in the religious affairs department of the BBC, Martin O'Brien, Bert Tosh and William Crawley. They will recognise many of the stories here as having originated as my reports for the *Sunday Sequence* programme. They are not, of course, answerable for the book itself.

I am grateful to my wife Maureen Boyle for her support, including tolerating my long retreats to the computer to work on this text.

The people interviewed for the book are almost too numerous to list. They include Richard Holloway, John Waters, Christopher Hitchens, Patricia Casey, Vincent Twomey, Breda O'Brien, John Brewer, Ciary Quirke, Kevin Brady, Paschal Scallon, Katherine Fitzgerald, Anna Hainey, Margaret Rose McSparran, Kaçpar, Justyna Pers and many others, some of whom are not named in the text but whose thinking has contributed much to it.

Suggestions for improving the text came from Evan Thornton, my agent Jonathan Williams and the patient editorial staff at Gill & Macmillan.

I am particularly grateful to Fergal Tobin of Gill & Macmillan for having the faith to commission this book when it cannot have been clear to him how it would turn out, and to D Rennison Kunz for overseeing the meticulous editing.

I received a grant of £1,000 from the Arts Council of Northern Ireland to help me write this book.

Introduction

Ireland is almost unique. It is losing its faith much more rapidly than any other European country has done before, without a revolution. Faith is plummeting in Spain too, but it has always been more complicated there. The Spanish have an anticlerical tradition. Socialists there put priests up against the wall and shot them. Any country with that degree of anticlerical violence in its tradition cannot be lightly compared to Ireland. We did not shoot priests or hang them in the public square. Most of us always respected them. Well, if we despised them, we kept it to ourselves. You could never have got a drink in a Dublin bar on the strength of your having garrotted a priest. And we did not undergo a revolution like France and Russia did and expunge religion by force.

We went the English way of gradual disillusionment and loss of interest. Only we did it with un-English haste. Where England appears to have lost its faith over a period of two generations, we have done it in one.

We have seen the collapse of religious authority from a far greater height than it had held in England for centuries. There isn't any country in the western world that has swung from such absorption in church life to such indifference so quickly. Yes, we still have high levels of religious attendance in Ireland, but alongside that we have seen the near total collapse of the religious orders and the priesthood. Religious observance is falling fast. And what is left is not to be justly compared with any other semi-religious country in Europe. You can fairly compare Ireland today only with its own past, because it was, for a time, uniquely devout. We have rejected more religion than anyone else like us because we had more religion to start with.

Even at an apparent high point, when Ireland was given its third cardinal, in 2007, that cardinal, Seán Brady, spoke of the need now for the Catholic laity to preserve the tradition of the church. He knows which way the trend is going. He expects there to be far fewer priests to preserve that tradition in the future. He's running out of them. He leads a church that won't ordain women, yet will soon have only women Eucharistic ministers to distribute communion to the rump of the faithful, most of whom will be women too.

This collapse of religion, in one of the most conspicuously devout countries of Europe, is both fascinating and pertinent to an understanding of the world we live in. If we understood how it has happened, we might better understand how—or whether—it might yet happen in other countries which are problematically religious today, particularly in the Islamic world. We are the evidence that Iran and Saudi Arabia might lighten up some day, that that kind of thing can happen.

And if we reflected intelligently on what makes people religious and what they get from it, we might contribute to the vigorous and caustic debate led by the New Atheists against religion. After all, we have been religious in our lifetimes. It shouldn't be strange to us that people commit themselves to God and religious institutions. We should be better placed to comprehend and explain religious behaviour than virtually anyone else in the secular west.

There is nothing more plain about the angry tone of the New Atheists than that they don't actually have any sense of what being religious feels like. We Irish are in a unique position to tell them, if only from memory. But we are not proud of that memory. We find it embarrassing. We have smartened up and become proud rationalists who agree that all that devotion and ritual and subservience was a bit like a belief in Santa Claus that went on too long. But it does matter. We are on the cusp of a transition from a religious preoccupation to a secular one, well placed to explain religious attitudes to secularists, and secular attitudes to the religious. If anyone is listening.

You can see the paucity of the understanding of religion almost everywhere. It was particularly evident in the media coverage of the funeral of Pope John Paul II. Most journalists in

Britain are simply mystified by Catholicism. They have no comprehension of its culture or its rites. Indeed, they have virtually no comprehension of Christianity at all. Nor do they see that as a significant deficiency in their grasp of the modern world. They trust that you can be a perfectly competent journalist and social commentator without any feel for religion. Yet the BBC would never send, to cover the funeral of a royal, someone with as little knowledge of monarchy and protocol as those they sent to cover the funeral of a pope had of the rites of Catholicism. We had commentators standing in St Peter's Square in Rome talking about the 'nice sacred music'.

On a Radio Five Live debate on whether or not the new pope might be able to change the law on contraception, one journalist argued that this was entirely possible since there was not a single reference to contraception or condoms in the *New Testament*. The programme presenter turned to the editor of *The Tablet* and challenged her: 'Is that true?'

But Ireland is in no mood to explain religious attitudes to the rest of the world, because it is embarrassed by its own. We are somewhat like those former Czech and Polish communists who speak perfect Russian but pretend they don't because they don't want to be thought of as people who once revered the party. Yet religion is what we must talk about.

Religion is now at the heart of a global crisis, and people who once took it seriously are ideally qualified to mediate between those who still do and those who haven't a clue. In November 2007, a Liverpool schoolteacher, Gillian Gibbons, was jailed in Sudan after sending a letter to parents explaining a game she had organised with the children in which each would, in turn, bring home a teddy bear called Mohammed. Much of the British media immediately expected British Muslims to endorse the action of Sudan. Fanatics were on the streets of Khartoum demanding that Gillian be beheaded, even offering to do it. Some journalists even said that Gillian Gibbons had been insensitive to the local culture and shared some of the responsibility for her plight. This, many felt, was in line with past incidents in which Muslims had taken offence at the parodying of the Prophet. That was their way of understanding it.

Yet suddenly Muslims were letting everybody down and talking sense. Practically every Muslim commentator who was invited to speak on the matter defended Gillian and criticised the Sudanese. Some said that they thought the Prophet would have been honoured to have children name a teddy bear after him. The media had expected British Muslims to respond as they had done to those cartoons published in Denmark which mocked the Prophet. British Muslims, however, were as quick as any people of good sense anywhere to see the difference between a calculated insult and the work of a conscientious schoolteacher.

A little readiness to compare modern Islamic religious fervour with our own past religious fervour, and the ordinary civil decencies that accompanied it, would have predicted that response. Instead, for many, religion has become an oddity to be handled with care. You must behave, as you go among the religious, much as you would among the mad. But we should have known better. Take the following statement in *The Guardian* in November 2007 from the philosopher and New Atheist A.C. Grayling. Most of us with a memory into our recent religious past know that it is wrong.

> Look at most Catholic countries until the 1960s and beyond, in South America or Ireland or Spain: the picture of the social, political and economic effects of Catholicism is in its essentials the same. Women enslaved to child-bearing, overlarge families perpetuating ignorance and poverty, backward social policies and the iron grip of a clergy acting like the Stasi in controlling the minutiae of private lives through the confessional and the influence of fear—fear of hell, among other things.

'Clergy acting like the Stasi in controlling the minutiae of private lives'? Well, yes in a way but no, nothing as plain and simple as that. How do you square that picture of oppression with the

Catholic provision of education? How do you square it with the divisions between the orders and the diocesan clergy and the diversity of approaches accommodated within that apparent monolith, the church? But you have to have lived through Catholic Ireland to understand it better than that. And then you have to have an incentive to correct the simplifications of a Grayling. For many of us, it is such an irrelevant discussion that we wouldn't bother; we are justly annoyed with the church and are happy to let him put the boot in, even though, in doing so, we let him tell us that our lives have been different from how we remember them.

Part One

The Big Change

Chapter 1

Ireland is losing its religion.

If you don't believe that, ask a young person to tell you what the first commandment is or where Jesus was born. According to a survey commissioned by the Iona Institute and the Evangelical Alliance of Ireland, only one in twenty teenagers and young adults (between the ages of 15 and 24) will be able to answer the first question and only a third will remember Bethlehem.

What's Easter all about then? A scrawny man with a beard nailed to a cross? About a third will make that connection.

Try this: Who are the three persons of the Holy Trinity? Well, nearly half of the young people will get that right, probably the same half who know that the first book of the Bible is *Genesis*.

And, granted, transubstantiation is a more difficult concept and more specifically Catholic, so you wouldn't expect many hands up from a class challenged on that. But it *is* the most fundamental theological difference between Catholicism, the predominant Irish religion, and all other Christian faiths on the island. If there is a difference that is significant enough to separate Irish Christians into different churches, then you'd think it was worth knowing about. About one in seven know what transubstantiation is. Not how it works—nobody knows that—just what the word means.

Sean Mullan of the 35,000-strong Evangelical Alliance suggested that the above-mentioned survey showed that the notion of Ireland having a Christian culture is becoming a thing of the past. That was to be expected.

And how does the church cope with the fact that most of us believe in marriage—one of the values it works hardest to promote—but that we want to live together and have sex together before tying the knot? 'Good news for marriage,' is how Willie Walsh, the Bishop of Killaloe, described a survey on the first seven years of marriage, which also found that three out of four couples are 'very happy' and would marry the same partner again. The survey was commissioned by Accord, the Catholic Marriage Care Service. 'It reassures us that the deeply held human need for a lifelong, loving relationship is alive and well,' said Bishop Walsh.

And one wonders how Bishop Walsh felt about some more of the findings. For example, the survey revealed that nearly a quarter of married couples first met in pubs. More than half had lived together before marriage. And 69 per cent of those surveyed described themselves as moderately (63) or very (6) religious. That's a large number of married religious people disregarding the church. Clearly we are living at a time in which neither religion nor marriage is what the church thinks it is; in which the church interprets the slightest adherence to its rules as a welcome endorsement. Figures like these would have been cited thirty years ago to the opposite effect, as proof of the collapse of interest in church teaching. Today it is the best news the church can manage to come up with.

Even if a couple is cohabiting, said Bishop Walsh, it should not be automatically presumed that they are sharing a bed. 'You may find a couple living in the same home for a period and might assume they are sharing bed and board, but they are not.'

Well, they might not be telling their priest or their mothers that they are sharing a bed but—they are! What the survey actually seems to show is that strict adherence to church teaching has no bearing on whether or not you have a long and happy marriage. The findings are good news for marriage but bad news for the church.

And what of those whose marriages don't survive? Well, the church is there for them, if they want it. The 1997 Family Law Act, which codified divorce in Ireland, recommends that solicitors refer couples to marriage guidance counsellors before going for a divorce settlement. How many couples were referred to Accord in 2006? By its own figures: none.

———

All other countries around us had gone through the same change before us. Something delayed secularisation in Ireland, but nothing is preventing it. Nothing prevented it in Germany or in England, so it is hard to imagine that anything will prevent it here. One interested body that can be trusted not to stop the generalised collapse of commitment to the church is the church itself. Under the pressure of its imminent demise it has not rallied its energies to make itself more relevant or appealing.

To understand how we lost our religion we have to first ask what religion is for and what else fills that need now. The strongest argument for religion appears to be that it binds communities, even binds nations. The strongest argument against it, perhaps, is that it pushes communities, even nations, into conflict with each other. And since people like war, they probably feel more supportive of churches that encourage war.

The father of sociology, Émile Durkheim, set out to define religion by studying it in its purest, most primitive form. He disposes of two theories about the origins of religion—the one that says we started imagining that we had a soul because we dreamed, and the one that says we attributed volition to natural forces because we named them from a language resource which, until then, had words only for actions. His best critique of these is that neither suggests a reality that people would be passionate about.

Religion, for Durkheim, had to be grounded on something that mattered and he didn't think that the sense that we have a soul would have mattered much. He is wrong. It isn't only in dreams that people may feel they have an un-embodied self. For some, the sense of having a soul can be awesome and worrying. Durkheim dismisses the notion that psychic insights would have persuaded people, because they wouldn't have had more than chance accuracy. But, apart from fortune-telling, some members of communities might have had decisive out-of-body experiences, such as are commonly described by people who have been near death. Many would have had occasional experiences of sleepwalking, which would have left an indelible sense of the body being amenable to a deeper spirit of which the waking person knows nothing. Drunkenness from eating rotting fruit would have been common, surely, and a very unpleasant form of drunkenness it would have been.

In those more dangerous times, more people would have bumped their heads or expressed epileptic symptoms. And it may indeed simply be that mystics are right when they tell us that sudden insights into a cosmic consciousness do occur. Durkheim may not have been right to exclude this from consideration of how individuals acquired or deepened their religious sensibility and inspired others.

Yet, however impressive the mystical experience might be for an individual, Durkheim appears to be right in not crediting it with the power to bond societies and motivate large numbers. Some individuals may have had massive influence through charisma or higher intelligence than those around them. Sociologists don't like theories that attribute revolutions to individual influence. But the major religious revolutions have all revered individuals, like Paul and Mohammed. The sociologists will say that they spoke for their time and the community rather than that they shaped that time and community and that this, therefore, does not refute Durkheim's theory.

They will ask: could we imagine a charismatic preacher emerging now and swaying Catholic Ireland back to the faith, or even forward to a new interpretation of it, or to a new religion? It is hard to imagine that this could happen. However, it seemed for a few days in September 1979 that it was happening, when

John Paul II addressed a quarter of the population of Ireland. But he appears not to have actually changed our minds about very much.

Durkheim said, let's find out what religion is, not by reading revealed scripture and God's instructions to his people but by looking at religious behaviour. He argued that the first religion traceable among the North American Indians and aboriginal Australians was totemism, the practice of making an animal, plant or element of nature, representative of the clan or tribe. If the totem was, say, the sparrow, then the sparrow would be represented in the sacred artefacts. Only rarely and sparingly, at sacred ceremonies, would members of that tribe eat the sparrow. The people of the sparrow would gather in large numbers together and chant their rhythmic prayers and achieve a kind of collective state of rapture.

This seems tentatively readable as a model of Christianity, in which the bread and wine are taken as emblematic of the totem, Jesus, and shared sparingly in ceremony. The difference, of course, is that Christians could eat bread and drink wine any time they liked, but it was only when these were consecrated by a priest that they became sacred. Then they belonged in the tabernacle, equivalent to the hushed cave in which the aboriginal tribe secured its holy artefacts. This type of ritual is seen also in Hinduism as Puja, when food is first offered in sacrifice and then shared out as Prasadim. Again, the food is sanctified by the act of offering it to God. Common among such rituals is the representation of blood, by red wine among Christians and by ochre among aborigines and Hindus.

Jesus broke bread and poured wine and said: do this in memory of me. If he had said: 'remember me when you do this', every meal would be a rite and no meal would be sacred because no meal would be profane. Durkheim noted that the religious approach divides the world into things that are sacred and things that are profane, and therefore a culture that made no such distinction would not be religious.

Durkheim believed that religion embodies a whole society and its universe, including the darkness and the danger. Hence,

Satan in Christianity is not a counter to religion or its enemy; he is part of the package. Perhaps when there is no darkness, the stakes are simply not high enough to engage most people.

So, our ancestors divided up into tribes represented by the sparrow or the lizard or the dog and felt themselves to be of a shared nature with their totem. Then they invented agriculture and developed an idea of God more appropriate to that. That would be a god who represented all of nature and not just an element within it. Such an idea required monotheism. We settled into communities at the beginning of the Neolithic age and turned towards One God. The totem was no longer to be a representation of our tribe but an explanation of the whole world. You would have been keen to find an explanation for the whole world back then because the ice was shifting back to the North and uncovering glorious, fertile valleys.

———

In *Genesis* we wove a myth that we had once belonged in a beautiful garden and had lost it through listening to evil promptings. Those promptings said that we could take a short cut to knowing the difference between good and evil. The story of Adam and Eve tells us that only trouble can come of women listening to nature and of men listening to women. It was all about putting the man in charge and treating nature as suspect and dangerous.

We had not been in a garden, of course; we had been hunting mammoths through blasted tundra. In fact, in Ireland we had not been doing anything because we had not yet arrived here. The land had been under that extended arctic ice cap. Iraq has had human occupation for 70,000 years; Ireland for not even 10,000. It was between the Ganges and the Euphrates that the great monotheistic religious ideas were developed; from there emerged the dominant religious cultures. Since people had lived on those plains tens of thousands of years before Abraham and the writers of the Vedas, it seems likely that their religious messages carried traces of earlier, forgotten cultures.

When people had a garden of their own making in the fertile valleys that remained after the last ice age, they feared they would lose that too, as they had lost Eden, if they were not disciplined and focused. So religion's job would be to discipline a society as it diversified. Religion, as we know it, is bound up with agriculture. Even in the New Testament we find an affirmation of agriculture. Jesus sanctified bread and wine, food of human manufacture, rather than fish, which he had also given to his disciples. In fact, in much religious art Jesus is depicted as a fish. Evangelical Christians wear a little lapel badge representing a fish, to let people know that they are friends of Jesus. They should really use an image of a loaf. The Irish School of Ecumenics at Trinity College incorporates a sheaf of wheat in its logo because Jesus defied the Pharisees by eating wheat grain from the stalk on the sabbath. By blessing bread and wine, Jesus appears to have been endorsing our garden.

The Irish have not been disciplined religious people throughout their history. They have not been centred on agriculture and a god of rules and rewards. Often they explored their spiritual intimations by imagining a fairy people close at hand. These were called the Good People, not because they were good but because you had to speak well of them or they would blight your land and turn your milk. But in nineteenth-century Ireland, after the spoiling of our Irish garden by potato blight, we turned more emphatically to religion once again, and elevated its strict sexual mores, to protect the legacy of the land against subdivision and loss. Christianity is agricultural. It was when Ireland began to move away from agriculture that it moved away from religion and its laws. A key boundary crossed in that journey was the admission of divorce, which would allow a spouse to take half a field. We found ourselves able to allow divorce only when fewer of us had fields to hold on to.

The farmers still don't like it. A series of workshops by the Irish Farmers' Association in December 2007 found that there was a strong interest among them in pre-nuptial agreements that would prevent a wife walking out with half the farm. Unfortunately the church doesn't approve of such agreements. A readiness to leave a marriage on pre-agreed terms would smack of defective intention, one of the grounds for annulment. All the better still for the farmer, but not what the church calls marriage at all.

———

In Ireland, religion was predominantly social. Church attendance expressed membership of a society. In the 1950s, nearly all Irish people were practising Catholics, aside from a large concentration of Protestants in the North and smaller groupings on the border, in Dublin and around Cork. But religion there too would have been a declaration of belonging.

Catholics lived by the seven sacraments through which they were baptised, brought into communion, confirmed, married or granted holy orders, were shriven and buried. They went to mass every week, often receiving communion after fasting beforehand. Their leader was the priest, and slightly below him in authority was the schoolmaster. The weekly focus of religious activity, the mass, was not only a religious rite but the bonding of the whole community. Your absence would be noted if you didn't attend. It would also be noticed if you came improperly dressed. Jesus might have been born in a stable, but you were expected to have your Sunday best clothes on, your hair combed and your shoes polished. You went to pass a social test, not necessarily to experience a spiritual frisson.

Durkheim believed that the communities of aborigines were bonded by the intensity of religious experience in their gatherings. The men would stamp their feet in rhythm and come to be possessed by a collective spirit. Few people expected profound religious experiences at Sunday mass. It might have been different at High Mass, with more incense and music. Catholics didn't sing hymns as often as Protestants did. But religious traditions that don't offer ecstasy threaten Hell instead. That does the job of retaining your attention when the call to social belonging is weak.

Everyone would be there, so there would be children crying; there would be excess people pouring out the door and down the steps. In big city churches, there would be first-aid workers from the St John's Ambulance patrolling the aisles, carrying out those who fainted. There would be surly men with hangovers, young women tending to their elegance, teenage boys and girls making eyes at each other, lightly touching hands in the pews, more considered frottage perhaps, among a few. There would be men and women of the Legion of Mary stewarding the crowd, passing around the plates for cash collections. There would be little old women kissing their rosary beads between decades, nominally present at mass but worshipping in their own preferred way.

In the 1950s, the mass was in Latin and the people in the congregation would follow it in their missals. For a children's mass, a priest in the pulpit might provide a running commentary, explaining the offertory or the difference between an epistle and a gospel. The sermon after the gospel would allow everyone to sit still for a while. Then the priest might expostulate at length about why Jesus had picked lowly fishermen for apostles or spared the woman taken in adultery. Hell was still a primary concern of the church in those days. A priest might remind his flock of the horrors that awaited them if they died in sin. After the communion liturgy, and a prayer for the conversion of Russia, the hundreds would flow chattily out of the church to stand in groups and exchange the gossip of the day, eyeing others surreptitiously, commenting on who was meeting their social and familial responsibilities and who was not.

There may have been occasions when it was the religious ardour generated by a compelling mass that enabled people to feel like members of each other, but more often they went there out of a sense of social responsibility, to stop neighbours gossiping about them, or at least to be on hand when they did. Just a few, perhaps, were there to feel elevated into a clear sense of communion with a God who loved them.

Or is that unfair? There were certainly times when people did share a strong religious sensibility. On occasions they may do, even now. The Irish still go to mass in huge numbers at Christmas, and feel, when the carols are sung, that love has actually come among them. They also used to go in large numbers to the annual Lenten mission, often to be berated and scowled at by the raging and eloquent Redemptorists, with their morality tales.

'A man left his family home and went to live in London, and when he parted from his mother she made him promise that he would get down on his knees every night in life and say three Hail Marys. That man fell into sin and into drunkenness but kept his promise, and on his deathbed he pleaded with God to forgive him his wasted years. That man is in Heaven today for one reason only, that he fulfilled his promise to his mother.'

No one seemed to question then how the Redemptorists could have known who was in Heaven and who wasn't. People seemed to understand that the story was not literally true and seemed not to mind.

'What has become of the woman you took in carnal sin? Do you know? There is no surer road to Hell than the squalid life into which you have led her. And do you think the Lord God will spare you your responsibility for her damnation?'

Going to the mission was a bit like going to a horror movie; you went to be scared witless and then to be redeemed from your terror. So, although the routine of religious life was almost profane and pedestrian, there were occasions that would have matched Durkheim's idea of a collective religious enthusiasm and that would have imprinted on people a strong sense of identity. The problem was that when the potency drained away from those few occasions, only the pedestrian routine was left and it was not enough to engage the interest or the commitment of those who did not need assurance that they were not being gossiped about.

The church itself must take some of the blame for changing the religious culture of Ireland. A generation ago, if you drove on a Sunday morning through the Irish countryside, you would have been hindered at every town by the crowds around the local Catholic church. An early change was a relaxation of this universal routine. The church determined that those who wanted to lie in on a Sunday morning and nurse a hangover could go to mass on a Saturday evening instead. That would also mean having to get scrubbed and dressed up only once, since the clothes you wore for mass would do for the pub or the hop afterwards.

The big theories of religion suggest that it is social, but there is also a strong personal and private element in religious belief. However collectively people pray, each prays secretly, too, and alone. Even the public prayer in a full church may be framed as a very private resolve in the heart of the individual.

Why do people pray? They pray in order to feel that they are not alone. They pray in order to focus their resolve, perhaps to know their own minds. They pray for a sense of inner coherence and peace. They pray to remind themselves that life is more than the turmoil of the moment. They pray to order their priorities around a sense of their having an eternal life. That was the personal and private side of religious life. But they can do that at home, even under the bedclothes. Perhaps that's where many do it now who would have you believe that they don't do it at all. Churchgoing, by contrast, is public.

People who lived on isolated farms and in small village communities valued church as an opportunity to be part of a wider circle and hear the local news. It might be the only time of the week that they would make contact with friends and relatives. They would go there to break from the drab routine, have an excuse to dress up. It might be all that kept them civilised. They would compare themselves with their neighbours and have some sense of their social standing. And they would go to pray, because prayer is gratifying. They would go to appreciate the beauty and mystery of the ritual; to take time to think about the dead. They were afraid to miss mass. They had been taught that it was a mortal sin and that to die in a state of mortal sin meant going to Hell to burn for all eternity. People believed that. And it is still those religions that threaten Hell—Islam and Evangelical Protestantism—that thrive most.

Religion fed a sense of communal superiority. The Catholic Irish felt that they were better than the other materialistic races of the world. Germany and Japan harboured similar notions about themselves at the same time. The southern Irish felt that they were better than the English; the northern Catholics felt that they were better than the Protestants, and they retained their Catholic conviction longer because the dispute with Protestants lasted longer.

———

Ask people what changed Ireland so suddenly and they will point, erroneously, to the wave of disclosures, through the 1990s, that priests and members of religious orders had been abusing children. Ireland did not give up on religion on account of that, however. There are undoubtedly huge numbers for whom this was the breaking point but it is not what precipitated the slide. Read, for instance, Gemma Hussey's account of religion in Ireland in her book *Ireland Today*, published in 1995. There you see the bald fact of the collapse in vocations, the radicalisation of the orders and the boorish obsession of the bishops with sexual morality. What you do not get is a single mention of child abuse by paedophile priests. That was a story that was still to break.

Hussey showed that between 1970 and 1990, the proportion of teachers who belonged to religious orders in Ireland had dropped from a third to a tenth. In the same period, vocations had more than halved, and vocations specifically to orders of sisters and brothers had plummeted. The orders of brothers were not taking in a tenth of what they had been at the start of that period. So the paedophile scandals did not start the flight from the church. That flight was already calamitously under way before the ordinary lay news-watcher had even heard of the fact that the church was covering up for child abusers.

And sex was already at the heart of the people's scepticism about the church. Hussey wrote that in 1993 Archbishop Connell of Dublin had offended many people by describing homo-sexuality as 'a disorder'. He was using only the words that the Pope had written in the encyclical *Veritatis Splendor*, but they were words that Irish Catholics did not want to hear.

The greatest irony was that when it was almost ready, if not to concede ground on sex, then at least to shut up about it, it was sex that rebounded on the church. The church in Ireland had, for instance, let a referendum on contraception proceed in 1992 without directing the people on how they should vote, commenting on it only afterwards. But priests of the church which had built a theology of family planning on the understanding that sex was only for procreation and had challenged everyone who wanted a planned family to exercise heroic restraint for their own spiritual welfare, and the rest to abstain, had been fiddling with the kids and lying about it. Who were they to demand heroism of anybody?

'Oh, I see,' said Irish Catholics in virtual unison. 'We are the ones who go to Hell but the priest gets a transfer to a new job.' Well, they weren't having it. Moral authority could not survive the exposure of the gap between what the church demanded of the laity and what it was actually practising itself.

———

Had Ireland retained a strong religious character, it would have found a religious explanation for the sex-abuse crisis, and would have endorsed a religious solution to it. It would have accepted, as argued by a few, that priestly paedophilia represented a worrying assault by Satan against the holiest men among us and that we had no choice but to pray more ardently for these same men to return to God. It didn't. We responded instead with a secular answer to a problem that seemed to be familiar in secular terms, and this was because we responded to everything in a secular way since we lived in and understood a secular world. It was the profane space, not the sacred, that was now responsible for the ordering of society and for providing explanations for human behaviour.

We knew why a man like Bishop Eamon Casey wanted sex with a woman and we didn't need to imagine a tempting devil. We knew it because we knew that all men and women want sex and that they are entitled to want sex. We might have been bewildered by men wanting to have sex with children, but we could reason that they might be more likely to want to have sex with children if they had been denied all sexual expression since they were children themselves. And worse, the horror of it, we could understand that the priesthood might be particularly attractive as a career to a man whose deepest sexual orientation led him to children. We didn't need to find a place for Satan in that story, at least not as an explanation, though we might be quite happy to imagine that Satan was there serving justice and stoking the flames for those we despised. That Satan was no longer the enemy but the ally. We liked that Satan.

———

People in Ireland in the 1960s and 1970s did not undergo so much a collapse of faith as a disruption of tradition. Had religious belief been at the core of their sense of place in the world and in the universe, its loss would have been personally critical for them. It wasn't. Had it been the foundation of the personality—the real explainer of life's meaning—they would not have given it up so lightly. And their happiness—even sanity—would not have survived the loss.

You could argue that the loss of tradition has been calamitous, in that children not adhering to the values of their parents produces drug use, crime, fatherless children, chaos and cynicism. The remedy for this needn't be a religious conversion, except in so far as religious communities would re-establish tradition and family order. Families can do that around some idea other than religion. Some family traditions are maintained within a trade or profession, even within the repetition of family holidays at the same resort or caravan site. Christmas, for instance, pulls families back together, not by virtue of its religious appeal but simply by the power of custom. It can be a slight to the whole family not to be at the dinner table that day. It is no light decision to waive Christmas—not because Jesus will be offended but because Mother will be offended. But she will be less offended if you're living and working in Dubai or London and can't get time, or can, at least, half-plausibly say that you can't get time.

Eric Kaufmann offers a theory for the rapid spread of religion which leaves out the appeal to the heart. In an article in *Prospect*,

'Breeding for God', he argued that religious people simply have more children and therefore outbreed those who are not religious. They hold families together in strong communities that are more protective of their young. This being the case, you do not have to posit the notion that whole populations of Africans and Indians were overwhelmed by the messages of Mohammed or the Buddha, in order to explain the rapid spread of Islam or Buddhism. It wasn't that the idea inherent in their teachings won people over; it was simply that those who believed the teachings, and adhered to the disciplines, replaced in time those who did not. The core believers did not have to proselytise energetically. They simply had to have more children and look after them better—which they did, as religious people tend to do.

Rome fell to Christianity in the same way. Religion, therefore, is not a heart-consuming message but a family tradition. We explain the collapse of religion, then, not as the collapse of the core idea but as the erosion of that tradition.

——

If the change in Ireland was from a society that had relied on spiritual and supernatural explanations for everything, that society was being challenged even 500 years ago to rely on reason, though in our own generation there are many who, by their simple vision, still explain events in terms of divine justice or predestination. Your marriage fails; your mother explains: 'It wasn't meant to be.' You apply for a job and fret about whether you'll get it; your granny reassures you: 'What's for you won't go by you.'

A secularising society easily lets go of an understanding that all events are part of a struggle between God and Satan. It may still cling to fatalistic superstition but that superstitious view doesn't hold a religious community together when the other bonds have gone.

Religious Ireland was a place in which core decisions about the ordering of society were taken by clergy. Married couples in difficulty sought religious advice on how to manage. Disputes in communities were mediated or adjudged by the priest. Secularisation includes an institutional shift away from the church towards the police and social services and secular counselling services and the courts.

Though we have the relics of a pre-rational society among us, in our superstitions, the Irish, even in their most religious phase, were people of simple common sense too. You can see that even in the superstition. It is always consolation, never a challenge. There always had to be something in it for them.

The bond that kept all those people going to mass on a Sunday morning was community. They were going there to meet each other and be seen by each other, not just to obey God's law. And if they didn't go, their absence would be noted. Clare Keegan described a character with precisely this attitude in her short story 'The Forester's Daughter':

> Deegan is not a religious man. He knows that beyond this world there is nothing. God is an invention created by one man to keep another at a safe distance from his wife and land. But always he goes to Mass. He knows the power of a neighbour's opinion and will not have it said that he's ever missed a Sunday. (From *Walk the Blue Fields*, Faber, 2007)

Once people felt free of the scrutiny of their neighbours and the collective pressure to conform within conservative and unchanging village communities, they felt free to lie on in bed on a Sunday morning. So, young people taking jobs in the city stopped going to mass. Their parents warned them that they were in danger of losing their faith, especially if they went to London or Manchester. When they got out of the habit of going to mass, but went home to the family for the occasional weekend, they might go to pass themselves or pretend that they had already been, or take a walk for an hour on their own to give the impression that they were going. And it was easier for them to stop going to confession than to stop going to mass, since that was less of a collective expression of faith. And what was the point? They stopped going to confession because they had sins that they did not think were sins. To be young and in love and up in Dublin was never to have to say sorry to God or a priest for having had sex. So it appears that urbanisation and the erosion of the influence of the village drove secularisation in Ireland, as they had driven secularisation in England and in Germany and all over Europe, as they will drive it in India and, some day, in Saudi Arabia and Iran. We are nothing special.

And, you know, we were always smart enough to see that that is how the world works and that you don't need God or Satan to account for most things. Ireland has never been a totally non-secular, religious society. Ireland was never theocratically governed, though there have been periods in the last hundred years when the Catholic church had undue influence over the running of the state. There was never a time when this church dominance was fully accepted, however. There were always strong voices opposed to it.

———

Religion filled a human need to bond communities together and that need was strong in agricultural Ireland, particularly after the trauma of the famine. It was nothing to do with explaining to us how the universe came into being or where we go to after death. Organised religion does not meet the needs of the pining lonely soul bewildered by the moon; it meets the needs of the organisation and the collective human need to be organised. Religion was about the lives we lived in the human environment, and it was always possible that that environment would change and that the relevance of religion would then change with it.

Chapter 2

It was an axiom of our thinking, during the religious years, that those who lost their faith lost a reason to live, that the alternative to belief and devotion was a life of sin and despair, much as many theologians still imagine it to be. Not only are they wrong about that, but they are wrong to suppose that a life without religion is an empty and feckless life. The fact is that we have negotiated the change without personal trauma. Hadn't we been conditioned and indoctrinated? Hadn't religion been deeply impressed on us by the church and the family? Surely it wasn't going to be easy to shrug it off. The Jesuits were said to believe that if they had a child by the age of seven and could 'bend the sapling' while it was young, they would have the child for life. Their experience for generations seemed to affirm that theory, until a generation came along that was able to walk lightly away from all that conditioning. The brothers and sisters in the orders had children to the age of 15 for six hours a day, to drill them in faith and devotion and, even with that advantage, could not prevent the secularisation of Ireland. So it can't have been they who had made us religious, since they were unable to prevent us from changing.

We take our conditioning not from our parents but from our peers. It's common sense really; every parent has always known it. Now Ireland is the evidence, as of course is Japan too, or

Germany, or Northern Ireland where just a decade ago the society seemed riven by sectarian animosity and now is a model to the world of harmony and reconciliation. People change. Well, who'd have thought it?

The change was easier for some than for others. Some discovered, when they gave up their religious routines, and spoke frankly to their parents, that their rejection of the church was fully expected. They discovered that many in the older generation had long ago become routine adherents to a faith that meant little to them and a church for which they even harboured quiet contempt. How could it have been otherwise, after all, when thousands upon thousands of people had suffered, with secret pregnancies, unhappy unbreakable marriages, indissoluble vocations? Yes, some of the tired and the cynical were priests, brothers and nuns, too.

For some, the challenge to reject religion was difficult, however. These were people who had been formed not just by the church and in the school but by intensely religious parents too. Their conditioning met them on all fronts. They felt guilty about not going to mass and confession. They felt guilty about sexual relationships of which Mother and Mother Church would not approve. And their struggle to rationalise their needs and resolve the contradictions was a replay of the philosophical struggle that made the modern era, a struggle to push God far enough back from day-to-day considerations to enable one to think clearly and put needs and desires and fears into manageable proportions.

The person who had given up religion would be known by those who hadn't as 'lapsed'. But you knew that your struggle to free your mind had not been a lapse, an accident, but a serious and considered resolve. You knew that the conscience grounded in reason and self-knowledge was a better, more mature, more informed conscience than one that simply took instruction or followed habit and tradition, for no better reason than fear of the anger of the da, the hurt of the mother or the disdain of the priest.

You knew that those who asserted religious belief still did not actually believe everything they said they did. In the 1950s, parents stood in the pews of churches and sang 'Faith of Our Fathers':

> How sweet would be our children's fate
> if they like them could die for thee.

Of course, they didn't seriously believe that it would be better for their children to be killed as martyrs than to live and be teachers and accountants, but the fact that they did not correct themselves when they sang such words suggests that hypocrisy was normal to them. There is a lesson for the New Atheists there. If people don't necessarily believe fully the things they say they believe, then attacking them for their professed belief may not address at all the passions and concerns that actually motivate them.

This is not to say that there were no people in that generation—say, the post-war generation—who were genuinely religious, though it is to suggest that many of those who profess religious belief in, say, Islamic societies may also hold private convictions very different from their public ones. There is no reason to suppose that there is anything uniquely Irish about this kind of dissonance. Those who flooded into the religious orders and into the priesthood were presumably motivated, at least in the beginning, by profound piety. But they were increasingly out of step with a society that would publicly honour what they had done and privately pity them.

Some priests still give an impressive account of the satisfaction in their job. Fr Kenneth Brady, a Passionist at Mount Argus in Dublin, says that he finds it in contact with people who are more devout than himself.

> It struck me that God's presence is in places where society doesn't look for him any more. What I often feel is that people evangelise me, or my own struggles with faith, or my own humanity; somehow or other, if you are going through something, people seem to come along; they don't know what you are going through but you are able to relate to them in some way.

He had worked in North Belfast during the worst of the troubles there.

> I was in some intolerable situations in the North where people were killed and to hear people say, 'Sure, Father, it's our faith, God's good.' And I'm saying to myself, if that was my brother that was dead, I don't know what I'd be saying.

This is the model of the modern priest, someone who is struggling to live a spiritual life and finding inspiration in ordinary people. It's a long way from the old idea in which the priest spoke and the people were silent, and it still doesn't suit many of them. No priest now can expect to keep a support group of priest friends around him because so many are dropping out. Fr Brady says:

> Some of them decided it wasn't just for them. For others, it could be they met someone and fell in love and it opened up a whole new area that wasn't opened up before. For others, it was that they wanted to help people but they no longer felt that you had to be a priest to do that, and I would also say that for some it could be that they were restricted by the limitations that others impose on what it means to be a priest; including the limits bishops impose. And I'd also say, to be fair to bishops, that many bishops would have sweated about these issues themselves.

The disjunction was obvious everywhere. Those called by God to become Christian Brothers or teaching nuns ran schools for turning working-class children, not into brothers and nuns, but into middle-class professionals. Even those teachers themselves would have thought that the child who took them seriously—and followed them into the disciplined and celibate life, dressed in black—had seriously misread the opportunities laid down. Those of us who went to such schools remember that teachers who drilled children of 10 and 11 in simplistic piety and obedience would let them in on the joke when they turned 15.

The best they could hope for was that we would later look back and think well of them.

Even Catholicism, when it seeks to offer guidance, in modern Ireland relies on psychology, that is on science, rather than on spiritual discipline. It has, in fact, lost any sense of the difference between the spiritual and the psychological. That is a victory for the secular perspective. It has colonised faith.

The church used to teach that the road to God led away from happiness in this world. Now it regards happiness—psychological well-being—as proof that you are moving in the right direction. You can't get into most religious orders these days without passing a psychological assessment that many revered saints of the past would assuredly have failed. If you turned up with chains under your shirt, you definitely wouldn't get in.

If priests and spiritual people now talk mostly of the psychological and spiritual as if they are interchangeable, there is occasionally a question that arises to divide these two perspectives. One was the news in late 2007 that Mother Teresa of Calcutta had been depressed throughout much of her life and that she had questioned whether she had been right after all to heed the call of the Sacred Heart since she had been mostly devoid of any sense of the presence of God in her life after hearing that first call, on a train.

The psychological reading must be that she was depressed. A diagnosis like that would indeed have confirmed her deep suspicion that she was in the wrong job. The spiritual diagnosis was that she had suffered the 'dark night of the soul', a stage on the mystical journey during which God seems entirely absent. This diagnosis would have encouraged her to stay with her vocation and would even have reassured her that she was making progress in it. But if she turned up at the door of an order in Ireland today to announce that God had spoken to her on a train, she would not be admitted. She first joined the Loreto nuns in Rathfarnham at the age of 18, having been brought to Ireland from Albania by a priest who had recognised her devotion. Today the Loreto order would not accept an 18-year-old. If they had observed the same rule in the past, Mother Teresa might never have become a nun and might, if those filtering processes have any value, have lived a happier life.

———

When J.H. Whyte wrote *Church and State in Modern Ireland* in the 1970s, he asked how deep Irish Catholic religious conviction really was. There was evidence on both sides of the question. On the one hand, he could see that Catholic Irish emigrants would often give up their religious routines. That suggested that those routines were not founded on a need in the person to express devotion through them. If you could forget about Jesus when you moved to London, as lightly as you could adapt to the Guinness served in English pubs, then Jesus clearly was about as important as good Guinness to you; not much more, not much less. This suggests that many were adhering to rituals like weekly mass attendance in Ireland out of a social rather than spiritual need, or, more extraordinarily, that moving to England had, in itself, met that spiritual need.

However, on the other side of the question, Whyte could see that Catholics in Ireland were not merely observing the rules of their church minimally but were enthusiastic in their practice. This suggested that their religious convictions were deep rooted. The church required them to go to mass once a week; many went more often, some every day. The church required them to attend confession and communion once a year; many went every week. Whyte concluded that religious devotion was therefore genuine and that adherence to Catholic religious practice was committed.

Faced with two ways of assessing the degree of religious devotion among the Irish, he chose to accept the version that said it was real. He could as easily and plausibly have argued from evidence that religious devotion in Ireland was no more than a social custom. He should have been more careful here in defining what was required of the ordinary Catholic before interpreting behaviour as reaching beyond requirements. Yes, the letter of the law was that a Catholic should go to confession once a year, but the requirements of teachers in Catholic schools or of energetic priests were much higher. It wasn't the book of Canon Law that the ordinary Catholic was up against but a busy church.

And Whyte may have read the signs of Irish religious enthusiasm simplistically. Though many went to mass every day, the majority did not. Those who went on weekdays to attend, for instance, the Nine First Fridays, or during the Marian month of May, would have been responding to strong urging from church campaigns. There is, indeed, plenty of evidence that people were embarrassed about expressing strong religious commitment and that they would have come under peer pressure to curtail it. For instance, Paddy Haughey, giving an interview to a BBC programme about his membership of Opus Dei, said that it had been difficult to be a daily mass-goer in Ireland in his youth, in the 1940s and 1950s, because people mocked him for it. His devotion would have counted as evidence of the kind of religious enthusiasm that Whyte saw as indicative of the character of Catholic Ireland. The mockery of his peers would have weighed on the other side of the argument. And there were more of them.

———

Which is not to say, of course, that Ireland was not really religious. In some sense, it was. Ireland was like no other European country. It was conspicuously and comprehensively religious in the way that India and Saudi Arabia are now. You can't travel in those countries without being struck by their religious culture.

In Ireland, a far higher proportion of the population was going to church every week than in the other great Catholic countries, Spain, Italy and Portugal. Those countries had lively anti-clerical elements to their politics; we hadn't. But what do we mean when we say Ireland was religious? Are we talking about the institutional structures and the degree of adherence to them or are we talking about devout feeling in the hearts of huge numbers of people? What is it that changed with secularisation? Was it the social organisation of society or was it the thinking of the people about who they were and what mattered most in life?

Part of the problem for those who tried to describe Ireland at that time was their want of any society with which to compare it. Today we are more familiar with countries that are as religious as Ireland was then, like India or Iran. Indeed, the United States is religious in a way that no European country now is. Perhaps we will get some kind of clue to religion in Ireland, whether it was primarily institutional or personal, by drawing comparison with those countries.

In India, everyone believes in God by some conception; everyone worships, and religious mores decide the life of the family, the character and ritual of marriage, virtually everything. And similarly, we find that many who leave India and come to live in the west often discard their religious customs. Now, it could be that it is those people who are less religious at the start who are more likely to move to the west. People who take seriously religious strictures against marrying out, or even crossing the Brahmaputra, are perhaps less likely to emigrate.

Londoners are familiar with Arab and Persian émigrés who live the high life in the city, gambling and enjoying call girls. All of this suggests that the restraints on moral behaviour are contextual or social, rather than engrained in a conditioned conscience. What we see is that the close regulation of social mores by a religious culture can affect all people in a country, yet can lose its hold on those same people very quickly. What we also, of course, see is that some people never give up religious belief.

What is it that tells us then that Ireland is rapidly secularising? Is it just the loss of social control by the Catholic church or is it a change in the way in which ordinary Irish people view life, destiny and personal responsibility?

Predominantly, it must be the loss of institutional control by the Catholic church. In a country in which a strong religious culture holds sway, there is a heavy incentive for everyone to participate, even when personal conviction might be quite low. Not to participate is to put yourself outside the prevailing culture, much as, today, a working-class man does when he displays no interest in football. England may not have a religious culture like Ireland had fifty years ago, but it has a strong parallel in those all-encompassing football enthusiasms by which people identify themselves with each other and with territory.

Everyone wants to belong. They even rush to change their clothes when fashions change. They regard that as a mature and cool action to take. There is no deriding conformity. Imagine an England in which football clubs run the hospitals and schools; in which it is football clubs that marry you, set limits to whom you may marry, and induct your children ceremonially into membership of the supporters' club. It would actually be more trouble than it was worth to stay outside.

The strength of the religious culture was that it inducted people in childhood through school, and retained them throughout life. Even still, in Irish cities where the old Catholic tradition is in decline, it is still to Catholic churches that merely nominal Catholics go to get married or to bury their dead. None of which means that they have well-formed Catholic consciences.

But if it is difficult to take the people of thirty years ago at their word, that they are religious, then it is as likely that the people of today, saying that they are not, are undependable too. Go to a funeral or a wedding and you see people at church who never go for any other reason, and yet they queue for communion. What does it mean? Thirty years ago, only a few went to communion; now you often see in church that nearly the whole congregation goes. Does this suggest an underlying religious sensibility in secular people, awakened by the sacrament? Or does it mean that people simply have no sense any more of the value of the sacrament? In the past, they were restrained from going by a sense that they were not in a suitable state of grace, but no such self-criticism or reverence restrains them today.

So, you can't easily judge whether people are religious or not, at heart, either by their actions or by what they say. Applying that to Ireland of the past suggests that those who have recorded our religious years may have wholly misunderstood them. The corollary of that—which we have to live with—is that those of us who judge Ireland to be rapidly secularising today could be wrong, too. Prayer is as private as masturbation and, for all we know, as widespread.

Chapter 3

There is plenty of evidence that Ireland in the past was a deeply religious country, but alongside much of that there is also the strong hint that a countervailing voice often had its way. Paul Blanshard was a strident critic of a kind of Catholic global imperialism that he saw emerging out of Ireland in the 1950s. In his 1954 book, *The Irish and Catholic Power*, he cites, as one example of the degree of control exercised by the Catholic bishops and theologians, their attempt to ban the use of tampons.

The Rev. J. McCarthy of Maynooth had written in an article in 1949 that tampons could 'easily be a grave source of temptation, especially to those who have strong physical desires', which by his understanding, of course, wouldn't have been everybody.

Certainly that is as glorious an example as one could hope for of the church prying into the private, intimate affairs of lay Catholics and ordinary people. But Blanshard goes on, 'The priestly ruling on the subject broke down, after a great deal of subdued laughter.'

So the story doesn't, after all, serve to prove that the people were dominated by the church or in awe of its teaching. It proves the opposite—that the church made itself the laughing stock of the people when it transgressed common sense. And that subdued laughter of the people is nearly always just audible on the fringes of debates raised by the church on intimate questions. The church seemed almost eager to make itself ridiculous, as when it proposed that a married woman faced with the prospect of 'condomistic intercourse' was as much obliged to resist with force as any virgin threatened with rape. 'She may not remain passive. This means active, forceful resistance which may be discontinued only in the face of the greatest actual danger.'

That suggestion was published in the *Irish Ecclesiastical Record* in March 1948. It appears to suppose that men often raped their wives but that the wife's right to defend herself was qualified by whether or not the man was wearing a condom. If he wasn't, she might accede more readily. What did the writer imagine was going on in Irish bedrooms that he presumed that a wife would need to prepare to use violence against a husband who wanted protected sex with her? Did the writer really suppose that a wife would feel more passionately determined to resist sex when the prospect of a pregnancy was reduced? Did he suppose that a husband had a right—if a conditional right—to rape his wife; that condition being that a prospect of pregnancy was there? Otherwise the *Irish Ecclesiastical Record* could simply have said that a wife had a right to resist rape in all circumstances.

Articles by priests in religious magazines of that period provide the researcher with many examples of naïveté and arrogance. Take Fr Peter Finlay, defending the right of the Catholic church to demand a legal prohibition on divorce that would apply even to non-Catholics. It had been argued by W.B. Yeats, among others, that this was an infringement of the rights of Protestants and Jews not to be governed by Catholic moral theology. 'As well say that prohibition of suttee is a denial of justice to the Hindu widow,' wrote Fr Finlay. So divorce was always an act of violence against a woman and it was as bad as killing her.

It is true that, at this time, the church was recruiting huge numbers of boys and girls into religious orders, and this attests to popular support. But, even at the height of that recruitment, it was not as simple as that a powerful church rallied devout and eager thousands through the gates of seminaries and convents. The religious orders were taking boys in at the brink of puberty. The Marists, the Franciscans, the Brothers of St Patrick and other orders were recruiting boys as young as 13. But Blanshard acknowledged also that many, even of those who were indoctrinated early, resisted the burden of chastity when they became aware of it. Even in 1953, one-third of recruits were dropping out of Maynooth during the seven-year course.

Blanshard was eager to prove that the depressed state of Ireland was a result of religious oppression, but he was aware of economic factors, too, and even argued that the weather had something to do with the apparently low levels of sexual energy accounting, in part, for fewer Irish getting married. Less than half of Irish men between 30 and 34 were married in the early 1950s. An amazing 65 per cent of the population was single. Blanshard showed that he knew about poverty and the weather as inhibiting factors but decided, without much evidence, that the predominant reason why the Irish were not marrying, at least at home in Ireland, was that their sexual interest had been suppressed by priestly ardour. Another part of the same problem, celebrated gloriously in Merriman's *Midnight Court*, was that many fine, red-blooded, heterosexual men were pledging themselves to celibacy in the priesthood and in religious orders.

> Is it any wonder the way I am,
> Out of my mind for the want of a man,
> When there is men by the score with looks and leisure,
> Walking the roads and scorning pleasure?
> (*Translated by Frank O'Connor*)

But what the quote from Merriman proves is that the Irish didn't need to be taught by outsiders to laugh at the church and its censorious teachings. Perhaps if the church seemed, at times, almost frantic in its Puritanism it was because the Irish were so impervious to religious censure. It is rare to find a priest being ridiculous without hearing a sneer from the laity in the wings.

Blanshard argued that priests were turning the Irish into moral infants. He was appalled at the tolerance of gambling by the church and even the church's use of raffles to raise funds. The outsider often commented on Irish drinking, which even the recruitment of tens of thousands into the Pioneer Total Abstinence Association could not reverse. How had the church managed to kill off the Irishman's interest in sex, yet failed to stop him getting drunk? Clearly Catholicism's power to suppress desire was limited. Or perhaps the truth is that the church had no effect on either appetite.

If the Irish were bound strongly to their church, the church's indulgence of their drinking and gambling suggests that Ireland was not a profoundly moral or abstemious country, but that some slack arrangement had been arrived at between Christian restraint and native, easygoing ways; perhaps an Irish solution to an Irish problem. And wasn't this inevitable in a church that sought to embrace the whole population? Smaller churches can impose more exacting standards and let those who can't live by them stay away. There is certainly a big difference between Catholic and Protestant conceptions of morality, and this confuses Protestants who try to assess the moral conduct of the Catholic Irish. A Belfast clergyman tells the following story about the behaviour of Catholic boys at a cross-community peace camp.

We were all settled in the big tent but there was no sign of the Catholic boys. They started arriving back at one in the morning and they were all drunk. They had been to the pub, which our crowd found disconcerting. But when I woke in the morning the same boys were all gone. They had got up and gone to mass. I have to tell you, that gave me something to think about.

That clergyman couldn't reconcile the sin of drinking with a religious approach to life. But then, maybe he had misread the religious attitude of the Catholic boys, too. Maybe their going to mass said no more about their hunger for God than their drinking did about their association with the Devil.

Blanshard cites delightful examples of convoluted moral theology, which permit what he sees as sinful compromises. In one, a theologian argues that a man who steals a half-sovereign, mistaking it for a sixpence, then loses it, need make restitution only of the sixpence that he genuinely thought he had stolen. In another, the morality of taking bribes is unpicked to show that the recipient of the bribe isn't always morally obliged to repay it. These are the sort of moral conundrums that schoolchildren once used to lure their teachers into debating, to break up boring lessons. Blanshard believed that they were evidence that the church had cheapened the moral character of the Irish people. And he had further enthralling evidence of that, too. When 3-D movies came to Ireland in the early 1950s, audiences were asked to return the coloured spectacles they were given for viewing the show. Audiences in Belfast generally obliged. In Dublin, they didn't. The proportionate loss of spectacles in Dublin, through cinemagoers taking them home, was ten times what it was in the more morally mature North.

But is that really the best interpretation that can be put on this—that Northerners had more responsible consciences? Could it be that the church, far from having infantilised the moral conscience of the Irish Catholic, had simply failed to impress it very much at all? Priests could make their silly rules about what couples ought to do in bed, but the priest didn't come into the bedroom and the people could work out for themselves whether to take him seriously, as some did, or to disregard him. Who was going to know if you masturbated or used a condom—or a tampon—if you didn't tell?

The morally infantile Dublin of 1950 that Blanshard sees is very like the rural Ireland that William Carleton saw a hundred years earlier, before the church had seriously begun to impose its censorious control. In some ways, it appears not to have changed things very much.

Blanshard believed that the Catholic church was stupefying the population in order to undermine democracy and, if not actually prepare the country for dictatorship, at least produce a pliant people who could be summoned to revolt if ever an Irish government turned against the power of the church. He makes his case by citing the numerous examples of Catholic-church regard for fascist dictators in Europe. The practical application of clerical power was to isolate those who criticised the church, as writer Hubert Butler was isolated and stripped of several public appointments after he dared to raise Catholic complicity with the Nazis in Croatia at a public meeting attended by the Papal Nuncio.

However, the theory that a uniquely Irish Catholicism had succeeded in dominating the entire population overlooks the lightness with which people will resort to a church when they feel the need of one. They don't enter the church in an attitude of apprehension and fear. They go there because there is something that they want to do and because that is the place in which it is done. Blanshard also overlooks the fascination and wonder with which many people approach religious ritual and the comfort that they derive from it. The most cynical reading of the institutional church would have to be not that it had mesmerised the population, but that it had won control over religious customs and ways that people valued and made its priests the gatekeepers to a spiritual resource that many people could not do without.

―――

But we can go too far in celebrating the mischievous Irish spirit and its immunity to humbug. People *were* denied the right to think for themselves. The great evil that the church inflicted on society was the curtailment of free thought and imagination. Many of us policed our own thinking as instructed by the church, especially in sexual matters.

To preserve its standing as the great explainer of life and destiny, the church had to oppose intellectual freedom and it did so. The young person who raised questions and aired doubts might be sneered at and patronised and told to go and pray for guidance. This was only in part an institution defending itself against reason; another part was the embarrassment of clergy at their own intellectual immaturity and educational impoverishment. There may be great intellectual theologians in the Catholic church but at the point of contact for most people it was anti-intellectual and obtuse. It was every smart Catholic schoolchild's experience that the priests, brothers and nuns would back off from an argument. That may have followed from their training in obedience. To a modern educationalist it would seem strange that someone who was forbidden to consider ideas might be fit to encourage young people to explore, but that is how it was. A teaching nun or brother would live by monastic guidelines of obedience and prayer, and yet that same person might be teaching schoolchildren to question.

The church played two major roles in people's lives. It regulated their conduct and it provided a focus for their sense of beauty and wonder.

A generation ago, most Catholics in Ireland had to take seriously the church's rulings on sexual conduct. Those who broke those rules often seriously believed that they might go to Hell but they knew also that they faced a social sanction. This was well past the stage at which a priest might read someone's name from the pulpit, but people broadly felt that if they were out of favour with the church, they were out of favour with their neighbours. The church provided employment for teachers, nurses, school and hospital cleaning staff. As a national institution with employment and property responsibilities it provided contracts to builders, solicitors, architects. It was simply too big to be openly contradicted. Young people looking for their first job would seek a reference from a teacher or a parish priest. It was important to be in good standing with the church, and if young people themselves did not understand that, then their parents did.

The Catholic hierarchy was a kind of royalty. When bishops toured their dioceses in the 1960s, the streets were decked with papal flags and bunting and huge crowds turned out just for the sight of a prince of the church in whom its authority and charisma were embodied. There was little space within which to dissent. Parents whose children were beaten at school had no choice but to resolve their differences with the school on the school's terms.

And it was, perhaps, out of a spirit of obedience and ingratiation that many attended mass, evening devotions, the sodality and the confraternity and the Corpus Christi procession. Many, however, perhaps all occasionally, approached the altar with genuine reverence and wonder. Mass, when it was in Latin, was mysterious. Catholics who have stayed with the church could argue that the ceremonies and rituals have been brought closer to the laity by being translated into the vernacular, but perhaps one of the things that was lost was the awesome grandeur of a rite that was enfolded in mystery. Once the words of the priest were understood, the drabness of the delivery had no cover.

People do feel better after prayer. Private prayer enabled people to articulate their deepest fears, if only in conversation with a favoured saint. Any psychologist will confirm that that is infinitely better than not articulating those fears at all. An imagined friend is better than no friend. Many articulated their deepest anxieties to a priest in confession, if only to have him reaffirm that their primary responsibility was to the family and to send them back to the routine of their duties a little refreshed for having shared a secret with someone who could be trusted not to pass it on.

The Protestant critique of Catholic life was that people were drilled and policed by a sinister clergy which dominated every aspect of their lives. In retrospect, it is easier to see that that was more or less true and not to feel that you are letting the side down by acknowledging it. Still, there was a kind of genius to it. The people were in on it. Where Protestantism theologically was about the right of the individual to reach a personal understanding of God, Catholicism was about a hierarchical institution laying down the rules for the laity. In fact, Catholics found their freedom to play the system, to a degree, if only by choosing the priest they might confess to, knowing that one was more compassionate than another.

The late Rev. Sidney Callaghan, a Methodist minister and a Samaritan counsellor, often told the story of how he could use the flexibility of the Catholic church to help people in distress. Faced with stricken and depressed Catholics, who felt the burden of guilt too strongly to be able to risk a dressing down in the confession box, yet who needed absolution, Callaghan, when he was at Dublin Central Mission, would tell them to go to the Franciscans on Merchant's Quay, whom he trusted would go easy on them.

'I'm not a Catholic myself and don't believe that the priest bestows God's forgiveness on the sinner, but if a sinner is hung up on the need to have that absolution, in which he believes, then it's best he have it,' he said. 'And if he was afraid that he was going to get a drubbing from his parish priest, I would say to him, "Would you not go down and see the Franciscans at the quay? They're the boys that'll sort you out."'

What Callaghan understood was that the Catholic system allowed for an approach to God on the penitent's own terms. Many was the backsliding evangelical, near suicidal with remorse, who had no such resort available. The church married us and buried us, often in a routine and somnolent drone, sometimes with such beauty and sublimity that we felt we were touching the very ground of our being. But it has lost out for not generating as much wonder and beauty now as many people find in football or at a U2 concert.

Chapter 4

We always knew at heart that we were not as devout as we let on to be, and that fact is reflected clearly in all our best literature. We lost our religion a long time ago, properly speaking, when practical reasoning overtook God as an explanation for events. And we lived a long time in an interim phase in which we honoured religion as if it were more important to us than it was. Now, that is not to ignore the many devout people who still take scripture literally, still use religious medals as charms and amulets and the many more who still pray with desperation when they are in trouble. But there was a time when the shared world view of the majority admitted God into all concerns, and that ended a long time before the collapse of the institutional influence of the Catholic church in Ireland.

We said we believed in God's direct management of the world but we conducted ourselves like people who expected the laws of nature to hold. The disjunction between what we said we believed and what the conduct of our lives implied we believed was the theme of many Irish writers, for example Edna O'Brien and John McGahern. The friction suffered by their characters was not between individual conscience and divinely appointed responsibility; it was between their free ideas and the assumptions of their community, or their elders, about the proper way to behave.

In O'Brien's works, the pregnant daughter agonises not about how she has offended God but about how she will survive practically now that her family has disowned her. The sons and daughters in McGahern's *Amongst Women* never doubt that they are right to escape, exercise freedom and discard tradition; they doubt only that their relationship with their father will survive the change.

It is a long time since Irish fiction produced a plausible character whose central crisis was a concern for what God thought. There was no weekly television drama about the struggles of a heroic young priest, or life in a parish priest's house, resolving our spiritual fears the way cop dramas raised and settled our anxieties about crime. For all that we had a huge commitment to the church and huge numbers among us joined the religious orders, nothing in the popular culture of the time suggests that we harboured a fascination with the saintly and their struggles. We had thousands of missionaries across the world, some doing heroic work among the poor and under cruel militaristic regimes. If we are to judge by the concerns of both literary fiction and popular television drama of the time, the people back home were indifferent to this.

Of course, that can't be true, can it? Beside every newsagent's till there was a collection box or three for the Medical Missionaries of Mary or the Holy Ghost Fathers. We knew about the church and its work; how could we not? And we were supportive. Of course we were, but we were not engaged in the concerns of those priests and brothers and nuns, not even to the degree that an ordinary working-class family in Britain is today with the work and fears of the police or of hospital staff. They read about the police. They watch police dramas on television. Their newspapers call every day for support for the police in the war against crime, urge readers to understand the humanity of the police, their struggle against bureaucracy and impossible expectations.

Police dramas are resolved by police methods, but what few plays there are about priests are usually resolved by human devices other than prayer. The cop show is there to tell us what a grand police officer the hero is; the play that features a priest is usually telling us what a sound bloke he is underneath all the trappings. The history of hospital dramas, in living memory anyway, goes back to *Emergency Ward 10*, *Dr Kildare*, up to *Casualty* and *ER*. Policing and medicine are among worlds of events close to us which can be framed by dramatists to fascinate us inexhaustibly. The church is not one of those worlds. It never has been.

We had our respect for the clergy, of course. We even loved them but we were not, even in the days when there were so many of them, envious of them. We did not think that they lived better, more interesting lives than we did, and we did not particularly empathise with them. Poor Fr Walsh, having to listen to all those confessions, having to genuflect on his gammy knee. No, if we empathised it was to say something like, 'What a lonely life the poor man must have, but I suppose he will have his reward.'

When priests did come to feature on television drama and in literature, it was not on their spiritual riches or their improved prospects of salvation that the writers and directors concentrated, but on the paucity of their daily lives. The consolation of their lives was not that they would go to Heaven and see God but that they might get out for a round of golf midweek.

Of course, it may be that the spiritual journey of a devout servant of the people could never be appropriate material for literary or popular fiction, since it is internal. But many books were written about holy people and holy endeavour; they simply never came to be of central importance within Irish culture. They went onto the shelves in the religion section of the bookshops and were enjoyed by a minority of people who were genuinely pious but were not representative of the broader strands of Irish society.

An exception, of course, is John O'Donoghue's *Anam Cara*, a book which claims to represent Celtic spirituality. This is a marketing triumph rather than a serious work of literature and has probably been bought more than read.

Occasionally a work of religious focus would be popular:
films like *The Song of Bernadette* or *The Bells of St Mary's*. And
there were also flurries of spiritual excitement which spread
beyond regular churchgoers, like the giddiness around the
moving statues, like the Clonard Novena in Belfast. But religion
was never mainstream, even in Catholic Ireland. Yes, people
went to church on Sunday; they might even go out in the middle
of the week to the Sodality or Confraternity; they would feel
honoured by the visit of a priest to their house, a house they
would have had blessed when they moved into it; but when they
turned on the television or picked up a book to read, they did
not seek a reaffirmation there that God was in his Heaven and
that they were safe within his Catholic church.

When people turned to popular entertainment for a
suggestion of spiritual realities, they sought out horror films and
magic, expressions of the mysterious other side of life in forms
of which their church disapproved, in forms which resonated
more with the belief in fairies held by their great grandparents
than with the picture of an afterlife they had acquired at school
or in church. In the divide between the sacred and the profane,
almost everything that they were interested in was on the
profane side.

And perhaps it was because mass meant so little that many
saw no need to stop going, when the authority of the church
collapsed. They had been called there by community and
comfort and habit, not by dogma, so the death of dogma's
influence had little bearing on their decision. When we turn out
for the funeral masses of our atheist friends and say words we
don't literally mean, we are doing nothing different from what
our parents did, thirty, fifty years ago.

————

One indication that the Catholic laity is not particularly fussed
about doctrine suggests itself in the autobiography of the
broadcaster priest Brian D'Arcy. D'Arcy has had a high profile
for decades as a chaplain to the entertainment industry and he

has shifted in recent years from being thought of as light and trendy to being a serious commentator, particularly on child abuse by the clergy and the church's response to it, but also on the relevance of dogma. He came out as having been abused himself and declared that he was opposed to the doctrine of priestly celibacy but that he would observe it while it was still in place.

D'Arcy's assent to the actual letter of Catholic doctrine seems remarkably slight. Yet when the media have cornered him over the years—and the media clearly like him yet still operate on a compulsion to undermine him—they have never done so on doctrine. He has often been asked embarrassing questions about whether he was ever in love (he says he has been), or had sex (he says he hasn't) or about his friendships with other controversial clergy. But no one in modern Ireland seems to mind that his stated description of his personal theology is merely Christian and hardly specifically Catholic at all. He obeys the rules of the church but does not actually agree with them. No one argues that that undermines his position; on the contrary, it makes him more attractive and acceptable.

In his book *A Different Journey*, he says that he has discovered a new way of thinking about God from Gerald Hughes's book *God of Surprises*. Hughes, a Jesuit, has re-conceived the contemplative exercises of St Ignatius for the modern Christian. In these exercises, you visualise one of the gospel stories and then place yourself in it to see what, in your imagination, happens next. For instance, you're on the banks of the Jordan when the Holy Spirit appears over the head of Jesus. John is pouring water over Jesus. A thousand people are watching in hushed fascination. They hear a voice from Heaven. What do you do? Do you hear it?

More prosaically, perhaps, you are with Martha and Mary in the house of Lazarus when Mary is doting on her lord and Martha complains that she won't help with the washing up. Jesus says, 'Leave her alone for she has chosen the better part'. Now, what do you do? Do you, like Mary, lose yourself in the contemplation of the face of Jesus or do you get up and help Martha with the dishes? This is undoubtedly a fresh and imaginative way of using the gospels for contemplation but it has nothing to do with taking them as literally true or even as doctrinally important. And why wouldn't one address the same techniques to Shakespeare or *Eastenders*?

You are having dinner with the king when suddenly he starts responding to a ghost at the table. You do not see the ghost. What do you do? Do you pretend that the king's behaviour is normal? Do you humour him and pour a drink for Banquo? Do you emphatically reassure the king that the ghost of Banquo is entirely of his own imagining?

————

There is an anomaly to be explained, that whereas Catholic Ireland was apparently universally devout, practically every significant Irish writer of the twentieth century depicted the church as a burden on the people and a restraint on their imagination and freedom. The television series *Father Ted* in the 1990s seemed to represent a breakthrough to a new nadir in the depleted reverence for clergy at the time of the sex-abuse scandals. In fact, nearly all depictions of Catholic clergy in Irish literature in the twentieth century represented them as stunted and narrow, immature people engaged in pointless preoccupations. *Father Ted* was not a revolution in the depiction of clergy as shallow and naïve but rather something else; it represented permission to laugh at a ridiculous clergy. Until then, the absurdity of their ways was worrying and fearsome and depicted darkly, not as comedy. In *Father Ted*, we were laughing at them and perhaps we were laughing obliquely at ourselves for having once taken the priests more seriously.

The most outstanding representation of a dark and terrible clergy is in the writings of James Joyce, and in particular in the character of the preacher from *Portrait of the Artist as a Young Man*, with his awesome depiction of the horrors suffered by lost souls in Hell—'they are not even able to remove from the eye a worm that gnaws it'. This is the priest as indulgent tormentor. But when Stephen comes out from the sermon, he overhears a conversation between a teacher and some boys, restoring a perspective from which the sermon is not to be taken too seriously.

> I suppose he rubbed it into you well.
> – You bet he did. He put us all into a blue funk.
> – That's what you fellows want.

When religion was heavy in the air, there was always a voice on the sidelines saying that none of this was to be taken too seriously.

There is a similar contrast in Joyce's *Dubliners*, in the first story, 'The Sisters', about the wake for a priest as witnessed by a boy who had been tutored by him. The sisters remember the priest as a sad and bewildered man who had lost his way after he accidentally broke a chalice. One day, when he was missing, other priests searching for him found him sitting alone in a confession box laughing to himself. This is behaviour that the sisters are entirely unable to comprehend.

Before Joyce, Gerald O'Donovan in his novel *Father Ralph* drew a picture of the relationships between priests and their bishop in which they were self-serving and sycophantic and he was petty and vindictive. All were contemptuous of free thought and difference. In some ways, O'Donovan's depiction of priests is even more damning than *Father Ted*, for it is not parody; we are invited to take it as a simple, accurate representation of how these men behaved among each other and what they thought of us.

Patrick Kavanagh, in his poem 'Lough Derg', writes of the diverse angsts and hypocrisies that draw the Irish to prayer.

> For this is Lough Derg, St Patrick's Purgatory.
> He came to this island-acre of limestone once
> To be shut of the smug too-faithful. The story
> Is different now.
> Solicitors praying for cushy jobs
> To be County Registrar or Coroner,
> Shopkeepers threatened with sharper rivals
> Than any hook-nosed foreigner.

Kavanagh is contemptuous of the traditionally religious and their smugness and gullibility. He is contemptuous, too, of the new religious, who want to barter with God for material gain and professional promotion. To him, they are all people who have missed the beauty at the heart of wholesome religious faith. Kavanagh, who tells us that he has not missed that beauty himself, is dated by the easy racism of his presumption that the 'hook-nosed foreigner' is a sharp dealer.

For Louis McNeice, in his poem 'Apostasy', Irish religion is mixed up with an unwarranted Irish sense of self-esteem, drawing as much on a canonical reading of history as on the stories of the saints.

> Take credit for our sanctity, or heroism and our sterile want,
> Columba, Kevin and briny Brendan the accepted names,
> Wolfe Tone and Grattan and Michael Collins the accepted
>   names …

It is too easy to imagine that secularisation in Ireland amounted to a change in the character of the people, that previous generations of people were pious and devout and that they lost that and became more anarchic and slacker in their morals. There is a nice corrective to that perception in a short story by Benedict Kiely, 'The Pilgrims', about a family travelling with a train full of others, probably to Drogheda, to see the relic of a martyr. At the heart of the story are two brothers, one in long trousers, old enough to appeal to the girls, the other still in short trousers and embarrassed by that. In every carriage in the train, pilgrims are saying the rosary.

The older brother explains the difference between an excursion and a pilgrimage. An excursion is 'all drinking and fighting', 'and a wee bit of coorting'. He says, 'I was a year in a seminary. You can't tell me anything about pilgrimages. I know that the people who go on excursions go on pilgrimages too. The only difference is that they don't fight and there isn't much drink.'

There is, as it turns out, plenty of 'coorting'.

The population didn't divide into those who were religious and those who were not. Most people were religious some of the time and irreligious at others. It's really the meeting of the ordinary human hungers and the impossibly formal demands of the church that fascinates most Irish writers and they all side with the human against the church because that is where, even in the most devout decades, they see the people.

You will see this also in Frank O'Connor's two short stories about confession. In both, the penitent comes to confession without guilt and the reader is left the option of approving that position. In 'My First Confession', a seven-year-old boy impresses the priest with a precocity that is more interesting than honest guilt would have been. The priest, in responding to this, is not acting in line with Catholic theology. His strength is humanistic, not religious.

In 'A Lesson for the Church', the priest who browbeat a young woman into seeing her sexual adventure as sordid succeeds in enforcing the church's view. But the reader is left feeling that he is cruel and shallow and has defended his righteousness at the expense of a young woman's morale.

The tension between the religious and the humane is a recurrent theme in O'Connor's short stories. In another, a family is embarrassed by a lavish wreath at the funeral of a priest. They know that people will think the dead man has had a lover. So the wreath has to be got rid of? No. O'Connor sides with the wreath and the mystery person who sent it.

Compare the quizzical eye that the Irish writer always raises to the church with a tone that survives in Irish America, which treats of religion entirely without irony. In the film *The Devil's Own*, Brad Pitt plays the part of an IRA man living in the home of a good honest cop, played by Harrison Ford, in Boston. When the cop realises that he has a terrorist under his roof, and confronts him, the Pitt character responds with pleas for understanding about how bad things are in the old country. 'Wee Annie, killed by a plastic bullet; God bless us and save us.'

In Ireland, this would be seen immediately as an implausible characterisation of a hard man. The script puts the words of a

1950s granny into the mouth of a young man of the 1990s. A massive contrast between mere stereotype and reality is made evident in the failure of an external perspective on Ireland to grasp what the country is really like and what the actual place of religion is in popular culture. Irish America had accepted that the modern Provo was a good Catholic. This proves the success of a propaganda endeavour. There is not a real affinity between a Catholicism there, which has survived like the French language in Quebec, and Republican militancy at home, which has competed with religion and, for some, become a viable alternative to it.

In the most religious days in Ireland, there was also a counter-culture of casualness, even anarchy, vented through music and dance and humour, which believed in natural and honest expression. This competed with the church. There were some for whom religious devotion was a gift, was their natural and honest expression, but the culture of respectability said that everyone had to honour religion, no matter what their inclination.

There was evidence of that counter-culture in the nicknames that children gave to priests and teachers: the Bat, the Boss, Kipperhead. These were common and often cruel. Those who needed to survive in the close shadow of churchmen often disarmed the latter's influence over them by speaking privately about them in this irreverent way.

———

Though literature in Ireland is humanistic rather than religious and devout, the same cannot be said of music. Outstanding devotional music is still being written, reviewed and widely bought. Some reviewers of Sinead O'Connor's album *Theology*, which drew on the Psalms, were keen to point out that it could be enjoyed for its musical qualities despite its religious content, but O'Connor herself is determined that it be understood as an act of devotion to a god she loves.

Mind you, when she sang Psalm 137, 'By the Rivers of Babylon', she left out the horrifically vengeful last lines that others skip over too: Daughter of Babylon the despoiler, happy who pays you back in kind, for what you did to us. Happy who seizes and smashes your infants against the rock (trans: Robert Alter).

In interviews accompanying the launch of the album, O'Connor described herself as a Catholic. Is this then evidence of a vibrant, creative Catholic tradition surviving in Ireland?

No. O'Connor is in the tradition of those who adapt the material of Christian thinking to their own concerns and disregard the church. Sinead O'Connor is the very model of the à la carte Catholic and, more, a brilliant subversive. Not that she articulates her position in speech as movingly as she does musically: '… there's a lot that's brilliant about the Catholic church. It's a beautiful religion—there's no getting away from that. But I think the boundaries are unclear sometimes, and that sometimes religion doesn't understand that God and religion are two different things.'

She told the beliefnet website: 'God loves everybody equally. In lots of religions, including Catholicism, there are people who are deemed less entitled to God's love than others. It's bad for business, and I wouldn't like to see the baby getting thrown out with the bath water, which is what I think is happening. Catholicism is really on the decline, certainly in my own country [Ireland].'

O'Connor is very clear that she follows an intuited sense of the will of God which contradicts the church. 'Sometimes when you love a thing, such as the Catholic church, it's really like a parent. Sometimes we want to challenge the people we love, and sometimes we want to rattle the bars because we see them going down the drain unless they face particular issues. And they may not want to face those issues. For example, the issue of sexual abuse by priests within the Catholic church.'

In another interview, O'Connor showed that, in making the new album, she was well aware of the need to tread carefully when expressing religious interest in song. 'I wanted it to be on the right side of the line between corny and cool. When it comes to religious music, there is a very fine line between cool and very uncool. It deliberately deals with the Old Testament. If you start writing songs about the New Testament, you're doomed no matter how you say it, people have such a prejudice about it.'

So, you can't mention Jesus or you'll just come across like a trite evangelical trying to be trendy. O'Connor recognises that it is a daring thing in Ireland today to say that you are a Catholic and that you love God. That's why she says it. It is part of her rebellion and no endorsement of Mother church. It does the bishops no favours but it is beautiful and heartfelt music.

One writer who does still explore the Catholic world with fascination is the poet Paul Durcan. He says: 'It was wonderful for any child to grow up in the richness of the Christian stories, as well as the particular Catholic liturgy. Too late in the day, I got to see things in a Protestant way, reading the Bible. In my childhood it was unheard of to read the Bible. Luckily, the poet Michael Hartnett introduced me to the Bible in 1962, to the King James Authorised Version and that's been with me ever since.'

He says that he would call himself a John XXIII man. 'I do recall vividly, as if it were yesterday, the excitement in the air at the time of the Second Vatican Council, when we thought ecumenism wasn't an airy fairy word up there; it was for real.' But he now regrets the decision of that council to restrict the saying of the Latin mass. 'When it happened, I was smart and sadly I thought it was part of the revolution, throwing out the Latin and bringing in the vernacular. I think now it was a regrettable step. I wish to heavens we hadn't thrown that away. For all kinds of reasons.' He says that he still takes out the old missal and reads the Latin mass. 'You know, it is so sad. Part of the old civilisation of Europe. No one could possibly understand the history of Ireland without steeping themselves in all that.'

But Durcan's Catholicism today, reflected in his poetry, is a cultural backdrop to a human world, not a pious one. His priest, the priest who has conducted all the christenings and funerals in his family, is Pat O'Brien from Mayo, himself a radical. Durcan describes Fr O'Brien in *Greetings to Our Friends in Brazil*.

When first asked for an interview for this book, Paul Durcan said that this poem said all that he wanted to say about religion.

In it he describes Fr O'Brien giving a sermon on his own friend, John Feeney, killed in a plane crash. Feeney, as editor of *The Catholic Standard*, had been severely censored by Archbishop McQuaid and had taken his revenge by submitting an editorial extracted from the epistle of James. McQuaid, not recognising it, had slashed it as unacceptable.

It is James who tells the disciples that if they discriminate in their respect for a man with a gold ring over a man of 'vile raiment' they cannot call themselves followers of Christ. So Fr O'Brien's sermon was a cheer of approval for Feeney, the good Christian who had shown up the archbishop as a hypocrite.

Not everyone who endorses Christianity endorses the church. How much consolation would, say, Cardinal Brady take from the endorsement of Christian teaching voiced by *Sunday Independent* columnist Eoghan Harris, speaking at the West Belfast Festival in July 2007. Harris said: 'I am a follower of Aristotle for the last thirty years. I believe that politics cannot change the heart of man. Each individual must make that change. That's part of the Protestant thing that I like and admire, that conscience thing. We used to have it too in Catholicism. I believe that the Christian tradition is a far more potent force in the long run, the Christian commitment to internal transformation.'

———

But if religion is dying out in Ireland, how do we explain the huge popularity of pilgrimage? On the last Sunday of July every year, tens of thousands of people climb Croagh Patrick in County Mayo. They do this in continuation of a tradition of penitential prayer devoted to St Patrick, who is said to have preached from the top of the conical mountain above Clew Bay. It may go back even further.

It is easy to imagine what the first people who came to Ireland in the Neolithic age made of this mountain. In its height they would have seen grandeur and in its symmetry and straight lines they would have seen design, the handiwork of a god.

Neolithic religions elsewhere had a fixation on the phallus and some may well have seen that big pointy mountain a little differently from how we do, filtered through that interest. The modern reading is that they addressed it in fertility rituals. Perhaps. There are still people who ascend Croagh Patrick, 'The Reek', in hopes of conceiving. Whatever its ancient provenance, the pilgrimage to Croagh Patrick is still an event bigger than, say, the twelfth of July parade in Belfast, when Orangemen march in commemoration of the victory of William of Orange at the Battle of the Boyne. And it is not a passive submission to religious teaching. This pilgrimage requires exertion and commitment. It is hard. You would not choose lightly to make that climb.

The pilgrims on Croagh Patrick must exert themselves to the limits of their endurance, and some take it further and make the climb barefoot. It is a long and arduous ascent, and the final part of it is dangerous. On the forty-degree slope, the route is covered with loose, broken rock that offers no secure foothold. Pilgrims stumble and fall; they stop every few yards for breath and relief. No technique suggests itself for the walker to get into a rhythm, for each step is different—stretched to reach a footing or shortened to avoid a trip.

So, this seems plain evidence surely of deep Catholic commitment; tens of thousands of eager pilgrims, climbing a mountain to pray. At the top is a little church, an oratory, dedicated to St Patrick. Some pilgrims, when they reach it, circumnavigate it like Buddhists round a stupa, as if they had not exerted themselves enough. And there are other challenges along the way. At the foot of the final ascent, they will walk seven times around a pile of stones, praying for their special intentions. This routine may have been devised to ease a bottleneck at the point where the climb steepens, where pilgrims might otherwise be stumbling over those slowed down ahead of them. But not everyone does the 'station'. Indeed, Croagh Patrick is unlike many other pilgrimages in that it is not really devout at all. Yes, some will walk up in bare feet, but ask them if this is a penance and they will—some of them—say that it isn't.

Jack from County Clare says, 'Och, it's a challenge. Why do I do it like this? Well, why not?'

His friend Gus explains why no one is praying, why people are not walking with their rosary beads or in reverential silence. 'The doing of it is the prayer,' he says.

Perhaps you can't take people at their word when they play down the religious part of their motivation, for faith is one of those things that many are coy about. Yet Croagh Patrick seems distinctly secular. At Medjugorje or on Loch Derg, prayer is conspicuous. On the slopes of Croagh Patrick, there is more cheerful social amity and banter. The exertion brings people together in a playful way. But it does this much as a marathon does.

Mary O'Reilly from Sligo says that she came along to accompany a friend who has now gone on ahead, leaving her struggling alone, but that it is turning into a pilgrimage for her, though she had not anticipated that it would. It reminds her of life, which has hard ways and easy ways and occasional little detours.

As in a city marathon, there are people taking part under sponsorship for a charity. Siobhan Gleeson, originally from Tuam but now with a tinkly northern English accent, wants to raise money for the Jennifer Trust. It is three months and 12 days, she says, since her baby died of SMA.

'The whole family is here. Mam, too,' she says.

Two men from a radio station have come for the eighteenth time since the start of the year to raise money for an autism charity. And another man says that he just likes the physical challenge. 'I didn't pray much at the top. I just sat and ate an apple.' In modern Ireland, many priests would be content to accept that solitary achievement as a spiritual act, and well it might be, but if so, it is derived from the man's own idiosyncratic liturgy and not from theirs.

One man from Cork says, 'I walked around the church and thanked God that my divorce had come through last week. And I met a man who'd been a priest and he had brought his wife. So where are you, when they're no different from us? Was it religious for me? Not a bit of it. I just like climbing mountains and there is no better crack than climbing this one with thousands of other people like yourself.'

Some articulate a spiritual or a naturalist love of the mountain and the walk. A woman from Keady says, 'I just love the feeling of being able to do it.'

Barefoot Jack says: 'It makes me grateful for being the created being that I am.'

So, spiritual rather than religious seems to describe the attitude of the pilgrims. But the destination is the top of the mountain and the church there, so up there it will become clearer if this event is a Catholic pilgrimage, which is what it ostensibly is, or a challenge of a different focus.

Three sisters say that they are climbing together for a special intention but don't say what it is. It isn't hard to work out from their tone and expressions that it is a serious one. Behind them comes an Englishman who says that he believes in Jesus but not in God, which is a bit odd since Jesus believed in God. But there is spiritual variety on the mountain. There are even Northern Irish Evangelicals handing out leaflets, calling people back to the Bible. They see this as a chance to win souls away from the Catholic church by proving that they are as fit and committed themselves.

The ascent of the main slope is difficult and treacherous. A man in an old black suit, perhaps a hill farmer, walks casually over the rocks as lightly as if he was strolling to church, which he is. Most people, relying on sticks, are panting and grunting and stopping often. You walk with your head down, not thinking of anything but the effort, and occasionally stop to look around at the astonishing glory of sunlit Clew Bay. It would be madness to attempt this in the rain. It is hard to work out why people aren't tumbling to their deaths all around you when you feel yourself to be in imminent danger. What is most frustrating is that some of your most arduous steps take you nowhere because you just slip back down through those loose rocks.

You sit, facing down, and wonder if a tumbling rock hitting your back would leave lasting damage. Perhaps the hill is not as dangerous as it looks and feels. No rocks tumble more than half a metre before the other rocks stop them. No one seems to fall flat forward and split their head. But the mountain rescue people stationed along the way, and more densely on the last slope, are wearing helmets, which suggests that the pilgrims, if they were to be as safe as they should be, would be wearing helmets too.

The people coming down encourage those going up. Some tease the younger ones: 'The worst is ahead of you still.'

Even at ten metres from the top it is impossible to judge that you're almost there. 'Not far now. Take it in short steps.'

A man grabs your hand and yanks you over an awkward part. 'There y'are; if you can't help a total stranger, who can you help?'

There are places where the soft soil under the stones is bare and even harder to get a purchase on. Every step takes you back a bit. No step takes you as far forward as you plan it to. It is hard, and it dawns on you that no one in their right mind should be here. Yet some have brought their children and pets. One man carries a baby on a seat strapped to his back. A red setter jaunts lightly over the stones as if bewildered that his owner is making so little progress. A bull of a man playfully scolds two teenage girls who have stopped for a rest. 'You're the biggest pair of sinners in County Clare; will ye up there now and get your confessions heard!'

And the girls giggle and rush ahead invigorated for a few steps.

And then, with a puff, you're at the top which is more spacious than it had appeared from below. And there it is the most natural thing in the world to say: 'Thank God!'

It is conceivable that those who devised this pilgrimage sought to convert that feeling of relief into religious enthusiasm. Other pilgrimages are arduous too. On Station Island on Lough Derg, pilgrims pray repeated rosaries while walking barefoot over stones that would be rough but for the thousands over the centuries who have smoothed them. The more people who do a pilgrimage like that one, the easier it gets. But nothing smoothes your way up Croagh Patrick; everyone who goes before you damages the path and makes your own way harder.

On top of Croagh Patrick, a few dozen people gather for mass in front of the oratory while most just wander around and take in the views of the bay and Mayo. The old oratory is painted white and is visible for miles. There is a little chapel inside from where the priest addresses the congregation, on this day in the open air. He stands in a little conservatory, speaking into a microphone, trusting that the loudspeaker outside is conveying his words, though, in fact, they are muffled and blown away.

There are four doors in the oratory, two entrances at the front, two exits at the back. Pilgrims file through on one side to have their confessions heard, on the other for communion. You could make a funny film from the back of more coming out than could possibly fit in. Fr Patrick Farragher from Castlebar is one of the eight priests hearing confessions and he says that people come to the sacraments at Croagh Patrick who normally don't bother. 'And strangely, though usually it is more women who come to confession, here the majority are men.' He can't explain it. Through a door beside him, a man in his fifties is crouched with a priest and they are both laughing, as if they were old friends. Perhaps they are.

Patrick Kavanagh, who was sniffy about the devotions of hypocrites at Lough Derg, was much happier to endorse the popular worship at Croagh Patrick. Kavanagh made the pilgrimage himself in 1940 and wrote a diary report on it for the *Irish Independent*. His enthusiasm was plain from the start. But he assumed that most people who weren't actually at Croagh Patrick, or in nearby Westport the night before, would have difficulty comprehending that enthusiasm.

> A sight like Westport tonight has to be seen to be understood. All houses are open and lighted. Everybody is up, everybody is gay with a gayness that is the ecstasy of the pure of heart.

He doesn't tell us how to distinguish between 'the ecstasy of the pure of heart' and an ordinary high old time, but he expects the reader to trust that he knows the difference himself. The enthusiasm for the scramble up Croagh Patrick that Kavanagh described in 1940 is as plain more than sixty years later. Croagh

Patrick is not a pilgrimage of solemn devotion; it is fun more than anything else.

'A stroll through the town', wrote Kavanagh, 'is a real tonic to bring the fire of religious emotion to the face of the toughest cynic. Not that the talk in the houses and along the streets is openly pious, but it is humour and light talk against an eternal background—the Faith.'

'There is nothing in secular experience', he wrote, 'to give an idea of this strangely beautiful excitement of the soul.'

Well, so far Kavanagh has described nothing but a carnival atmosphere and if he has detected a refined spirituality at the heart of it, he has been, for him, unusually inept at communicating it. 'Croagh Patrick is not a place to which tourists may come in pursuit of pleasure. Tonight we seek joy. Pleasure can be bought with the coin of the realm, but joy can be bought only with the coin of the heart.' This is trite stuff.

Kavanagh, in 1940, perceived that on the top of Croagh Patrick he was surrounded by 'crowds of inarticulate saints', who are 'physically weary, spiritually exhilarated'. Perhaps that is exactly how he would perceive the mood of the pilgrims on the summit this year.

> Something that is solemnity is here. And there is a sense of the dramatic. It is this sense of the dramatic which marks a difference between Croagh Patrick and Lough Derg. Lough Derg represents the meditative, hermit-like quality in Ireland's faith, but Croagh Patrick is the glorious, singing, laughing climb of an Ireland young in spirit and truth and enthusiastic in performance.

Everybody should do that climb at least once, if they can, and decide for themselves if it is a spiritual event or just a great day out.

Chapter 5

The church has misread the secularising trend in Ireland. It regards it as a moral collapse on the part of those who have given up being Catholic. It imagines that there remains a core of good Catholics still and that these are being neglected and excluded from society. It fails to see that the division between the devout and the secular does not divide a population in two but runs through all—or most—individuals. It is helpless to communicate to the religious notions in the secular because it does not believe in them and it is unable to represent the practising Catholics of modern Ireland because it imagines that they are alien to the wider community rather than part of it.

The Catholic church in Ireland set itself up as the enemy of imagination. Those, like Edna O'Brien and John McGahern, who wrote of Irish sexual and religious hypocrisy had their works banned by a censorious government, serving a constitution which gave the Catholic church a 'special position'. Are a country's writers representative of its people? Certainly not by any democratic arrangement. But writers who nail the hypocrisies and easy barbarisms of the country can expect to be reviled and disowned, not for slander but for betrayal of the family secret. The writers who released the secret that we were not as devout as we pretended to be, that our clergy were not as wise and venerable as we allowed them to pretend, may not have been speaking with the consent of the mass of people, but their creative merit rests on their integrity, and had they all been lying, none of them would have survived as artists of repute.

The priests in the drama of Brian Friel are negligible characters, or they are cruel. Two feature in *Dancing at Lughnasa*. One is a legalistic and patrician member of the school board who wants to sack Kate. The other is a returned missionary who has been converted to paganism by his contact with Africa. Mad Father Jack is this family's dark secret. Nowhere in the works of Friel do we find a priest represented as a wise, spiritual man, or even as a mature adult with a decent, compassionate nature.

It is not easy to find Irish writers of the last century who were both avowedly religious and brilliant in their appraisals of Irish life. Paul Durcan is subversively Catholic. Mary Kenny is the real thing. She defends Catholic values in the terms in which they might be articulated by a bishop. Kenny, in *Goodbye to Catholic Ireland* (1997), has mapped our transition away from deep commitment, through telling milestones like naïve articles published in the *Sacred Heart Messenger* or quarrels around Gay Byrne's *Late Late Show* on RTÉ.

A correspondent to the *Messenger* asks if it is still possible to receive the grace from blessed rosary beads while handling them with gloves. This woman seems to stand for the unabashed ignorance and simple faith of the peasantry which takes the word of a priest on everything. A bishop erupts in rage against the *Late Late Show* after a guest, challenged to remember what colour of nightdress she wore on her honeymoon, suggests that she perhaps didn't wear one at all. But how telling are these incidents really? The woman asking if her gloves might insulate her fingers against God's grace is, after all, only one person, and perhaps even a practical joker at that. The bishop, appalled at the thought that a woman might share with a television audience the news that she sometimes sleeps naked with her husband, even then spoke for a narrow conservatism that was not shared by the studio audience who laughed and applauded.

Where the role of television in the transformation of Ireland
has been recorded and even exaggerated, little account is taken
of the role of radio, which is perhaps more significant still.
Religion is a medium for collective emotion. That is what it has
been for thousands of years, the prevailing emotion changing
sometimes, but the function of providing emotional and
imaginative coherence to the community always its constant.
Radio and television emerged as new media playing the same
role. That is how they competed primarily with religion, even
before there was a clash of ideas. They took over religion's job of
encouraging people to reflect on human sorrow.

In most countries, the media serve fairly shallow emotion.
Radio works to a grammar that requires short items and quick
changes of mood. Yet, radio in Ireland found a space for the long
confessional interview. Gay Byrne, who was credited with the
television revolution against old Ireland, was the founder of this
format, too. Since his day, the mark of the great Irish broadcaster
has been empathic listening, and the high point of programming is when a hush descends over the whole country to listen
to, say, a man tell Ryan Tubridy about his wife's miscarriage or
Nuala O'Faolain tell Marian Finucane that she is dying.

It is hardly noticed in Ireland how culturally specific this is; it
doesn't happen even in Northern Ireland. You would expect that
individuals would come forward and open up to the whole
country, to this extent, only out of the anonymity you can have
in London, yet it is a particular feature of little village Ireland,
where everyone knows everyone else, out of a culture that was
conformist and controlled by the churches and the busybodies,
where to be distinctive was to be getting above yourself.

One of Gay Byrne's last radio programmes featured an
interview with a woman whose clitoris had been desensitised by
surgery. Who in Catholic Ireland would have foreseen a woman
wanting to talk so personally and the nation being absorbed in
her suffering? And this being a particular feature of radio
programming in Catholic Ireland raises the question of whether
something in the Catholic culture survives within this type of
broadcasting. We are candid, it seems, and we respect emotional

intelligence. A church should be able to thrive in such a culture. It doesn't. The church's failure as a medium for collective emotion is primarily in the quality of service it provides. It can't compete with radio and television. It is not primarily that the message is different—the message of religion can be virtually anything—it is that the management of collective emotion is done badly by those who do it on behalf of the churches. If Marian Finucane had been a Dominican nun with access to the God slot, she would have excelled there too. But those who do take God slots are invariably inept.

Part of the problem for the church is that the media take up most of the message. They deal with personal sorrow, politics, practical advice for living, health and finance and leave religion with only the scripture and the liturgy, the core. In the days when nearly everyone went to church, the church's job included commemoration of the dead, the organisation of dances, bingo, bus runs and pilgrimages. The church was almost the whole of the media, and people turned to it for those things that the media provides now. To suggest, as the theologian Vincent Twomey does, that the media have damaged religion through the activities of a vocal liberal minority is to overlook the scale of the transition from one medium to another, as radical as the shift from gossip to the newspaper as the key provider of information.

When church was the medium of collective emotion, it had the capacity to cover all of life; to lead people into conformity on justice, on their reflections on illness, on love and sex, on anything and everything. The emergence of other media defeats the church not on oppositional ground but on its own ground.

But something remains distinctive about how this has happened in the Irish Republic. BBC producers in Belfast used to marvel at how RTÉ could provide forty-minute interviews with a woman in Carlow, who would tell Gay Byrne that her husband had left her, and who would hardly seem to notice that the entire country was listening. The BBC would have made the same kind of programmes itself if it had had people who were capable of being so candid and presenters who could be so trusted. It hadn't. That combination occurs only in the remains of Catholic Ireland. Everywhere else, radio programming is constructed around the idea that no one can hold an audience's attention for more than a few minutes.

———

When we say that we have secularised in a generation we mean, perhaps, that we have loosened the hold of institutional religion over us rather than that we have radically changed our own private perspective on life. We have stopped going to church in huge numbers, but how many still pray under the bedclothes is anybody's guess. And if people of a generation ago really were as religious as they appeared to be, then the fall from that has been a steep one; but if they were basically humanistic underneath, then the change has not been so radical.

So what do we mean by secularisation? In state terms, secularisation is the decline of the influence of the institutional church so that it ceases to affect greatly how laws are made and how people conduct the routines of their lives. In personal terms, secularisation, properly speaking, is a kind of growing up. The individual learns that truth is not passed on by a priest caste and that nothing can be believed that is not tested by reason and experience. There will be some whose own reflections will lead them to religious or spiritual conclusions. Most, it appears, will not want to join a church. How secular are the Irish by this definition? Have they really acquired, most of them, freedom of thought? Or are they just worshipping other hand-me-down gods instead?

At one end of the conceptual spectrum is a country in which all believe in God and all assume that events are governed by God. In this society, legal determinations must be made with reference to God's law as interpreted by the church. At the other end is a country in which all people are atheists and scientific rationalists who live entirely without any conception of the Deity bearing on their lives. Ireland was never the one and will probably never be the other. But it was more religious a generation ago than it is now and it appears to be on a continuing progression towards being less religious still. And the rate of change is, as noted above, faster than in any other European country.

And yet secularisation is not about just the loss of religious faith. Most people still believe in God but many of those who believe in God do not go to church. They will say that their belief is a personal thing and that it finds no expression in an institution or precise set of teachings. Many prefer to call themselves 'spiritual' these days. Being spiritual seems to amount to agreeing that there is a spiritual or mystery context to human existence but feeling no particularly strong need to comprehend that context or make any great sacrifices in acknowledgement of it; you don't need to fear it or placate it. Sometimes just wearing a crystal is commitment enough. It is somewhat akin to the kind of religion that Durkheim concluded might have emerged from primitive reflections on dreaming, enough to make you wonder but not enough to make you want to live by strong laws.

You can be free to be spiritual when it feels nice to be spiritual and free to be a hardened realist instead when a spiritual consideration might cost you something. To be spiritual is to be moved to stop and listen to 'Silent Night' sung by carollers at Christmas—on your way home from the pub—and to have no concern at all to know who the Virgin, Mother and Child are or what brought the three of them together.

By secularisation, we mean the process of emerging from under the influence of institutional churches towards the exercise of individual conscience. The country in which most people don't go to church is a secular country. A country in which most people never pray, never think of God, a country governed by a totally materialistic culture is a secular country all right, but secular to an inconceivable, unprecedented degree.

———

Is a total unreasoning hedonist secular, though? The bishops and theologians are right to observe that some people just don't care for any moral law or to consider by what principles they ought to live. Not everyone discards a church after serious thought. Some just go and have a beer. The modern Irish secular rationalist probably doesn't want to be lumped in with the drug addicts and the bag-snatchers but wants to be regarded as a thinking and civilised being. Indeed, some may have found the escape from religion difficult. They will have had to argue their way out. But the difference between the rational ex-Christian and the hedonist cannot be so sharp in a society that has left religion so far behind that it isn't even part of the public discussion. Ireland isn't there yet; many other European countries are.

One simple sign of secularisation is the reduction in the numbers of people going to church. A more stark one is the reduction in recruitment to the priesthood, ministry or religious orders. Another is the relaxation of the felt need in government to defer to the institutional church or the religious sensibilities of the electorate. All these trends are strongly evident in Ireland. It doesn't mean that we are all atheists, yet. If we were, the contemplation of atheism that drives the sales of books by the New Atheists would not excite us as much as it does. They would not be telling us anything that we feel is new.

But we are getting by without God, most of the time. Someone who was raised a Catholic and who moved out from under the influence of the church is commonly called, in Ireland, a lapsed Catholic. The language supposes that we leave the church only by accident or by neglect and not after serious consideration and even, perhaps, painful struggle. At a debate on secularisation at the McGill summer school in Glenties in 2006, you could see that same presumption of neglect and lack of thought in speeches made by the Archbishop of Dublin, Diarmuid Martin, and the theologian Fr Michael Paul Gallagher. Martin described the secular position as immature. Gallagher regarded it as 'sadly adolescent'.

Both pastors argued for a society governed by strong religious values and principles. They saw morality in religion; among the unreligious, they seemed only to see unthinking and irresponsible behaviour. If there was a reasonable basis upon which a thinking, intelligent person might opt for a secular life, they couldn't see it. By this vision, those who left the church simply fell away. They were one day just too lazy to get out of bed; they lost the resolve and the discipline to attend to their religious duties. By this vision, a secular person is only a religious person who has lost direction, like someone who has stopped exercising and put on weight.

We read this argument constantly in the sermons and tirades of religious leaders of all faiths. Rarely do we hear a strong, secular reply. Rarely do we hear a secular voice saying that this is a profound insult. Do not unreligious people love and protect their children too? Do they not also behave with honesty and consideration towards their neighbours? How does Archbishop Martin explain why all the people who don't go to church aren't in jail? Why do secular people do decent, generous things? Plainly something other than belief in God gives them a sense of moral responsibility and compassion, but the church is content to be oblivious to that side of human nature.

Were the case made against any other religious group that they have no morality, it would be regarded as discriminatory and inflammatory. Religious people would be the quickest to defend themselves against such a charge, or even to defend other religious traditions against such a charge. But you can say anything you like about secular people. And that's fine. Secular people are not banded together to assert their secular thinking as a brand of identity. They have, for the most part, simply withdrawn from the discussion.

When the religious seek to imagine the secular world, in which others do not believe in God or derive their moral values from the church's teachings, they see the secular represented in drug-users, prostitutes and teenage delinquents. They don't conjure up the image of a young family taking the children to the ice rink instead of church, and then point to that and scowl—'evil!' They have no answer to ordinary human decency so they harbour the fantasy that it doesn't exist, though it is all around us.

It is true that the drug-users and the alcoholics are outside the church but anomalous that a church tracing itself back to Jesus Christ, who would have had them on the inside, defines itself by that reality. It is reminiscent of the Pharisee in the temple proclaiming, 'I am not like this publican.' (Luke 18: 10–14)

Archbishop Martin defended the use of the term 'prostitute' as distinct from 'sex worker'. Things should be given their proper names, he said, and undignified work should not be endorsed with a dignified name. Presumably, then, an office cleaner should properly be called a 'skivvy'. Those who use terms like 'sex worker' do so to drain moral censure from the label and to spare the feelings of those engaged in such work so that they might be admitted into the discussion. Isn't that a compassionate and civil thing to do?

The religious world sees a barrier between itself and the secular. On one side are decent, religious people struggling to adhere to their values; on the other is a seething morass of indulgence and chaos among those who are divorced from God and guidance. The barrier that religious leaders see between the proper religious life and the chaotic secular life is one that distinguishes people who live by principle from people who live by moral relativity. The secular person is reviled as a moral relativist who applies different moral principles to different occasions, not because that is a practical way to manage and because morality has to be educated by experience but simply because the person has no dependable centre and doesn't think. Fr Michael Paul Gallagher argues that it is a mistake to put morality before God. 'Put God first and the context changes and morality falls into place because there is a reason for it.' By this reasoning, only belief in the existence of God prompts a person to behave in a moral way.

The theologians and bishops of Ireland are reciting a favourite theme of Pope Benedict when they attack moral relativism and claim that the only viable morality is one that derives from belief in God and in what Catholic theology calls 'objective morality' or 'natural law'. By such grand titles for their moral and religious perspective they side-step any charge that what they believe is mere opinion.

Vincent Browne, in his *Irish Times* column on 10 October 2007, took a swipe at the bishops for closing their annual conference with a statement grounded on the assumption that non-believers have no morality. The bishops had said: 'With [recent economic success] has come an increasing experience of secularisation and coinciding with this has come a decrease in the awareness of the importance of moral values.' Browne wrote: 'The inference that secularisation is moral-free, that those who believe in a secular society are morally indifferent or that morality exists only in the context of religious belief, is an insult to all those who do not believe in any religion but who struggle, however inadequately, to live moral lives, lives that respect the equal rights, entitlements and convictions of others.'

Some theologians do much more than imply that non-believers have no morality; they state it plainly.

———

At an earlier McGill summer school in Glenties, in 2005, Fr Vincent Twomey attacked secular efforts to impose order and good conduct. He described as 'nearly futile' those restraints that a secular society uses to defeat corruption in public life. Ethical guidelines and accountability had their place, but only nature's 'own school of virtue, the home' could actually counter corruption and cultivate morality in public life. No good at all can issue, apparently, from the efforts of secular-minded people to create a functioning social order.

Twomey exudes a confidence that he knows how to sort out modern Ireland, and it's not with these tribunals and account-ability measures but with 'objective morality' and the family. He said: 'Objective morality is no longer the criterion by which positive law is measured. Morality is reduced to whatever happens to be useful, or whatever is perceived to be the view of the majority, usually by some kind of questionnaire.'

He appears to seriously think that people are consulting questionnaires for guidance on what to believe or how to behave. Where are these questionnaires published? By this view, it is the secularists who are looking around themselves and trying to ascertain the right way to behave, not the docile people in the pews. Where does Vincent Twomey imagine the secular atheists are taking their moral prompts from—some central committee interpreting those questionnaires for them?

Does a woman have a right to choose to terminate a pregnancy? Well, there must be a questionnaire somewhere that provides the right answer. Anything is possible, from Twomey's perspective, but that an intelligent-thinking person might address a moral question responsibly without asking a priest for an answer to it.

> It's not enough. Judges who interpret the constitution in the light of the prevailing ideas and concepts, may in fact be simply reflecting a passing view, perhaps the so-called progressive views of a vocal minority supported by a media that is often partisan on moral issues.

So now it is the vocal minority that is the enemy. The vocal minority publishes the questionnaires, presumably. The vocal minority has the impressionable masses in its thrall. It is a sinister cabal doing the job that the church used to do. One of Twomey's favourite targets is an imagined coterie of atheistic journalists who have nothing better to do than sneer at Catholicism. He appears to imagine that they are the generators of secular ideas rather than a reflection of the proliferation of such ideas. Market forces, he suggests, work in entirely the opposite way to that in which most economists imagine. People buy what they are told to buy, believe the ideas that they are told to believe. Where can Twomey have acquired such a vision of Irish society? From a past, perhaps, in which individual thinking was sneered at, in an Ireland which was all the better for that?

And the moral condition of a secularising Ireland, which will have no principles and no direction, is critical. The crisis, he says, is a big one.

When moral relativism meets the utilitarian needs of the multinationals then the result can be particularly lethal, such as the approval of experimentation on human embryos, human beings, stem cell research and the creation of some human beings to provide organs for others, as recently advocated by our own government-appointed commission. There was only one dissenting voice.

The marvel in Twomey's world view is in how he matches crises of different scales together, as part of the same overhanging horror. It is as if a US president were to preach at once on the twin evils of climate change and children's television—not so unlikely really, when you think about it.

For Twomey, the threats of our time are the annihilation of mankind through the commoditisation of human life and the restraints on the freedom of academics to sit and think and write books. Well, that's what he says.

> Government insistence, for instance, on quality assessment in the universities is one example of the ways such distrust is creeping into what should be communities of scholars, a concept which for similar reasons has been radically undermined by a top-down administrative process suitable for business, not for the cultivation of the mind.

There is no crediting the damage done by teachers being made to prove to those who pay them that they spend time teaching.

> Since, apart from the churches, the universities are the main source of spiritual values, such as the development of the critical sense, an invitation into the great intellectual tradition of humanity and the cultivation of a need to know the truth, the undermining of the universities can only leave society all the weaker and open to, ultimately, totalitarianism.

So it is our academics who save us from tyranny?

If you don't have a thinking people, if everything is geared
to exams, if teachers now have to prove what they are doing
and can't just sit for four or five years thinking about and
producing a book—you know this is all because money is
going into universities and the people want to know what
you are doing with the money—it is very hard to quantify
what is essentially a spiritual entity.

So, critical thinking is now a spiritual value, except, presumably,
when it is a secularist who is doing the thinking.

But Twomey is not concerned just about the spiritual condition of the modern thinker, hampered by the need to fill in
forms. He is concerned about morality in government and is
convinced that legislation is not the answer. His formula for
rooting out corruption in public life is vaguer still than his
prescription for academic freedom, leaving thinkers alone to do
what they want. It is done through the cultivation of virtue.
Catch a councillor taking a backhander and what do you do?
Quick, cultivate virtue!

All the wisdom traditions of humanity agree that the
cultivation of virtue, the cultivation of personal integrity,
is the only solution to corruption wherever it is found. And
trust is restored only if people are perceived to be trustworthy. And how do you make people trustworthy? I don't
think by having them all the time accountable. You make
people trustworthy through acquiring personal integrity
or virtue.

Perhaps it is fair to suppose that Twomey has tangled up his own
thinking here and would be clearer if he had taken four or five
unaccounted years to sit and think. Or do you make other
people more trustworthy by acquiring virtue yourself? One
moment he is talking about how to address the corruption of
others, and the next moment the solution is in personal change.
Then it is in the raising of children, something that there
mightn't actually be time for, once a crime has been disclosed.

The reform of society by cultivating virtue in all its members is surely a long-term project. Is it really an alternative to the monitoring and regulation of public servants? He does seem to think so.

> The acquisition of virtue presupposes many things: above all, a stable family life and the witness of upright parents and teachers. These provide the ultimate conditions within which virtue can normally flourish, since it is primarily caught, not taught. Here too is where all those little civilities and politenesses which make society bearable, as Thomas Aquinas said, the basic thanks and holding the door and smiling, this is what you learn at home.

This is what who learns at home? Everybody? And if not everybody, what use is this theory for transforming a society that already has corruption, incivility and people who don't smile and open doors for you? As far as Twomey is concerned, the answer is in the family. And we all know what a family is or should be.

> And here one must look with alarm at some suggestions being proposed for the redefinition of the family and for new forms of childcare outside the home, economy seeming to be the main concern there. These will effectively weaken human nature's own school of virtue, the home.

Twomey is an idealist. He believes that families in Dublin and Limerick can be schools of virtue through which society can be so transformed that no regulation of public servants will be needed and everyone will appreciate the need for academics not to be accountable to those who pay them.

> Healthy families in turn create healthy environments where a genuine sense of community including a sense of local identity is experienced.

So no lesbian couples if we are to have a stable society; no single mothers; no working mothers; only families that function as schools of virtue. It is hardly credible that someone could find a platform from which to deliver such ideas in Ireland today, but a title in a theological college endows chauvinistic views with an air of authority. But even he, clearly, didn't feel free to state plainly the implications of that last paragraph, that heterosexual marriage produces good children who become good citizens and that if we could restore that we would have no need to worry about crime and corruption. Of course, he knows himself that something more is needed. That more, in his view, is the state's endorsement of God.

> Virtue finally needs faith in God to flourish. Trustworthiness is not exclusive to believers but it is rarely found in abundance outside of faith communities. Atheism is not an option for a healthy state or a healthy democracy.

If this is true, then old Ireland must have been a wonderful place with happy, moral children being well cared for and growing up to be responsible and decent citizens. One wonders what he thinks went wrong. Fr Twomey's claims would be of some value if he could show that Ireland in 1955 was free of crime and alcoholism. Most families then had two parents of different sexes and everybody believed in God. So surely the ideal conditions which he commends for the eradication of corruption and crime were in place. Is he not curious himself about why they failed?

There is no mystery in these ideas of Fr Twomey's being disregarded by most people in Ireland; the mystery is in a man of education in the modern world still holding onto them.

In his book *The End of Irish Catholicism?* (Veritas 2003), Fr Twomey expands on these ideas in a slightly more coherent fashion. He believes that there is one absolute moral law. He identifies it with the Tao in Chinese philosophy—which is very eclectic of him. Politics is the field of compromise but morality must never be compromised on, says Twomey. There is only one moral law and it must govern our politics too. Twomey sees politics and morality as separate. We must be absolute in our moral judgments and we must compromise in politics. There seems no place in his vision for politics which is ideological or principled. Politics is always simply about agreeing pragmatic solutions to 'the exigencies of the economy and social welfare'. He seems to think that political parties are nothing but groups of people with shared ideas about how roads should be built.

It is not possible to adhere to the moral law privately and to compromise it for the sake of others in politics or public life, he says. If, for instance, abortion is wrong, then there can be no compromise on laws on abortion. Fr Twomey would apparently have stood firmly and confidently beside the tyrannical Archbishop John Charles McQuaid who is remembered today as the most daunting symbol of old Catholicism, a Catholicism that even much of the institutional church is happy to be rid of.

People, he says, will debate moral law, of course, and it is right that they should, but this debate must be brought to 'some kind of closure by the authoritative intervention of the Magisterium'. So, on the one hand, the moral law is universal and written into our human nature, but there is only one authoritative interpreter of it, the Pope. Being universal, of course, it binds all people and not just Catholics. Twomey appears to believe, therefore, that the Pope has the authority to pronounce on the moral choices that all should make. Without religion there is nothing, he says, only nihilism. This is a more extreme position than the one he took at the McGill Summer School in which he at least acknowledged that some few atheists do have integrity.

So the Ireland he would have us live in is one in which practical decisions on the economy are taken by a government that refers all moral questions to the Catholic church and in which the Catholic interpretation of moral questions is enshrined in law. It is an Ireland in which only one type of family is worthy of constitutional protection. Other types of family will be inefficient schools of virtue. Fr Twomey spoke as a professor of moral theology and, until recently, taught priests at Maynooth. He is editor of the *Irish Theological Quarterly*. He is not an eccentric. He is a Catholic.

———

Fr Twomey is not the only one who harbours a fantasy that the church is confronted by an organised secular enemy. The Redemptorist magazine *Reality* asked in the September 2007 issue if Catholicism is the new sin.

> It has become fashionable in Ireland to sneer at religion and religious belief, but given that our religious tradition has been predominantly Catholic, to be anti-religion in the Ireland of today usually means being anti-Catholic. And anti-Catholicism is on the rise.

The evidence for this was three jibes against the Catholic church of the past, made by Dave Fanning, Brian McFadden and Gabriel Byrne, and a story about a little girl altar server who had been told by her parents not to be alone with the priest in the sacristy. Those who regard that as 'open season on Catholics' will hardly bear up well when the debate gets more robust. Beneath notice, again, are thoughtful people who have decided, for what they regard as good reason, to stop going to church and taking their moral guidance from men in black.

There was another example of this simplistic thinking in a speech made on the media, in July 2006, by then Archbishop [now Cardinal] Seán Brady, the Catholic primate of Ireland. Archbishop Brady was urging people not to buy newspapers that do not cater for the non-secular, religious reader. This suggests a vision of Ireland in which those of strong religious commitment live separate lives, with separate interests from those who are secular. What it overlooks is that religious people themselves have a strong secular bent in their thinking and, of course, that many secular-minded people have the remnant of a religious tendency in theirs.

Churchgoers do not open the *Sunday Independent* and feel alienated from it because they can't find a sermon there. If Archbishop Brady was to define the religious Catholics of Ireland as only those who would rather read a sermon than a political column, he would have to concede that their numbers are small.

Archbishop Brady wrote, in a foreword to the annual report of the Catholic Communications Office:

> In Ireland, where many are deeply committed to marriage, family, religious faith, religious practice, and community, as key values which sustain the common good, it is peculiar that not more people in the media and not more opinion writers, in particular, reflect the values of such a large section of their readership.

He added, 'While the secular media in Ireland quite legitimately claims to be motivated by the noble ideals of freedom of expression, objectivity, investigation and diversity of opinion, the notable absence of those providing opinion and analysis from a specifically religious perspective suggests that no such choice really exists.'

Again, there is a hint that some areas of interest, in this case, family values, are the exclusive property of the church. Secular people value families too and they often read and write articles about family values. What is the Man Booker winner, Anne Enright's *The Gathering*, about if not about family values? If Cardinal Brady was more honest, he would emphasise that it is the specifically Catholic understanding of family values that he wants promoted and that there are many decent people, even in the pews in front of him, who do not share it.

The fondness for secular newspapers among churchgoing Catholics surely indicates that even those Catholics themselves are more interested in news, features and social and political commentary than they are in the teachings of the Catholic church. And if they want to read an article about child-rearing or sex in marriage, they are more likely to want to read it in the *Sunday Independent* than in the *Sacred Heart Messenger*. In fact, the actual teaching of the Catholic church appears to be something that even regular mass-goers—even priests—have little interest in. Ireland is plainly not divided into groups who live by these opposing principles.

Within Durkheim's perspective, that a religious attitude divides the world into the sacred and the profane, England might be said to be a highly religious society, even today. There, the cultural and political worlds demarcate strict boundaries between the populace and the divine figurehead, the monarch. A religious society may be one in which the sacred and profane spaces are well separated, but a lot depends on who does the separating. In England today, there remains a reverence for monarchy as a remnant of a religious culture, but that reverence is maintained by the people rather than by the institution, and the people make free with the right to sneer at the monarchy sometimes and at others to celebrate it. The monarchy is at the mercy of a public mood.

In Ireland, there was a time until recently when the church determined what were sacred times and spaces, but vast numbers of people have chosen to disregard those rulings entirely. Religion, for them, has to be grounded on something that matters. The sacredness of a time or space has to be potent. The potency of royal events in England is weak, except at moments that actually clash with the traditional reading of monarchy, like the death of Diana. The potency of the average mass is similarly weak, yet there are times when acts of public worship pull huge numbers of enthusiastic people.

The church survives, like the English monarchy, on nothing but the occasional interest of the people and must endure the occasional derision of the same people if it is to survive at all.

Chapter 6

Let's talk about sex.

At the beginning of our secularisation, people started moving from the country to the towns and cities where they had wider social circles and did not need to go to church to redeem themselves from the loneliness of the week, as they might have had to do had they lived in a hillside cottage in Donegal or Kerry. Imagine how important church was in the 1950s when you mightn't have had electricity in your home or a neighbour you could visit without putting on Wellington boots.

The agricultural basis of religious custom diminished as we moved to the towns and cities, and found work that did not depend on the ownership of land. In the cities, people went to dances and the cinema and they could dress up for these, so they didn't need church as a platform for their occasional, hard-earned stabs at elegance. In the city, their sense of social standing was now related to their jobs and to the pecking orders within their employment and social circles. They might still pray, but sometimes praying alone is more intense anyway than praying in a crowd. And when they prayed ardently, it was because they were missing Mammy or feared they were pregnant or would get sacked. These were solitary, shameful individual concerns, not to be shared with the people in the pew, or even the priest in confession. At home, people stood in churches and prayed for a good harvest or a spot of rain or the Fianna Fáil candidate— concerns that bound them together.

And just at the time when the social underpinning for church attendance was shifting, the Vatican changed the liturgy and the drama of the mass. The ritual was pared of its beauty and mystery when it was translated into English. Some older people still say that that was the most important change cutting them off from something they had known and loved since childhood.

The church had anticipated that the city would open sexual temptation to the young, but instead of accepting this as inevitable, it tightened the rules against contraception and lost influence over people who could not accept those rules. If the church had accepted the reality of sex before marriage, and recognised the occasions for compassion that arise from relationships going wrong, it might have secured the loyalty of the young in the cities. Instead, it chose that moment to reaffirm its commitment to St Augustine's strange ideas about sex and was going to be of little use or interest to young people who were just discovering it.

And the church did a strange thing. At the moment at which it chose to try to police our sexual conduct more rigorously, by formalising its ban on contraception, it threw away the whip in its own hand and stopped preaching about Hell and damnation. (This will be a lesson to the newly ascendant One True Faith religions: give ground on your absolute position and you don't gain followers; you lose them.) We were told that it was a sin to use a condom—in Dublin, they were called 'frenchies' then—but we were no longer told that sins had painful consequences for us, apart from making God a wee bit unhappy. And, when you think about it, just how unhappy is an infinite, omnipotent being likely to become?

The church also at that time adopted an ecumenical approach, acknowledging that people of other faiths were entitled to think of themselves as right in their own way and not merely as mistaken and lost. So how could it be much of a sin for a Catholic to use a condom if it wasn't a sin for a Methodist who was going to Heaven too?

But if people once needed religion and then ceased to need it, presumably something else was beginning to fill the space in their lives vacated by their rejection of it. So, what is it that replaces religion for the Irish who have given it up? You might as well ask what replaced it for them before the long century of Catholicism. Ireland had not been as universally committed in the early nineteenth century as it was in the first-half of the twentieth. Sean Connolly, in *Priests and People in Pre-Famine Ireland*, writes of how out of touch the Latin-educated priests were and how little control they had, to restrain fair-day faction fights, for instance. This was a people with a fairy culture that included infanticide on a scale that cannot now be measured. The sickly child, presumed to have been swapped for the healthy one by the fairies, was taken out and exposed to the wind and rain. Connolly argues that the Catholic church, after the famine, with the consolidation of farm holdings, found a coincidence of interest with the farmers, imposing family values more rigidly, giving the farmer power to preserve the land against bastard claims. We were back to trying to preserve the garden, and Jesus, the God of poverty and simplicity, had become—as gods will— the God of landed inheritance.

A hundred years later, and those who lived without land in the cities were beyond these concerns, and put down religion as lightly as if it had never really mattered. The world now came to us through radio and television. It had been possible to be anti-Semitic in Ireland in 1950 and not know how out of step that was with the wider world. We were introspective and arrogant, but all we had was the radio and the newspaper, Radio Éireann and the *Irish Press*. Our ignorance was excusable.

Suddenly, in the city, our sexual immaturity became socially untenable. The woman who thought that she could form relationships without sex found that the man she wanted moved on. The man who thought he could relate to women through the assumption that those who had sex were slags or sinners found, too, that he could make few friends among them, not even among the virgins. These changes weren't just Irish; they were reflected in Hollywood, which hardly noticed Ireland. Doris Day's cute virginity expired because the western world changed. Films that in the 1950s were seen as plausible accounts of relationship stresses, between adults who never undressed together, suddenly became merely quaint.

———

However, there was another factor in the early 1960s that changed the religious climate of Ireland. That new mood that reached the country and suggested individual freedom had coincided with the Second Vatican Council. Vatican II had seemed, at first, to be hugely liberating. The sudden hope of Irish Catholics was that they could be radical and free and stay in the church. It was the 1960s and the church was going with the flow of the times—or that's how it seemed. And that coincidence was exciting. It encouraged many religious people to feel that the broader social change was in line with a spiritual revolution. Hopes were then raised to giddy heights and those hopes were dashed. Both sides of that swing produced flights away from the religious orders.

Some, inspired by the liberal hopes and the elevation of the laity, felt emboldened to leave the orders and, fired up by the new mood, wanted to experiment with ways of religious living on the outside. Still more of these liberals left the church when their hopes were later suppressed, but in the meantime there had also been a conservative flight following Vatican II. These were the nuns and brothers and priests who had lived ordered and regular lives according to rule and custom for decades and now felt that the life they had known and loved was being denied them. So Vatican II, remarkably, drove out both liberal and conservative Catholics from the religious orders.

Fr Kenneth Brady of Mount Argus recalls the excitement of that period, though he was not yet ordained:

> Vatican II gave us an ideal. We fell in love with the ideal. There wasn't an awful lot of realism in terms of the steps to

get there. I think for me there was almost an element of magic rather than an understanding that things are achieved by hard work, struggle and self-denial. And from an institution that held things tight, there were people expressing different views and perspectives.

So the Catholic church in Ireland was torn between young priests and nuns who felt that a revolution was under way and bishops who wanted to preserve as much as they could of the old ways of doing things. Fr Brady was 18 in 1965, and recalls:

I was part of the old and part of the new. What I would say is that the ass had fallen out of the old. For many it had been sterile for years. Our provincial sent me to university and a big concern among some of our men was how we would cope with university. The university actually made it more difficult for us to be here, because the internal life hadn't adapted, hadn't changed; most of the men belonged to a previous formation and it created difficulties for us because we were looking for more from here than it could actually deliver.

He says: 'I remember a priest saying to me as a student, "Well, there is one thing you can be sure of: the canon of the mass will never be in English."'

And in such a period of transition, some were afraid. They didn't know for sure if the trend was towards a more liberal church and they wanted to guard their backs.

I suppose there was a fear. People were inclined to look over their shoulders in terms of saying what they thought. I often heard that from some theologians because the possibility of getting a bishop's hat meant that in a lot of official meetings they didn't often say what they felt or thought, because they'd lose the mitre.

A relic of that period is the changed character of the much-reduced religious orders in Ireland. Within those orders now, strangely, it is the liberal-minded radical Catholics who prevail. One of them is Sister Finbarr of the Sisters of Loreto, or Sister Kathleen Fitzgerald, as she prefers to be known now.

Kathleen entered the Loreto convent in Rathfarnham in 1963. She had worked with a firm of accountants in Dame Street and made up her mind to become a nun after she was offered a well-paid job with Guinness. Her boss joked with her that the odour of sanctity was clearly more attractive than the odour of stout. She was an eager young nun, inspired by the serenity of sisters she had seen at mass during her schooldays, but not strongly attracted to the traditional convent life.

> At times there were things that would annoy you and you'd say, 'What in the name of goodness is this about?' And we were right. I know the Mistress of Novices said that we were the first group that really questioned everything: why we had to wear this, why we had to do that. I think there was a real sense of there being something new about, at the time of the Vatican Council. There was an enthusiasm and a life, and I would say really that one of the sadnesses of my life would be that that didn't get a scope to develop.

She says that Pope John XXIII was her hero. 'The church's familiar face of unfeeling perfection was somehow changed by the face of John XXIII. It gave great courage to the younger people there to think, this is how we should be.' This revolutionary optimism coincided with the sunny mood of the 1960s in which young people felt that institutions were adapting to their preferences. A generation whose mood was not darkened by the memory of the Second World War, which saw less need for obedience and conformity to the ways of a preceding generation, felt free to criticise and to demand change.

Fr Kenneth Brady recalls the enthusiasm around Vatican II as a difficult period for older clergy who were settled in a fixed way of imagining God's role.

The faith of the world that I came out of was the jigsaw faith where all the pieces fitted together. I then discovered that the world is more like the front loader of a washing machine and that, somehow or other, faith has to make sense of that reality. I think that in the Irish church and in many other churches there wasn't sufficient theological reflection; you couldn't be ahead of the posse.

Some people were exploring radical, new theological ideas that excited the young and appalled the older generation.

Take a theologian like Rahner—I saw him in Dublin, a wee pudgy fat man—he said it was a myth that priests and religious had made a personal commitment to Christ. John XXIII took us out of our cocoon. It opens up the world, all sorts of things come in and everything is challenged.

Some were able to negotiate that change and even to feel more comfortable within it. For many priests it actually put them on a personal journey of faith and a personal journey of themselves and I suppose in some of the orders lots of things were begun like communication workshops, getting people in touch with their own emotional life and I think that was a big area of weakness that there wasn't training in emotional and psychological life.

Sister Kathleen says: 'I think the great mistake was that Vatican II wasn't followed up. I feel there was a fear that battened down the hatches.'

———

The crisis for many came after Vatican II when expectations of a reformed and more open church seemed dashed by that papal ruling on contraception. Some in the clergy then were thinking that in their lifetimes they would be free to marry, but it wasn't their own sexual freedom that was at issue here; it was the question of whether the church was listening to the people, and the ruling on contraception showed that it wasn't.

Pope Paul VI followed Pope John XXIII and deliberated over what the church's stand on artificial contraception should be. He rejected the advice of a commission that included married laity and penned the encyclical *Humanae Vitae*, endorsing the ban on contraception and ruling that only 'heroic abstinence' was permitted by God as a means of controlling family size.

'After *Humanae Vitae*, I worked in a disadvantaged area of Dublin,' says Kathleen. 'Before that I would have believed, yes, this is the right thing, but afterwards I realised: oh dear, they have no idea of the lives of the people.'

Kathleen is one of those who thinks that the Vatican had panicked at the sight of the liberalising of the church that the Council had prompted, and sought to block it with a hard-line statement on sexuality grounded in that old boor, Augustine.

The encyclical envisaged only 'continence' as an alternative to an ejaculation inside the unguarded womb, all other means of expressing semen, at least while conscious, being sinful. It was a very odd message to be sending to the women of Ireland who were discovering new freedoms through education and employment.

Whereas many young Catholics thought that Vatican II was validated as the work of the spirit by having been so much in the spirit of the times, *Humanae Vitae* was a message that the Catholic church didn't do 'the spirit of the times'. And Irish-born philosopher Elizabeth Anscombe explained that the Pope had had no choice but to affirm the basic truths articulated by Augustine. She wrote:

> If contraceptive intercourse is permissible, then what objection could there be after all to mutual masturbation, or copulation *in vase indebito*, sodomy, buggery (I should perhaps remark that I am using a legal term here—not indulging in bad language), when normal copulation is impossible or inadvisable (or in any case, according to taste)? It can't be the mere pattern of bodily behaviour in which the stimulation is procured that makes all the difference! But if such things are all right, it becomes

perfectly impossible to see anything wrong with homosexual intercourse, for example … You will have no answer
to someone who proclaims as many do that they are good
too. You cannot point to the known fact that Christianity
drew people out of the pagan world, always saying no to
these things. Because, if you are defending contraception,
you will have rejected Christian tradition.

Humanae Vitae is read then as defending the church's teaching
not just on sex inside marriage but on masturbation and
homosexuality too. You can't argue that masturbation is a sin if
you don't hold the line at contraception. You cannot allow that
that which causes sexual arousal in you determines what is the
appropriate sexual behaviour for you. If the expression of semen
for personal pleasure is to be admitted, then the entire edifice of
Catholic sexual morality collapses. That is what Paul VI and his
interpreter Elizabeth Anscombe believed. Better that unwanted
children be born than that someone somewhere should be
masturbating and feeling good about it! Paul VI wrote:

> The right and lawful ordering of birth demands, first of all,
> that spouses fully recognise and value the true blessings of
> family life and that they acquire complete mastery over
> themselves and their emotions. For if with the aid of reason
> and of free will they are to control their natural drives,
> there can be no doubt at all of the need for self-denial.
> Only then will the expression of love, essential to married
> life, conform to right order. This is especially clear in the
> practice of periodic continence. Self-discipline of this kind is
> a shining witness to the chastity of husband and wife and,
> far from being a hindrance to their love of one another,
> transforms it by giving it a more truly human character.

Strange stuff indeed! Once you have learned to overcome the
need for sex in your marriage, your love will deepen and take on
a more 'human' character. What can he possibly mean by the
word 'human'?

Pope Paul's expectation was that those who regulated their families would achieve heroic mastery of their bodies and feelings and would also achieve 'continence', the avoidance of not just intercourse during the fertile period but of all sexual expression including, apparently, involuntary ejaculation. Within the terms of this theology, if a man trying to abstain from sex for two weeks each month, to avoid impregnating his wife, found that he could hold out no longer, he would have to call in the 'debt' (Augustine's word) of sexual access to her and then take the risk of conception, that being the lesser moral danger for them both. Most Catholics hadn't read *Humanae Vitae* and therefore hadn't realised how petty it was. Most priests hadn't the nerve to explain it to them.

In fact, priests no longer assert the importance of dogma, though they are at the bottom of a hierarchy that does. They seem happy now to serve those who have a basic faith in something that might be called God, people who are as content to pray in a Catholic church as in a field. The great embarrassment of sex is avoided. Few priests want to talk about how Catholic teaching clashes with common sense. The church, tracing from Augustine, says sex is for procreation. Any sexual activity not conducive to this is a sin. By Augustine's reasoning, it would be acceptable to copulate while hanging by the feet from a chandelier, since gravity would gather sperm into the womb, but not standing up, since gravity would work in the other direction. As for oral sex: well, surely there is a question about whether it is legitimate foreplay—if foreplay at all is legitimate. The trouble is, there is no Catholic *Kama Sutra*, but if there was, it would probably tell us that fellatio is morally more dangerous than cunnilingus since it presents the greater danger of seed being wasted. Strange how this concurs with New Atheist Richard Dawkins' theology of *The Selfish Gene*. The one sense in which Dawkins may be right about our being able to escape the selfish replicator is through contraception.

———

Even the hierarchy seems content to avoid sexual issues today, though there is no predicting what might yet issue from the pen of Pope Benedict. He recently urged the Namibian ambassador to the Holy See to recognise that Catholic teaching on the family is the answer to the AIDS crisis in Africa. He expressed the hope that Namibia would enshrine this teaching in state law.

But the church, so far, avoids sexual questions in the modern world which are of a type that would have prompted a response in the past. It is hard to imagine that if Viagra had been invented in the 1960s, the Catholic church wouldn't have banned it, and it is intriguing to consider that the church's ignoring it is a global phenomenon and not just a local Irish one. Viagra meets all the criteria of sinfulness that the contraceptive pill did. It is an unnatural interference in the conjugal relationship. Well, one reason the church might not mind it is that it leads, potentially, to more children being born, and sexual measures that facilitate that are usually thought of by the church as less of a sin. Viagra would have interested the moral conscience of St Augustine if it had been about in his time. Augustine believed that the fallen state of man was evident in his lack of control of his erections. Perfect man, in Heaven, would raise and lower his penis with the same will with which he could control his arms. Viagra cheats the Fall. It is hard to imagine that Augustine could have allowed that to pass.

––––

The enthusiasm of Catholic Ireland was briefly revived by the visit in 1979 of the new pope, John Paul II. But we had misread him. He was a narrow conservative. We can infer that he would not have approved of Viagra. He taught that it is sinful for a man to look on his own wife with lust in his heart. John Paul was one of those who had helped embolden Paul VI to adhere to strict Augustinian theology on sex. The Irish Catholics mistook him, on first sight, for a new kind of pope. He was far from it. They responded to John Paul II with a sense that he was, potentially, a leader for the new kind of Catholics that they were. They were wrong about this.

Yet here was this youngish Pope with a vigour that they had never seen in that office before. He had a voice with a gravelly pitch that John Gielgud would call perfect. It was a deep, charismatic voice of easy command. The new pope was humble. This did not mean, however, that he was deferential. When he kissed the tarmac of the runway on landing, this was not a gesture of putting himself at the disposal of Ireland, to hear Ireland's needs and adapt to them. The Irish didn't know it yet, but this was an old-school Catholic of the most conservative kind. That wasn't what they expected of a man who, before he was a priest, was a poet and a playwright. His vocation—for a man of his generation—was a late one. He had not decided to be a priest until he was in his twenties. He had trained in secret during the Nazi occupation of Poland. So perhaps he had had girlfriends; perhaps he was a red-blooded man with a bit of dash about him.

The Irish had loved and revered priestly men and knew how to be spiritually inspired by a personality, and John Paul had the gifts that they expected to find in an inspiring pastor. The only problem was that he would try to teach them to hold on to the bits of Catholicism that they were discarding.

The type of the new priest that the Irish wanted was the confessor who would understand them on a personal level and not bind them rigidly to the rules. If a woman told her priest that she was on the contraceptive pill and didn't want another baby, she expected him to say something like this: 'Well, this is ultimately a matter for your own conscience, my dear. And the Lord knows your heart and knows that you are a good person. Now, will you promise me you'll pray for his guidance on this?' And then he'd give her absolution. And if he didn't, she would go to another priest who would, or she would stop going to confession altogether.

John Paul would turn out to be a man who knew the rules and knew that the rules were right. He expected priests to adhere to those rules. He promoted priests who did and hounded out of work those who taught liberal interpretations of Catholic theology.

—

Fr Kenneth Brady says:

> *Humanae Vitae* introduced a crisis in terms of the way that
> authority is exercised. The Pill in confession? It doesn't
> arise. Most people don't mention it because they don't
> think of it as a sin. I have never found it to be a problem.
> *Humanae Vitae* presupposes a whole background of
> perspective that I don't think many people actually have. So
> if they don't have that—it's plumbing.

In effect, the priest as moral sheriff who would direct people
back towards obedience is gone. Yet the sexual conservatism of
the papacy was as strong in successive popes John Paul II and
Benedict XVI.

John Paul's ideas about sex had been developed when he was
a bishop in Poland. Not that there was anything novel about
them. Contraception was wrong—for one thing, because it
broke the intimate concentration on the act of love and
introduced the ugly practical. This was the observation of a man
who had never had sex, who didn't know that, for instance, a
lover might break off to rub a cramped foot or have a pee, that
sex is not a mystical state, outside the mundane.

Kinder biographers suggest that John Paul developed his
thinking by listening in confession to the wives of Polish workers
who took their women abruptly and greedily. Perhaps his
insistence on abstinence through the fertile days, as the only
legitimate contraception, was a way of claiming a rest for those
women. But his suggestion that abstinence is the only method
worthy of human love is a bit hard to comprehend. Some of his
sayings might have come across more abruptly in translation
than was warranted. He said that it was sinful for a man to look
on his wife with lust in his heart. Had he said that it was sinful
for a man to treat his wife as a sex object, fewer might have
dismissed him.

In his encyclical *Veritatis Splendor*, John Paul spoke of
contraception, homosexuality and masturbation as 'intrinsic
evils'. The big difference between him and the cultural climate of

modern Ireland was that he was an absolutist and Ireland was morally relativist to the core. If there was a single way of defining the moral and cultural revolution in Ireland from the 1960s, it would be to say that the people were eschewing absolutism and evolving a morality that made judgements against circumstances and with an acceptance of human norms. Only eccentric diehards were saying by then that masturbation was evil. And if they conceded that it was in some sense wrong, few would have conceded that it was very wrong. Yet the current Pope, Benedict XVI, continues to emphasise rules of sexual conduct and an understanding of natural sexuality that are odd in these times.

The Catholic church teaches that all its rules for sexual conduct are grounded in reason and natural law, but the Catholic church is defending some odd stuff and believes that all of it is totally compatible with reason. It has ideas about nature and reason which would have made for a much more colourful argument with the New Atheists than many of the others they chose to attack could have come up with.

The Catholic church preaches the 'natural law', or a moral law grounded in nature—not nature understood as the observed behaviour of humanity but as a route to God. Material contraception is sinful, not exactly because it interferes in a natural process. Shooting a lion that is attacking a child also interferes in a natural process, for nature allows lions to eat children. And the church has no problem with human endeavour being applied to preventing that, protecting children being natural, too. The lion would do as much. But sexual lusts provide a focus in our nature for our discipline and spiritual growth; tinkering with that is what contraception does.

Benedict XVI is clear about one thing when he is talking about nature and the need for us to live according to nature. Nature is not a description of what we do. You do not ascertain the nature of humans by watching what they do, the way you would with lions or spiders. What we do in marriage, for instance, is expect that we may divorce in the future. That isn't natural, says the Pope. To understand our nature, you have to understand the *Book of Genesis*.

This would clash with an understanding of nature from an evolutionist, who would argue that nature wants the male seed to be spread as widely as possible, to maximise the conception of offspring. Nature squanders semen like a drunk on pay-day because it wants fresh and fit young women to get pregnant and have strong, healthy children. Some of the modern thinking about evolution is a bit more complex than that. Nature doesn't leave procreation to rapists and the strong and, Steven Pinker argues, has an investment in peace and reciprocal harmony. The offspring of a pillaging army are not likely to be cherished by the chosen spouses of those raped women, and you'd expect nature to prefer that they were. But the Pope's understanding of nature credits it with far greater sophistication and generosity still.

Nature dictates in *Genesis*, he says, that we should not divorce. This strange claim was reported from a question-and-answer session with priests when Benedict was on holiday near Lorenzago di Cadore in 2007. He said:

> It is no longer simply nature that speaks, but *ceteri homines*—other people. What *ceteri homines* do is to get married with the idea that one day the marriage could fail and therefore one could enter a second, third or fourth marriage. This model of 'what everyone else does' becomes a model in contrast to that dictated by nature.

To help couples truly prepare for marriage as the Church and the Creator intends it, we must, the Pope said, recoup the ability to listen to nature, which speaks in a way much different from this modern way.

What is he talking about? He clearly doesn't understand nature as the natural world. To be true to nature, as he has it, is to live by Catholic church rules, even when those rules direct you against your own natural inclinations and happiness.

Humanae Vitae put it like this: 'No member of the faithful could possibly deny that the Church is competent in her magisterium to interpret the natural moral law.'

Pope Benedict said, 'Canon law assumes that man as man, even without great learning, intends to carry out matrimony according to human nature, as it is written in the first chapters of *Genesis*.' Man, being man, and thus possessing human nature, 'knows what marriage is'. Well, yes. Everyone hopes that a marriage will be for life, but how is it being more true to your nature to stay in a failed marriage than to seek happiness elsewhere? It is not recorded that any of the priests in Lorenzago di Cadore asked him that.

> But today this axiom, according to which man intends to do what is in his nature—one faithful marriage—is transformed into a different axiom.

The Pope also said that he 'recognised the suffering' of couples who lived together without having been sacramentally married. He was talking about the increasing number of people who want to stay in the church and receive communion but are barred from it because they have left a sacramental marriage for another relationship. 'A very specific kind of love in these situations is of great importance,' he said.

> And I think that only this love of the Church that they experience, which is made present through various forms of accompaniment, can help these people to see themselves as loved by Christ, members of the Church, even if they are in a difficult situation.

So, once a priest has told you that you can't have communion in his church because you are sleeping with someone other than your spouse, and that this is unnatural, he has an obligation to keep in touch with you and reassure you of Christ's continuing love, presumably in the hope that you will either go back to your sacramentally endorsed spouse or commit to a celibate life. It is hard to imagine that many people would receive this continuing attention in the spirit in which the Pope imagines it can be delivered.

Benedict, as Cardinal Ratzinger, had a reputation for legalism, but his encyclicals are more pietistic and even folksy. This is from *Spe Salvi*:

> There used to be a form of devotion—perhaps less practised today but quite widespread not long ago—that included the idea of 'offering up' the minor daily hardships that continually strike at us like irritating 'jabs', thereby giving them a meaning. Of course, there were some exaggerations and perhaps unhealthy applications of this devotion, but we need to ask ourselves whether there may not after all have been something essential and helpful contained within it. What does it mean to offer something up? Those who did so were convinced that they could insert these little annoyances into Christ's great 'compassion' so that they somehow became part of the treasury of compassion so greatly needed by the human race. In this way, even the small inconveniences of daily life could acquire meaning and contribute to the economy of good and of human love. Maybe we should consider whether it might be judicious to revive this practice ourselves.

Our grandmothers would have approved (you can't help supposing that sexual desire is one of those 'jabs' that Benedict would prefer we 'offered up').

Nothing demarcates the difference between the teaching of the institutional church and the actual relationship between the remaining clergy and the people the way sex does. The papacy and the hierarchy continue to imagine a world in which Catholics follow their prescriptions for sexual conduct, despite all the embarrassment and failure that have followed from past prescriptions proving untenable. Sex more than anything breaks the flow of influence from the hierarchy to the people. Moreover, since the priests understand this and need to preserve a relationship with the few people who still listen to them, they cater more for the laity's common sense about sex than for the hierarchy's strange conception of nature and what is natural.

However, there is one sexually related issue, surely, on which the church and the people agree: abortion. It is not so simple as it was, however. An *Irish Times* poll of attitudes of women in 2007 showed that 54 per cent of Irish women believe that the government should act to permit abortion. The figure goes up to 69 per cent in cases where the life of the woman is in danger. Right enough, it is pretty shocking that 31 per cent agree with *Humanae Vitae* that therapeutic abortion is wrong and would, by inference, rather see a woman die than have a foetus removed prematurely from her womb. A steep age gradient in attitudes, with older women being more conservative, shows that that thinking has changed over time and that the greater tolerance of abortion is recent.

Gerald, an anti-abortion campaigner, argues that Ireland is no longer pro-life. He says: 'We didn't get through to Irish mothers. The fact is that every mother's fear is that her daughter will get pregnant and, when it happens, no matter what her religious principles, she will see the attraction in a quick fix.'

Gerald might be reading the attitude of Irish mothers from their own history of managing the unwanted pregnancies of the past. Mothers who shuffled their daughters into convents in Belfast and Manchester, to have their babies and give them up for adoption, dispensing of the shame, do not, on reflection, seem ideal recruits to the pro-life cause. Ireland has always wanted rid of inconvenient babies and has always inflicted huge pain, if not actual death, on daughters and their babies in pursuit of this. Indeed, so cruel was the dismissal of the daughters and the severing of the babies that we could hardly be confident that the same hearts that urged that would have stopped short of murder. Indeed, the pregnant girls often did not stop short of suicide for fear of facing those mothers.

But suddenly, in modern Ireland, the unwanted baby, so long the focus of our disgust and rejection, has become the core symbol of our Catholic generosity. The unborn child is spoken of as a precious life from the moment of conception. The test question of whether you are a Catholic or not is your commitment to the prior rights of the accidental foetus, a being that had previously been shifted quietly out the Irish back door without the remotest concern for its happiness.

Had we really come to love the foetus, or was this concern fundamentally about something else? Go back to the nineteenth century and the Irish are killing babies in uncounted numbers. There are folksongs about how to get rid of the changeling, the sickly child that the fairies had left with you in exchange for your own bright, healthy baby. If you put it on the fire, it would leap up the chimney and your real child would return. And if that didn't work, at least you had killed only a fairy, and one who had already been rejected by its own. God knows how many sickly or handicapped children had that experiment tried out on them. The changeling was also left to die of exposure in the field. And how many died that way? It's impossible to tell, but the lore itself is proof that Ireland, like most rural societies, had found a way to rationalise the expedient of infanticide. And the manner in which it did that suggests that old religious injunctions were often permission to do what you'd like to do anyway, a surrogate motive for a material interest.

Irish Catholicism was so committed to the right of every sperm to have a clean run at an egg that there were bound to be casualties to be managed. And there was a kind of justice in people dumping their unwanted babies on the church which had led them into such difficulty with arguments against contraception, against masturbation and the injunction to 'render the debt' of sexual gratification on a husband, to spare him the sin of 'incontinence'.

It would, incidentally, have seemed implausible to the Irish Catholic bishops that *women* might also need to be spared the temptation to masturbate. Sales of vibrators on O'Connell Street were as unforeseeable in the 1950s as sales of the mobile phone.

Irish writers saw that the people had a use for the church and understood that use in human rather than spiritual terms. Dermot Bolger develops that theme in his novel *A Second Life*. Who else would have taken in the fallen women and disposed of the unwanted babies? In this novel, an adopted child in later life confronts the nuns. One of them says to him: but without us, you would have ended up in a bog hole. The old, the pregnant, the crazy got put in the home—as did the unwanted children. Who, this book asks, was using whom?

The church reinforced the view that the pregnant women were 'fallen', but the families of these women eagerly sought out the nuns to get them to take those girls and get rid of the babies. Were those families acting out a vision of the good life as taught by the church or was the church merely mopping up the mess created by the values inherent in those families? Or was it a cycle, the church reinforcing the 'holy family' conservatism and then dealing with the mess that followed such beliefs and their clash with nature? There was stern commitment to an idea of respectability, and conspicuous religious attendance was part of that, but did the church initiate that or serve it or find a symbiotic relationship with it?

———

Nature is evoked in Catholic theology as the basis of morality. So, homosexual intercourse cannot be right, says Gerald, the anti-abortion campaigner, because nature has clearly provided the vagina as the proper receptacle for the penis. Yet who but nature has erogenised the rectum and provided for a neat fit there, too? Why couldn't the rectum be a dual-purpose orifice, like the mouth, which serves both ingestion and speech, indeed even kissing too? Surely Gerald wouldn't say that kissing is wrong since it is plain that it is not what the mouth was made for. Maybe he would.

And those who evoked nature in defence of moral sex had little thought for the natural bonding of mother and child when they determined that many babies should be nurtured to full term in convents and then given away. These were the people most vulnerable to the charge that they cared nothing for the inconvenient baby, and suddenly they were howling across the land that nothing mattered so much as the survival of that foetus. This had been the class of people most embarrassed by unplanned pregnancies—illegitimate pregnancies—and suddenly, here they were saying that this foetus, from the moment of conception, must live, must be allowed to live, must have its right to life enshrined in the constitution; that recognition of its right to life is a test of your decency and moral worth. This new fervour cannot have been unrelated to the past anger. That the baby who had meant so little now meant so much says something about the heart of Catholic Ireland, primarily perhaps that it is rank with guilt.

The focus of the anti-abortion campaign was on the idea of the worth of the foetus, not on the practical measures by which its life might be preserved. There was no campaign to produce new adoption facilities, to get the church behind the care of the unwanted child, not just because this would have been impractical but because it would have resonated too much of the past failed way of doing things. There were no longer enough people in the religious orders to take these babies. There never had been enough families to adopt them. The church—where it had the sense to consider it—didn't want them. And any call from the pro-life campaigners for the nuns to take the young mothers and their babies would have been laughed off as too redolent of a scandalous past in which pregnant women and babies had been abused. A society that was now reflecting on the experiences of those abused by the orders wasn't going to buy the idea that the orders were the answer to the problem—even if there had been enough people left in the orders to do the job, and there weren't.

So, perhaps the pro-life campaign can be seen as a shriek of panic from the moralistic Catholics who had always wanted rid of inadvertently conceived children, faced with nothing but a final solution, but aghast at their own distaste for children having led them to it.

'When it comes down to it,' says Gerald, 'the Irish mother wants a quick fix, and we can't beat that.' But she wanted the quick fix traditionally, in part, because Catholic Ireland had always told her that babies not morally conceived were a disgrace to her. That doesn't matter any more.

Catholic Ireland needn't panic. The modern woman who wants an abortion is not agonising before God and St Joseph.

She is not acting in fear of bringing the taint of sin and disgrace on her family. She is not afraid of going to hell. In short, she could say to all the conservative Catholic moralists squirming in guilt, 'It's okay. It's not your fault'. She could say, 'I'm just not ready for this baby and that's got nothing to do with you or your Catholic morality or sin.' If the howling biddies could but see it, secularisation lets them off the hook. They don't have to go on pretending that the babies they never wanted either really mean so much to them.

Chapter 7

The Second Vatican Council must be seen in retrospect by many as a calamity for the Catholic church. It promised a liberalisation that was reversed by *Humanae Vitae*. There was a widespread sense among both liberal and conservative Catholics that their vision of the church was being trifled with. It brought, at first, a general sense among Catholics that a shadow was retreating from them. The status of the cleric was no longer to be higher than that of the lay Catholic. Those who liked the status of the clerical life felt that they were losing it. Disheartened conservatives and disillusioned liberals both walked away. The backbone of the institutional church in Ireland was broken.

Andrew Greeley, writing about the collapse of Catholicism in the United States, goes so far as to describe the return to dogmatism within the Catholic church since then as a 'restoration'. The greater damage was done by the collapse of liberal hopes. But there is also a conservative interpretation of where the council went wrong.

In 2007, John Lamont of the Catholic University of Sydney addressed the question in an article, 'What Was Wrong with Vatican II?', in *New Blackfriars*. Lamont establishes from the start his credibility as a devout Catholic. He asks whether it is indeed legitimate at all to look for flaws within a Vatican Council and cites as the precedent the Third Lateran Council which declared that the evidence of a Christian was always to be accepted before the evidence of a Jew, this being something that no Christian today would accept as reasonable. Freed up then to seek similar flaws in the reasoning of this Second Vatican Council, Lamont finds two which he blames for the collapse of religious ardour among Catholics.

The Council had declared that it was no longer necessary to be a Catholic to be saved. God himself might reach out and save people by direct methods of his own. The only people who were surely damned were those who knew that the Catholic church was a sure route to salvation but still rejected it. Logically, then, a missionary might do more good by *not* telling people about the Catholic church, so that they would not be tempted to an informed rejection that would condemn them to Hell.

The other thing that the Council had done, which had damaged faith, was to ignore evil. This failing was as much in the behaviour of the so-called pastoral bishops and their interpretation of the intentions of the Council, according to Lamont, as in the Council itself. It stemmed from the redefinition of mission. Liturgy had been rewritten to remove references to Hell and the threat of damnation. The Divine Office, centred around the Psalms, was edited to remove references to threats of punishment. From Psalm 62, the bloodthirsty ending was cut:

> But those who seek my life to destroy it will go into the depths of the earth. They will be delivered over to the power of the sword; they will be a prey for foxes. But the king will rejoice in God; everyone who swears by him will glory, for the mouths of those who speak lies will be stopped.

Not only was the church no longer telling people about Hell, it was failing in its own duty to punish, and this explains in part its later leniency towards clergy guilty of sexual abuse.

Lamont says that the pastoral bishops, who were understood to be unwilling to confront the churches, ducked final and moral teachings but would instead treat rejection of dogma as an acceptable option for Catholics. And the Council had left us with 'sappy liturgy' whose contrast with bloodcurdling scripture must have been obvious to many. The new approach to evil carried the message to Catholics that they were doing well enough in obeying the rules and that the days of arduous striving for perfection were over.

Lamont is perplexed that European bishops who had just witnessed the worst war in history less than two decades earlier should have virtually ignored the problem of evil. He wonders if many of those bishops had themselves been personally shamed by collusion with the Nazis. He does not consider the possibility that the war had actually frightened the bishops away from moral absolutism, having shown them the atrocities to which it can lead. If Hell is the consolation of the virtuous, rather than the scourge of the wicked, perhaps the Vatican II bishops let it go because they no longer felt so certain that they deserved such consolation, after the Second World War. They had seen evil, sure enough, but they were no longer so sure that there was a clear distance between it and themselves.

Anyone reading Gitta Sereny's account of the Holocaust, *Into That Darkness*, drawing parallels between the moral retreats of Treblinka Kommandant Franz Stangl and Pope Pius XII, will conclude that the church had had a harsh lesson in how the good are corrupted when they adjust to circumstances, and how it might have become more forgiving of those accused by others of absolute evil. It had been as forgiving itself when it had helped Nazi war criminals to flee secular justice after the war. Could this experience have produced the equivocations about evil in the heart of Vatican II? It would be a strange irony if it had.

The understanding that evil had overtaken Europe in 1940 would have to include the understanding that it had corrupted the Vatican as well. The only way out of that would be to argue against the comprehensive reality of evil, and that's what the good bishops did.

Chapter 8

It is usually assumed and widely accepted that secularisation came late to Ireland. Neighbouring England was perceived throughout the twentieth century by Irish Catholics as a dangerously pagan country. Those who travelled there would lose their faith. This was the core message of mission sermons and pep talks from Christian Brother principals to young men seeking work in Liverpool or London.

That there was a major difference between Ireland and England cannot be doubted but it is not as simple as that England had lost its faith earlier. What alarmed Catholic Ireland about Britain in the 1940s and 1950s was not that it was atheist but that it was Protestant. And it was Protestant. Callum Brown, in *The Death of Christian Britain* (Routledge 2001), has reassessed the secularisation of our neighbouring island and contradicts not just Irish prejudice—of which he, of course, took no account—but also the views of British sociologists. Social scientists had traced the decline of religion in Britain from the nineteenth century. They had seen secularisation as a product of the shift from the land to the cities of millions of people, into squalid slums and lives regulated by the factory horn. These people had identified the church with the hated establishment that had destroyed their rural ways, and they wanted nothing to do with it.

Brown shows that, by some indicators, religious faith was actually increasing in England, Wales and Scotland in the 1940s and 1950s. Nearly two million people went to see the evangelist Billy Graham during his 1954 crusade in London. This was one in twenty British adults—an awesome number until compared to the one million, or 50 per cent of Irish adults, who went to see a new Pope, John Paul II, in Knock in 1979. Religious belief in Britain then was deep and resilient, though the turnout for Graham might not be the best evidence of that, since everyone loves a show. Brown traces the turning point to the early 1960s. That was when England lost its faith. This has implications for our understanding of secularisation in Ireland, for, if it can be shown that the loss of faith occurred in Ireland and in England at the same time, then we must ask seriously if the cause was the same too.

The turning point in Ireland, in the 1960s, is widely credited to the Catholic church's assertive stand against artificial contraception. Catholic women could no longer be honest with their confessors or accept their right to dictate their sexual behaviour. So they ceased in huge numbers to pay any serious attention to the clergy. No such stand against contraception was taken by the Anglican church in England or by the Church of Scotland, and yet both suffered the same collapse at the same time.

Brown traces that collapse to the desertion of the church by women, 'the simultaneous de-pietisation of femininity and the de-feminisation of piety from the 1960s'. Women, he argues, had until then defined respectability by adherence to Christian values. The woman's responsibilities included the defence of the respectability of the family, which was a common-sense consideration anyway. At some point, she decided that her good sense applied to herself as much as to her children and her home. And when she turned on the priest and the church with the same scalding and rooted 'catch yourself on' that she had until then applied only in the home, the church withered for want of her collusion. She looked at what was expected of her, that she be a moral icon, morality having most to do with sexual probity, saw it clearly and simply shrugged it off. The ease with which she shrugged it off raises doubts, as it must in Ireland, too, about whether she had ever really been committed on her own behalf at all.

Men had 'chaperoned' women to church, but as soon as women stopped going, men stopped going too. New values replaced the old ones. Whereas previously, sexual responsibility had been defined as marriage and obedience, it came to be defined as the independence of a woman making practical decisions about relationships which she would enter into or leave as she saw fit. Now a woman who left a marriage would find herself in a community that respected and accepted her decision, and even admired it, while her mother, had she made a similar decision twenty years earlier, would have been reviled as a loose woman of no character.

Did contraception play a part in this transformation? The English Protestant woman would not be barred from using contraception, in the way the Catholic woman would, but she would be freed by it from the need to attend to the church's definition of respectability. She could protect her daughter now from a binding pregnancy by means other than imposing church-centred notions of responsibility and respectability on her; she could do it by teaching her to use the contraceptive pill. Was this really any different from the revolution that was occurring in Ireland at the same time? In Ireland, the woman would have to resist the church's bar on the contraceptive pill to secure the same freedom for herself, but it was the same freedom, enabled by the same pill.

No new religious faith supplanted Christianity in England, Scotland and Wales. The core values, Brown says, came to be expressed in different forms. Whereas abstinence from alcoholic drink had previously been a religious value, it came to be expressed, in the post-Christian era, through the practical need to drive safely. Thrift became an environmental value. Love of all God's creatures was now animal rights. Steven Pinker, in *The Blank Slate* (2003), has described how even in secular societies behaviours come to be moralised in new ways. The intriguing thing is that many of the things that we have moralised in our secular age—diet, smoking, alcohol and safe sex—replicate closely the concerns that the churches had previously tried to impose on us.

Brown observes that this rapid secularisation was a phenomenon within the white native Christian churches of Britain and that other religious strains coming into the country were not affected by it. He also questions, strongly, the argument of the social scientist and the historian that the decline of religion is an inevitable by-product of industrialisation and urbanisation. These cannot account for a change that came as suddenly as did the decline of religion in Britain, he says.

Whatever does explain it, there are priests now who say that they are glad of this change. It means that people come to church not because they are afraid but because they seek the spiritual riches that are there. But the church did not lightly give up its authority and showed little sign, when it had it, of understanding that life would be better for all when this authority was gone.

Chapter 9

Catholic people themselves decide now what it is to be Catholic, and it may include a strange diversity of ideas and practices. The Catholic church no longer regulates the lives of most people in Ireland. There are many fewer clergy and religious among us. Those nuns who remain are no longer dressed in conspicuous habits. One of the biggest changes anyone today would notice, if transported back in time forty years, would be the greater number of nuns and priests and brothers they would pass on the street, or see at bus stops. And those people would be treated with respect and reverence wherever they went. People would suppress their own frivolity as they passed.

The modern church is supported by some who find spiritual and psychological refreshment within it and by some who are simply called back by habit. The Irish have still not, by and large, found a better way to be married or buried. The fact that many of us who are drawn to church for weddings and funerals are not impressed by what we hear produces an increasing tension between the institutional church and the secular world.

The church asserts its right to have its norms acknowledged by those who require its services. It is entitled to do that. This produces amusing and painful anomalies: the couple who have lived together for years before marriage having to submit to a premarital course, conducted by a celibate priest; having to confess their living together as a sin, though for them it is the foundation of their confidence that they are ready to commit to each other.

We bury our atheist dead in holy ground, rarely having asked them if that is what they wanted, because that is the easy way to deal with something that has come upon us suddenly. So we see the embarrassed priest enunciate promises of sure and certain salvation that he knows few in his congregation take seriously. Of course, many people perhaps don't mind what words are spoken. Between the rump of committed devotees and the few atheists, there are the à la carte Catholics who take the bits they like and live with or ignore the bits they don't. Perhaps they concede that this is poetry and not to be taken literally anyway.

The assumption now must be that most Catholics are à la carte, taking from dogma what suits them and discarding the rest. But when weren't they à la carte? What is a table d'hôte Catholic? Is it someone who accepts without reservation what the church provides in spiritual teaching? Are there any of these? Were there ever any table d'hôte Catholics who preferred to ask a priest what was right or wrong than to work it out for themselves?

Dogma isn't important to people; it isn't important even to priests any more. It *is* important to bishops. If the Catholic church announced tomorrow that it accepted the reality of reincarnation, many Catholics would find that interesting but not disruptive. There would be a few television debates about the subject and some reassurance from a bishop that we are not compelled to believe in it but no longer forbidden to. Something like 10 per cent of people who call themselves Catholics already do. For many ordinary believers their sense of what it is to be a Catholic would not have radically changed, certainly not as radically as when the vernacular liturgy was introduced.

The ambivalence to doctrine became clear in 2006 when an Augustinian priest in Drogheda concelebrated the Eucharist with a Church of Ireland minister, in clear violation of church rules, and newspapers were inundated with letters of support for him from Catholic laity who rejected the hierarchy's ruling against intercommunion. Fr Iggy O'Donovan had invited Rev. Michael Graham, Church of Ireland rector at St Peter's Church in Drogheda, County Louth, to share with him in a gesture of unity at mass in the Augustinian priory. Few, if any, among the laity saw this as anything but Christian decency in practice. But when the church made its position clear, the laity accepted that too.

The laity did not feel that being Catholic required them to comprehend dogma. There appeared at first to be a change in their willingness to allow the hierarchy to comprehend dogma on their behalf. For a moment, it seemed as if their preference for civility over dogma would prevail. In fact, the church did what it had always done and reminded the errant priest of his duty of obedience. He took that to heart and apologised as ordered. And the laity who had supported him did not rise up to protest against his humiliation.

———

The à la carte Catholic is everywhere. Some of them are looking for spiritual consolation in other churches, without giving up their own. This reflects the ease with which they shop around in the modern spiritual supermarket. Attachment to a church is no longer like attachment to a spouse. It is not seen as infidelity to cross the road and hear what the pastor there is saying. And when attachment to church is drawn from family tradition and neighbourhood, rather than from spiritual gratification, it may be necessary to stray, to find endorsement of the person you feel yourself to be.

Many spiritual revolutions in the past have started among working-class people who were not impressed by the over-bearing theology of the church into which they were born, and sensed a class tension between themselves and those educated people who were explaining God and the afterlife to them. They wanted to be free to intuit and understand these things themselves and to work under the leadership of people who thought as they did and did not patronise them. Hence Methodism, Quakerism and the whole revolution of evangelicalism that produced house churches and city missions all over the country.

The same instinct produced in England the spiritualist churches. These churches taught the simple theology of an afterlife in which the soul found reward or retribution. There is no Hell, but there are lower regions in which sinners suffer but are still loved and not denied the chance to evolve. The souls are reborn—as in Hinduism—to try again and ascend the planes to perfection.

One of the stars of the spiritualist circuit in England was the clairaudient Doris Stokes, who preached and demonstrated her mediumistic skills in Morecambe and Lancaster in the early 1970s. Doris had the distinctively homely manner familiar within the spiritualist churches and passed messages to members of the congregation, often rebuking the spirits for clamouring around her and telling them not to be talking over each other. She presented the other world as a plane of domestic and simple concerns.

There is currently only one spiritualist church in Ireland, in Belfast. It is a small, brick-built church hall on Malone Avenue, next door to a similar building used by the Baptists. There, mediums are trained to develop their ability to commune with spirits of the dead, and hundreds of people are packed in to hear the messages in the hope that there might be one for themselves.

On one Sunday night, the medium is Diane Mitchell, a soft-spoken Scottish woman, probably in her sixties. Diane has that same warm approach that reassures the congregation that she is not a charlatan and that the spirit world is not a scary place. 'I'm feeling a gentleman close to me and I am smelling cigarette smoke. He's your father or grandfather. I think he is your father—is that right?'

The observer suspects that it would not be difficult to replicate these intuitions with a close attention to the responses from the person to whom the messages are addressed.

'I feel he was a strong man.'

What son doesn't feel that his father was a strong man?

To another, Diane says: 'Your mother passed over after a long struggle, a painful struggle? Does that make sense? No? Well, perhaps this message is for the woman beside you. I am drawn to that part of the room. Does it make sense to you, dear? Yes. Good. Then we're on our way.'

The advice is always general: 'Hang in there, dear. Things will settle down. These dark times won't last forever. You will find yourself on a more even plain, and you'll be able to see your way more clearly.' And people in the congregation sometimes gasp with relief and gratitude.

It is easy to sneer at this. But what differences are there between this and the consolations of the other churches? All promise the survival of death. It is equally easy for other churches and those who don't believe in any church to sneer at the spiritualists and their ostensibly amateurish religion. But spiritualists have much in common with others—too much for those others to be smug about. They provide what all churches offer, the assurance of life after death. And they do it with a frankness that others can't match, because they deliver the proof.

Yes, but only to the impressionable? Well, what churches don't address the impressionable? All ask for faith in mysteries. What exactly is it that other churches expect of reasonable, mature believers but not of the spiritualist—that they believe in saints in Heaven who work occasional miracles but don't turn up in little halls for mediums? Why would they expect the saints to observe such limits on their conduct? The spiritualists actually challenge the other churches to own up to whether or not they really believe in what they preach. There isn't a lot of difference between the Catholic bishops calling on the faithful to solicit a miracle from the late John Paul II or Mother Teresa, in the cause of their canonisation, and Mrs Johnson from Plevna Street asking Diane Mitchell for a message from her uncle George. Is there?

It is the spiritualists who usually get blamed for making contact with the famous, but it seems that the church is only interested in the famously religious, while telling us, all the time, that all survive.

At a funeral in Donegal for a boy killed in a road accident, the priest said: 'When Peter and Jesus met in the early hours of last Sunday morning, each will have recognised the other as a friend.' This priest believed clearly that Peter dead was still the person he was before he died; that he might even answer prayers and draw close to those who loved him. Why not then ask him where he left the remote for the video or his credit union book? The embarrassment about spiritualism is that it restores the simple faith of the simple people at a time when thinkers in the modern church are becoming more psychological and secular in their thinking.

People are defecting from the churches both to the more concrete and to the more abstract. At a meeting in Taney Road Parish Hall near Dundrum in south Dublin, the Open Christianity Network meets to hear Bishop Richard Holloway tell them that you can still be a Christian and not take the scriptures too literally. And the audience is gasping for that message as eagerly as the congregation in the Spiritualist church was gasping for an affirmation of the proximity of the other world. Holloway tells them that they can be secular without ditching their attachment to church. Scripture is now poetry rather than reportage and instruction—regardless of the fact that for 2,000 years that's all it was.

'What use is it to me to know that Christ rose corporeally from the dead?' asks Holloway. 'What's important is that his ideas live on.'

Ideas aren't enough for the people of simple faith. The spiritualists, for all that they are almost Neolithic in their simplicity, are the ultimate in à la carte believers. Many of those who go to their church are also practising Catholics. The relaxed rule of Sabbath observance, that allows Catholics to go to Sunday mass on a Saturday night, leaves them free to go to another church on Sunday—and in Belfast a few go to the spiritualist church and see no conflict between their Catholic observance and their spiritualist beliefs, including the belief in reincarnation.

Were it left to the church authorities to define who is and is not a Catholic, who is and is not a believer of the system they expound, there would be mass expulsions of the kind of people who visit the likes of spiritualist mediums and Bishop Holloway. There would also be a mass defection of nuns.

———

In the aftermath of the Second Vatican Council came the liberation of nuns within the orders, the throwing off of old habits—in both senses—and mass resignations from these orders. Karen Armstrong has described that revolution in her autobiographical books. With such a flood of nuns out of the orders, you would expect that what was left inside was only the most conservative of Catholic women, committed to the old ways. You would be wrong. In many cases, it was the conservatives who could not adapt to the new ways and left. Visit a home of sisters in Ireland today, meet nuns about their work, and you're likely to encounter women of strong, radical thinking. There are fewer of them but they are in a happier position than the diocesan priests because they do not have to answer directly to the bishops. Sister Kathleen Fitzgerald of the Loreto order says:

> There has been a huge change in the way our whole society operates. Television brought into our houses another vision of other things happening. Then more people moved out of their home and away somewhere else to work and I suppose really change happened very, very quickly and things began to be questioned in a much more open way.

The modern sister has a more independent life, if she wants it. For the past five years, Kathleen has lived alone in an apartment. She was given the job of maintaining the Loreto Archive in a house on Stephen's Green.

> I was offered that life and I was happy to do it. Now I have a foot in both camps. I live in my apartment for part of the week, when I am working here on the archives, and I am also responsible for a community, in Loreto in Dalkey.

Old Church—new use. (*Above left*) Tourism centre, Dublin. *(Mel Boyle)* (*Above right*) Methodist Church HQ, Belfast—to let! (*Below*) Sligo Library.

Derelict church, Ormeau Road, Belfast.

Crumbling icon. A gravestone in Strabane seems to symbolise more than the sculptor intended.

Religious and spiritual imagery still has marketing value. Ornamental Buddhas for sale in Dunnes (*above*). Yoga with chips (*below*).

Dance with the devil (*above*). Souvenir shop, Westport (*below*).

Fr Brian D'Arcy.

Sr Kathleen Fitzgerald ('Superior to whom?')

Poet Paul Durcan, a subversive Catholic.

Justyna Pers, says she was more Catholic in Poland.

Soline Humbert, called by God to be a Catholic priest.

Croagh Patrick. (*Top*) Mountain rescue on Croagh Patrick. Shouldn't the pilgrims have helmets too? (*Above*) Pilgrims scrambling to the top of Croagh Patrick.

A fallen pilgrim is taken to safety from Croagh Patrick.

A hopeful beggar appeals to religious sentiment on O'Connell Street. *(Mel Boyle)*

Nuns' graves; who will tend them now?

The Cardinal's hat hanging from ceiling of Armagh Cathedral
will fall when he gets out of purgatory.

The new face of religion in Dublin.

Sunlight through stained glass, Carnlough.

Shop window, O'Connell Street.

Cardinal mocked by media.

(*Above*) A statue and holy pictures dumped in a Connemara shed. (*Mel Boyle*)
(*Below*) An old church in Connemara is a relic of our religious past.
(*Mel Boyle*)

There are seventeen sisters in the community house. At 62, she is one of the youngest.

> I am the community leader. Years ago they would have called me the superior, but superior to what? To have been asked to come there as a leader was a gift to me because they are very fine women.

But won't her generation be lumbered with the job of looking after the older ones and then be stranded without carers in their turn? Shouldn't she have got out for her own good? She doesn't think the order is dying out. 'There have been times before when it was like this,' she says.

However, there will have to be new ideas and new ways. Even if there *were* young women wanting to spend their lives the way Kathleen has spent hers, they would not be welcome on those terms.

> I would be hoping that anyone who was thinking of joining us was coming with an idea, that they weren't coming to be like me. I would hope to be able to encourage them and support them in the idea. That's my hope.

And the old way is dying.

> I don't think I made the wrong choice in staying in, not that I wasn't at times angry with something. There were times of crisis, you know.

Has she ever had a lover?

> No lovers, I wouldn't have let myself go that far. There were people that I liked. There was someone and I felt I could see myself with this person. My rationalising was that I had met this person through my work as a Loreto sister, and if I wasn't a Loreto sister I wouldn't have met him, and somehow in the providence of the Lord I could accept that.

I didn't fall madly in love. I was able to put the brakes on a bit. And I was enriched by knowing him.

The Sisters of the Cross and Passion were a teaching missionary order. They worked with the factory girls of the North of England. Many Irish girls joined the order and some of them came back to teach in schools or to run retreat houses. At a little primary school in Ballycastle, in the shadow of Knocklayde, the nuns in their billowing robes taught children of four, five and six the story of Jesus, their first catechism and the alphabet. They laid down rules for good order, as they saw it. The girls in the mixed class were not to wear slacks. The nuns did not use proper canes but had little wooden strips of the light wood off an orange box to slap their wee hands with, without hurting them too much.

The sun shone in from the playground, which was a more anxious space for a little boy. At the end of term, the nuns invited the children to bring in orange juice and buns for a little party in the classroom and supervised them to be sure they weren't spilling crumbs onto the floor. This was a simple start to Catholic life, and the parents and, perhaps, grandparents of these children had known it the same. Who made the world? God made the world. Who is God?

Later, some of the girls in the class would go to Belfast or Manchester or London to be nuns or nurses or teachers. The Sisters of the Cross and Passion would seek to support them in their faith, inviting them to retreat houses, like the house at Drumalis, on the Antrim coast outside Larne. Drumalis had been the home of a rich merchant family called Smiley. It had been lavishly designed by the Scottish artist Walton with individually crafted fireplaces, a different doorknob for every room, marble and stained-glass in the lavish art deco style. The house has recently been restored with a grant of nearly £1 million from the Heritage Lottery Fund.

During that restoration, workmen took down the panelling with which the sisters had divided splendour into little cubicles for those on retreat. Those working-class women from the cities had been brought to a mansion for prayer but were shown very little of its style. Some of the women may have been perplexed to see a stained-glass dome depicting the Red Hand of Ulster. The Smileys had been Ulster Unionists. The importation of guns for the UVF in 1912 had been planned in the Smiley drawing-room and some of those guns had been landed at the bottom of the Drumalis garden.

Nearly all middle-aged Catholic women from Belfast have memories of Drumalis, of the silent retreats some had as schoolgirls, of the more open retreats they had as adult women, when the sisters decided that the violence in Belfast had changed their requirements from spiritual silence to a safe place to talk. It wasn't a retreat from the temptations of the city now, but a retreat from the dangers and stresses of a sectarian civil war.

The liberalisation of the regime at Drumalis coincided with a relaxing of attitudes within the order. The sisters were giving up the robes and headgear. An advantage of that was that they were not so conspicuous in a Protestant town. But with the further radicalisation of Catholic attitudes, fewer women came on retreats and fewer sisters were available to run them.

Today Drumalis looks more like it did when the Smileys owned it. Only two Sisters of the Cross and Passion live there, Margaret Rose McSparran, who grew up in the Glens of Antrim, and Anna Hainey, a Scot. Anna and Margaret Rose do not own up to being religious rebels but if Joseph Ratzinger, in his former role in the Congregation for the Doctrine of the Faith, had visited Drumalis, he would have seen much that would have perplexed him, from classes in Zen Buddhism, led by the co-abbot of the San Francisco Zen Centre, Paul Haller, to gatherings of the devotees of Gaia. Zen Buddhism may be a worthy pursuit but it is not Catholicism and it cannot easily be theologically reconciled to Catholicism.

The alternative, however, to running Drumalis as an open conference and retreat centre, catering for a diversity of interests, is that it would close, as other monasteries, convents and similar centres around Ireland have closed. There is insufficient interest among Catholics to keep them going in their old form, and therefore some other interest has to be found to sustain them.

Of course, many of those who go to Abbot Paul's Zen classes regard themselves as Catholic and do go to mass; they just don't define Catholicism in the same terms in which the Pope does. He may be the head of the church, infallible in his pronouncements on faith and morals, but that doesn't mean you have to pay any heed to him at all, other than as a titular head or symbol, a bit like the Queen—and you wouldn't want the Queen telling you what you could or couldn't do.

Zen and the Gaia are nice, almost neutral, theologies, however. Abbot Paul explains that Zen is an approach to life, not a system of teachings. It does not require any agreed lore or body of knowledge. It does not even require the reverencing of Buddha. This meditation is not prayer—it is the emptying of the mind, not the focusing of it in devotion. Gaia sees planet Earth as the mother. Well, so long as you are only actually thinking metaphorically, why couldn't you believe that and be a Catholic too?

The real change at Drumalis is that it no longer prescribes spiritual solutions in line with doctrine, but makes itself available for others who are seeking spiritual consolation and inspiration according to their own needs and ideas. The sisters are not into running it as people who know better than those who come to them what is good for them or what God wants of them.

———

The radical change in religious thinking in Ireland today tempers the importance of belief. Faith, as the church had sought to teach us, included assent to theological principles, church doctrine. You were not properly a member of the church if you did not declare your belief in things that you often could not even understand. The modern à la carte Catholic negotiates doctrine with blithe disregard. The tensions created by the demand for assent were played out in the novel *Father Ralph* by

Gerald O'Donovan, discussed above. Writing in 1913, O'Donovan described a Catholic clergy in Ireland which was sycophantic and cynical. The bishop has returned from Rome with a copy of the encyclical which will affirm papal infallibility, to demand of the young priests in his diocese that they declare their support for it. Young Father Ralph refuses and is suspended from the priesthood.

Here we see the differing attitudes to Catholic dogma. Those who assert it most strongly are the ambitious priests and bishops within the hierarchy, seeking to ingratiate themselves with Rome. Below them are the priests who want an easy life and simply do what is expected of them without any sense of their consciences being compromised. 'Sure no one ought to mind about signing a thing like that,' says Father Dempsey. 'What is it but a little bit of paper? There isn't much meaning in theology anyway.'

Then there are the devout churchgoing Catholics, like Father Ralph's mother, and Ann, his housekeeper, who take the word of the church on what is right and what is wrong and fail to comprehend that Father Ralph's individual stand against the church can have any merit or decency in it. Still, Ann the housekeeper concludes that there is goodness in Father Ralph and determines to pray for him so that he might, in the end, do the only conceivably right thing and submit to the church.

Perhaps Father Ralph's housekeeper Ann is the model of the table d'hôte Catholic who does not trust herself to please God with her own judgment but relies on the guidance of a priest. Surely even priests nowadays prefer that people think for themselves.

All Catholics are à la carte now but some go to church and never hear anything that offends them. If the church's rejection of artificial contraception was embodied in the liturgy, perhaps they would still go.

There is a word, of course, for a Catholic who relies on conscience and reason, rather than on the Pope, to interpret the will of God. That word is Protestant. Although it has not been formalised as such, Catholic Ireland has passed through a reformation. Protestant is the proper term for an à la carte Catholic. This has implications in the North, where much of the sectarian animosity towards Catholics has been predicated on the assumption that they were docile and ignorant people who took instruction from Rome and were therefore not qualified by maturity and responsibility to participate in a democracy. If people were not thinking for themselves, then they were not voting responsibly. A Catholic populace, however, which exercises that most protestant of freedoms, the freedom to think, to deflate the authority of a monolith like Rome, is the best possible example to people anywhere who are indoctrinated and manipulated.

But the Catholic reformation has not split the Catholic church, has not produced a European war, as the last reformation did. People could stop acting like Catholics, obeying like Catholics, and could still carry on going to church; the difference now would be that the church would be a facility to which they would resort as they pleased, not a dominant force in their lives.

In the Republic, this would mean that, where no ardent communal division between Protestant and Catholic existed, people could feel more free to move between churches, without feeling that they had surrendered core principles or even family allegiances. The trend until then—because of the Catholic church determination that children of mixed marriages should be raised as Catholics—had been that, where a Catholic and a Protestant married, it was the Protestant who converted. This trend slowed down when the Catholic church relaxed that rule. After the Catholic reformation, of the mid-1960s, we started to see Catholics, in small numbers convert to Protestantism, join Protestant churches, send their children to Protestant schools.

It is still more difficult for a Catholic to switch churches than it is for a Protestant. The Protestant has Protestant alternatives and many shift from staid and stuffy Anglican or Methodist congregations into upbeat evangelical ones. Catholics, by contrast, tend either to stop going to church altogether or to hang on in the pews but disconnect intellectually from the preaching there. A Catholic congregation is, therefore, more likely than a Protestant one to be a disconnected congregation. Catholics are more likely to go on describing themselves as adherents to their church while observing a diverse range of spiritual interests, from spiritualism to Gaia, Bishop Holloway's unbelieving belief and Zen Buddhism.

Yes, many formerly religious people have decided that they don't believe in God and don't care what the church wants them to do. But change affects more than them. The shift has been throughout the whole believing community. Some would say that it is more properly described as a liberalising than a secularising, and that those who stand with the New Atheists like Richard Dawkins, in the total rejection of the idea of God, are still in a minority.

Part Two

The Great Debate

Chapter 10

The decline of religion in Ireland is so far advanced that it rarely excites the Dublin commentariat, many members of which happily sneer at faith. Not all of them are the radical atheists that Vincent Twomey fears, and those who are must surely admit privately that he wildly exaggerates their impact on the spiritual character of modern Ireland. Some are religious.

In March 2007, the *Irish Times* columnist John Waters responded warmly to an attack by the then Taoiseach Bertie Ahern on what he, Ahern, called 'aggressive secularism'. Waters was pleased to hear a political leader say that we should do more than just tolerate the religious but that we should also engage with them.

We are suffering at present, the Taoiseach said, from 'a form of aggressive secularism which would have the state and state institutions ignore the importance of the religious dimension'. These secularists, said Ahern, argue that 'the state and public policy should become intolerant of religious belief' and confine it, at best, to the purely private and personal, without rights or a role within the pubic domain. 'Such illiberal voices would diminish our democracy,' said Ahern. 'They would deny a crucial dimension of the dignity of every person and their rights to live out their spiritual code within a framework of lawful practice which is respectful of the dignity and rights of all citizens.'

Furthermore: 'It would be a betrayal of the best traditions of Irish republicanism to create such an environment.'

Here was an Irish leader, in supposedly secular times, saying plainly that religious belief was 'a crucial dimension of the dignity of every person'. The churches didn't whoop for joy, perhaps because they are too tired, but 'lapsed agnostic' John Waters wanted to underscore the importance of Ahern's speech and took it for being more than the normal platitudinous stroking of an audience by a politician.

Whereas the secularist argues that the state should treat religion as a private matter for individuals, Ahern was saying that it would be a denial of the republican tradition to do so. If that was what he meant, then the doors of government were open once again to archbishops and cardinals. Waters was delighted and perhaps read more ardour into Ahern's speech than was really there. He used the speech as a springboard for his own claim that the religious notion is inherent in all of us, an appetite as real as the sexual instinct.

This was a claim that John Waters did not substantiate, and it would not be easy to substantiate it. Waters may be appalled that people give up faith, which he says they need, but he would have to concede that they appear to do so without any great sense of loss. Religion seems easily set aside. Where people attempt to suppress the sexual instinct, it rebounds dangerously. Church tradition has taught us that much, though it set out to teach us differently. It is plainly obvious that many people today walk the streets of Cork and Limerick oblivious to any need for God or faith and showing none of the tension or unease that is conspicuous in those who repress more demanding instincts. They don't linger around churches, wrestling with the urge to pray the way deprived lechers betray their interest in passing young women.

Still, Waters argues, the social symptoms of loss of religion are clear, and they are the same symptoms to which the bishops point when they make the same argument: alcohol, drugs, consumerism and sex crime. These all follow from the desperation to fill the God-shaped hole with things that can't fill it.

Increasingly, our society manifests an erosion of hope, a misdefinition of freedom and a collapse of meaning, and all of these phenomena are directly related to the disappearance from our culture of what we know as religion. This is not simply because the Catholic church has lost the authority to tell us what to do, but because, in the absence of a religious consciousness, there is, ultimately, no hope, no meaning and no freedom.

Vincent Twomey might have written that but is it true? Don't millions of people around the world live happily with the 'absence of a religious consciousness' and raise their children and take holidays in the sun and enjoy a beer at the weekends?

And it is not a simple matter to credit any social change in Ireland to the 'disappearance from our culture of what we know as religion'. What is it that we know as religion? Is it church attendance, which is down, or is it belief in God, which is still almost universal? Is it a sense of there being some indefinable spiritual context to our existence which feels stronger and clearer when you are listening to Beethoven or having an orgasm?

In a follow-up article, Waters attacked the secularists for their lack of 'philosophical rootedness' arising from a 'neurotic response to a bad experience of Catholicism'. He was saying that those who reject the church are doing so with a chip on their shoulders rather than with a coherent case. Now he had identified the enemy of religion as the grievance of the unthinking, but he had not yet defined religion as anything other than an innate hunger that once had greater cultural expression in Ireland.

Was there some other experience of religion in Ireland once, that was better than the bad religion to which so many of us were responding neurotically? What characterised Irish Catholicism was not the freedom to express innate human needs like the sexual instinct and religious devotion. Irish Catholicism was expressed as an authoritarian culture which belittled human needs; which would have celebrated neither the sexual instinct nor even the idea that the tendency to seek God was 'innate'. Its actual teaching was that if anything was innate, it was sin and that only by the acquisition of grace, mediated by the church, might one develop a pure and devout heart. Yes, it had ideas about nature which suggested that to be truly virtuous was to be truly human, but it had never trusted people to find this virtuous humanity within themselves, unguided by the church. Waters is clear that the religion of which we are bereft is Catholicism but he sounds more like a naturalist than a Catholic.

He accepted that damage was done in Ireland by 'a dysfunctional church' and that an extension of that damage is the 'widening gap between society and belief'. But he seems to be saying that we were better off with 'a dysfunctional church' than we are now without it. Better a warped church than no church at all?

Waters goes further and claims that even the sense of hope that atheists feel 'derives not from their own philosophical resting-place but from the residual background radiation of a once intense, if flawed, cultural faith'. So even the atheists show symptoms of having faith? But if so, that would seem to be evidence in favour of the argument for innate belief rather than for the merits of the Catholic church. Waters would have made his case better if he had traced that faith he detects in atheists back to the innate religious tendency he had claimed is in us all, but he didn't; he identified it as a survival from our past religious culture.

Waters lost his own argument in other ways. The dichotomy in Irish society is not between believers and atheists. The believers are no longer wholly convinced. There are very few atheists at all, and we all go shopping and drinking—atheists and believers alike. We are not separated by the materialist consumer society but united by it.

'In the absence of a religious consciousness,' he says, 'there is, ultimately, no hope, no meaning and no freedom.' But if the religious tendency is innate, then, presumably, religious consciousness can be made absent only through heroic denial or cataclysmic ignorance of human nature. There is another possibility, perhaps, and that is sublimation.

What is a religious consciousness? Is it belief in God? Obviously not in all religious cultures. Buddhists don't believe in God—or at least the theologically sound ones don't. How is a religious consciousness different from the aesthetic sense which finds uplift and hope in music and art? Is a music lover, stirred to tears by Bach, experiencing something different from what the worshipper feels at a Bach mass? Is there really any difference between that and the sense of transcendence which overcomes the opera lover listening to Puccini? If it is belief in God, then most Irish people still have that, even if they are not engaged passionately with their idea of God. If it is transcendence, then many atheists have that. Not even John Waters is saying that it is found best expressed in adherence to a church. So what is he saying?

Well, he gives us his definition of religion, as expressed in a reply he wrote to an atheist who took issue with him.

> I shared with him my favourite definition of religion, from the writings of Fr Luigi Giussani. Imagine, he demanded, that, at this very moment, you have just been born—but with all your faculties, emotions, intellect and other powers of apprehension intact. What, he asked, is your response to reality?
>
> The answer: it will be an intense and radical attraction to reality, combined with a profound sense that you have not yourself created one atom of it. That, he said, is religion.

No, it's not. That is a sense of wonder, a sense of belonging in nature but being humbled by it; that is a sensibility described also by Wordsworth. None of it presupposes a creator God. It raises a question. It doesn't provide an answer. Many non-believers would agree with Waters that that is a good starting point, but they would give it a different name. Waters is defining religion as a response to the world as not of one's own making. This is not Catholicism. But his argument is predicated on a decline in religion as measured by a decline in Catholicism.

There is, in fact, no evidence that religion, as he defines it in the end, is in decline at all. Is anyone measuring our sense of wonder at a world not of our making? Waters has thrown his own case away. He attributes the secular attitude to a grievance against a dysfunctional church. Yet it is perfectly possible to harbour such a grievance and still be religious by his definition—to reject the church and still respond with wonder and humility to a world not of your making. Indeed, many people would think that that is a definition of poetry rather than a definition of religion.

If the church was not the embodiment of religious sentiment in Ireland, then the collapse of that church cannot be read as the death of such sentiment. You cannot presume that a decline in a church has led to a decline in a particular type of sensibility, particularly if you acknowledge that that same church was dysfunctional and for many did not foster that sensibility. The decline of a dysfunctional church may indeed speak of a refinement of sensibility among people who were previously amenable to it.

The anomaly in the case against secularisation is that even those who most ardently bemoan it do not want the old church restored. They agree that it was dysfunctional. What they need, and lack, is a coherent, new spiritual vision that will be strong enough to motivate powerful cultural and social change. Without it they are as secularised as the rest of us.

———

Waters started out by citing a speech by the Taoiseach, Bertie Ahern, calling for dialogue with believers. Ahern went further than Waters to add, not that atheists were in denial of their real nature, but that many were good people who had helped to shape modern Ireland. So, as usual, he was stroking everybody.

> Many have contributed to building up Irish society and to the quality of our democracy, and the humanity of our society, from a philosophical basis which owes little or nothing to religious faith or practice. The dialogue process which we are inaugurating today includes, as a core and defining feature, engagement with that important and growing section of Irish society.

Waters appears to have missed this injunction to treat atheists as people with beliefs as valid as his own. He appears also to have mistaken a Taoiseach who was simply bending to please both sides for a radical new spiritual force in Ireland. But he has opened an important debate on the question of what, if anything, Ireland has really lost by walking away from the church. John Waters is not the only public figure ready to confess that he has been surprised by the value of a religious tradition he had previously disdained.

Graham Norton is a modern Irish comedian, wholly freed from authoritarian church restraints. He appears to be fully liberated from any sexual inhibition and submissive only to his own nature. He grew up a West Cork Protestant and, in his memoir, *So Me*, expresses no attachment to church or faith until his father dies and he finds himself grieving at the funeral. Now he is at a church service, joining in the prayers, listening to music, encountering the whole Irish cultural response to a bereaved family in the community, and he sees this culture in an entirely new way: 'All the things I had thought were there to hold me back I now found were there to hold me up.'

He has discovered the value in a religious culture without having actually conceded anything to the church's teachings which inform that culture. It wasn't Christian doctrine that Graham Norton was held up by when he visited Cork for his father's funeral. It was a more diffuse, more humanitarian culture of generosity, which was religious in its form but totally inclusive. But that contemporary culture has more in common with liberal à la carte-ism than with any dogmatic religion which, in a previous generation, would have barred his supportive Catholic neighbours from this Protestant funeral.

Viewed this way, it is the à la carte-ism that is traditional, civil and instinctive, and dogmatism that was the problem and an aberration within a more generous culture. And liberalisation is actually a restoration of a more humane and inclusive way of managing rites of passage. And this culture is religious. One of its strengths, as Norton observed, is that it does death better than the English do it.

Where then is Graham Norton to be located in the spiritual map that John Waters has drawn of modern Ireland? He is not a practising Christian but he accepts spiritual support within a religious culture, at least when he needs it, and shares with his readers his experience of the value of it. He concedes that religion is good for us, occasionally anyway, regardless of whether or not we buy the whole package. In that, he is more in tune with the mood of modern Ireland than, say, the bishops are.

It is the refusal to buy the whole package that distinguishes the liberalised Irish Christian of today, rather than the rejection of the whole package. But are these à la carte followers really Christians at all?

The northern poet Eoghan Walls illustrates a modern Catholic's ambiguous relationships with the church and faith in his introduction to his poetry in the collection *Incertus* (Netherlea Press 2007). He is describing his wedding:

> The wedding showed me that church cannot be viewed only as a charming anachronism. My relationship with Catholicism is fraught yet fondly retained, but there was an obligatory confession at which contraception was presented as one of the sins. It felt like an imposition of power ... Five minutes down the beach we laughed it off and said it was bollocks, but only after mutely reciting our penance. At our wedding we swore that there would be three people in our marriage, and maybe I did nod silent thanks to the clouds.

There are two ways to define a Catholic. One definition is a person who has been baptised, comprehends Catholic laws and, believing in the theological basis of those laws, sincerely seeks to adhere to them. The other definition is one who has been baptised and then likes to feel Catholic but regards the strict letter of dogma and doctrine as unimportant.

It is not just formal Catholics of the first kind who take issue with the relaxed Catholics of the second kind. Atheists and

secularists have problems with them too and accuse them of
inconsistency and insincerity. The trouble is, they are probably
the greater number of Catholics in Ireland today. They go to
mass the odd time; Christmas and maybe a few more occasions.
They want to receive some of the sacraments: they'd like to be
married in church or have their children baptised. They have no
intention of going to confession, except perhaps just once more
before they die. Ask them what it means to them to be Catholic
and they will say it is good to belong to something, to have
values. Do they believe in God? Yes, of course. Do they believe in
the physical assumption of the Virgin Mary into Heaven? It's a
nice story; they can't imagine that it would matter to anyone
whether they believed in it or not.

The secular critics of the à la carte Catholics argue that they
should just simply admit that they are not really Catholics at all
any more and give up pretending. The table d'hôte Catholic may
argue that a shallow faith is better than no faith at all, and will
hope—and pray—for a deepening of that à la carte faith and a
renewed commitment to the church.

The secular view and the à la carte Catholic view were
represented in a pairing of articles in the *Sunday Independent* in
April 2007. Pope Benedict had just reminded his flock that Hell
really exists and that human guilt cannot simply be set aside.
Emer O'Kelly took this as a cue for an attack on the à la carte
Catholics, telling them that they should admit that they are
living a lie. Beside this, an article by Antonia Leslie recounted
how she had recovered her sense of being a Catholic while
arranging for her daughter to have her first holy communion.
The daughter, in fact, took three sacraments in the one day,
having had to be baptised and shriven too.

Antonia Leslie had rejected Catholicism years earlier. But she
had retained a religious inclination and expressed it through
various new-age cults, some of them directed at well-intentioned
aliens. But now, in church with her little girl, she realised that she
could love God in a Catholic church too. And where was the harm
since, 'the only part written in stone is the 10 Commandments'.

Well, Antonia had set herself up as Emer's target. Being a

Catholic wasn't about having nice feelings at Catholic ceremonies, said Emer. And she was right. Antonia would have to read only one encyclical like *Veritatis Splendor* to be reminded that she is outside the church's teaching and that the Pope is not really the sort of person she would want to have over for dinner. He regards himself as God's lawmaker on earth, with a particular responsibility to curtail her sexual conduct. Has she no problem with that?

The à la carte Catholics find themselves in trouble with the institutional church when they want to get married. Some liberal priests are simply happy to have non-practising Catholics in front of them for an hour. Others bristle at the hypocrisy. In the Redemptorist magazine *Reality*, Fr Gerard Moloney wondered if it wasn't time for the church to start turning people away from the sacraments if they were not committed churchgoers. Why should they be able to avail of a marriage service in the church when they never turned up for any other service? The church was often just a backdrop for a wedding photograph, a fashion accessory. The Protestant churches have the same problem. A northern minister is known to have recently refused to marry his own niece because she isn't a regular churchgoer. The *Reality* editorial said:

> Clergy know that increasingly they are just being 'used' and the sacraments not taken seriously at all. Maybe it's time to consider whether something as important as the sacraments should be 'dished out' willy-nilly to whoever seeks them, or should be restricted only to those who have a genuine faith commitment.

Fr Moloney was thinking the unthinkable. Croatian bishops, by contrast, were cutting up rough.

The problem is that à la carte Catholics don't just want to get married in church; they often want to get married in a Croatian church. And they have been turning up for these ceremonies with all the practical arrangements made but having conspicuously failed to complete the spiritual preparations. The

Croatian church has complained to the Irish bishops about this. A letter from the diocese of Dubrovnik, in October 2006, disclosed that most weddings of foreign nationals there are of Irish couples. It complained that some couples and their guests do not go to Confession at all 'and still go to receive Holy Communion'. 'Many of them do not observe an appropriate dress code, especially ladies.'

Monsignor Ivan Simic, chancellor of the Dubrovnik diocese, said that he did not see any pastoral reasons for weddings in the city and diocese, 'though they clearly advance the touristic promotions of certain wedding agencies.'

> Very often, wedding candidates put our parish priests under a lot of pressure arranging wedding ceremonies and booking plane tickets and hotels before getting all the necessary wedding papers done, but if they want to get married it is hard to deny them.

His proposal was that, in future, if Irish Catholics couldn't meet the standards expected in Croatia, they should bring their own Irish priest with them and let him marry them. Monsignor Ivan Simic appears to have understood very well that Irish priests work to more relaxed standards.

Chapter 11

John Brewer, a sociologist of religion, argues that secularisation theory is now dead. What we have been witnessing is not the transition of religious communities into atheistic communities, he says, but a liberalising of religious attitudes. Picking up a term coined by Grace Davie, he says that people now believe but do not belong. And because they believe, they would like the rites of passage in their lives and the lives of their families to be conducted through church. Unfortunately, since they are neglecting the church in the rest of their lives, they are in danger of killing the institution itself and leaving themselves bereft of structures through which rites might be administered.

This annoys the church, of course, which wants greater commitment from congregations, not least because those who come to church every week, as they should, donate more cash to the upkeep of the church and the clergy and those who come rarely contribute almost nothing. The church is caught on a hook: it would like to tell the half-hearted occasional Catholics to take the church seriously or bog off, but even those who pray only when they are desperate or at turning points in their lives are better than no congregations at all.

Those in the churches who don't want the half-hearted imagine a day just gone when all Catholics were devout and committed, but did many of us ever really take seriously the teachings of the church about God's intentions? If you believe that a hurricane is coming your way, you make immediate and serious plans to protect your life and your home. The people who, Brewer accepts, believe but don't belong show no sign of urgency in meeting the demands that God makes of them. Then perhaps they never did, even when they belonged. He says:

> The church does require there to be believers. Believers tend to be happier in a church that requires less and less of them. So we find a declining church that requires more and more of its church goers, and believers who want less and less engagement with the church. That paradox will mean that the mainline churches will die out, unless they are successful in keeping their young.

Ironically, the believers in the mainstream churches, who commit so little to those churches, are strangling those churches of resources and will wake up one day to find that the church they rather like going to at Christmas or for funerals isn't there any more. He says:

> The areas where there is growth—the liberal charismatics, the Pentecostals and conservative evangelicals—these are churches which tend to be more staunch in what they believe and I tend to think it is that staunchness which is attractive to all sorts of Christians who don't like complexity, who like a God who permits very little ambiguity.

But it might not be a very good survival strategy for the mainline churches to turn conservative, strict and simplistic in the hopes of exacting more commitment from the liberalising Christians who are losing interest. It might just switch them off altogether.

Perhaps their new way of being religious is simply a phase people go through on the way to being wholly secular. While they are still engaged in the argument with the dominant tradition, they may seek to subvert that tradition's understanding of God.

But when the argument itself is over, many of those same people feel no need of a church at all.

———

Richard Holloway is an example of a radical voice and an inspiring speaker, telling many of the disaffected Christians what they want to hear, that the dogmatic church is wrong, that he stands with the anti-clerical Jesus and that you can too. He is ideologically close to the secularists and seems to provide a way of being a churchgoing Christian while retaining a secular approach to life. 'It wasn't Christianity that gave us feminism or many of the important moral teachings of our time; these are secular ideas.'

Still, Richard Holloway wants to be a bishop and to have standing within the Anglican Church: 'I speak the God language for people who take it literally, but I understand it differently myself, as poetry.' But why bother?

> I might have learnt the need for love from Wordsworth or Mohammed but in fact I learned it from Jesus.

This seems a creative compromise for people who want to retain connections to a religious tradition in a secularising world, but who needs it? For most Catholics, it seems easier just to be à la carte and to go to church when you have to, or the notion is on you, and to seek no ideological compromise. They have already made their compromise and don't need another. Their compromise was to work it all out in their own heads and not to bother too much about the preaching or the words of the liturgy. And since the institutional church has so little power, it is not a problem; they need neither cower from it nor overthrow it. They are not hungry for Holloway's creative adaptation or they might take it. In their heads, they already have. 'It's nice to go to church sometimes, especially at Christmas. I like the music. Oh, that priest does go on a bit, doesn't he?' That is the voice of spiritual revolution in Ireland today: tepid and innocuous because that is the character of the church that it confronts—tepid and innocuous.

———

Some studies of the decline in congregational religious practice in England suggest that societies like ours are moving not towards total secularisation, but through a spiritual revolution. What people have turned away from is religious authority which would prescribe how they live their lives. What they are moving towards is the authority of the voice within, the individual's subjective intuition of what is the right way to live. The evidence of this is that if you ask strangers if they believe in God they come out with answers like: 'Well, I do in a way but not the way you mean.' They assume that there is a shared sense out there that the word 'God' describes a singular, conscious, authoritarian entity, and they do not believe in that but might have subtler notions of their own which they presume are private and individual to themselves.

They take it that you are asking if they believe in the patrician creator who lays down the law, and they want to say that they have a more personal notion of God, individual to themselves, maybe best not even called God at all. The point these evasive answers fail to make is that the people who offer them are, themselves, part of a widespread reconsideration of religious ideas. Those who answer the God question with 'I do in my own way' are speaking for more people than they know. They are part of a broader revolution in society away from the self being defined by duty and an inherited role, towards people being free to think for themselves. They don't take on the jobs their parents did and they don't take on the belief systems to which their parents subscribed either. And neither do they cherish an idea of God as a rule-maker who requires duty and subservience.

This change was explored in *The Spiritual Revolution* by Paul Heelas and Linda Woodhead. They conducted a study of religious practice in Kendal in Cumbria and concluded that types of religious practice can be divided into categories, according to whether they discipline people in obedience to authority or encourage them to listen to the voice within. And they conclude that the ostensibly obvious decline in religion in England is actually a shift away from duty-centred obedience, expressed in congregational worship, towards a concern for the integrity of the subjective life.

But just how religious is this concern for the integrity of the subjective life? Is the voice within really the spirit at all or is it, at best, an intuition guiding your own welfare, part of the ordinary human make-up, and, at worst, a delusion? Those who celebrate the value of the voice within make little distinction between psychological well-being and spiritual salvation, for they find no contradiction between them. The patrician God, on the other hand, was well able to command you to do things that you felt were against your own nature, as Pope Benedict will happily remind you; though he would say that obedience to God's rules, as understood by him, *is* adherence to nature; it's just that he understands your nature better than you do.

What was distinctive about the traditional, authority-centred worshippers to whom Heelas and Woodhead spoke was that they thought it improper to agonise about subjective experience and feelings. They felt that the right thing was always to set those concerns aside and get on with meeting your responsibilities. People who thought like that, of course, did not, for instance, see it as good and proper to walk out of a marriage in search of personal fulfilment. The subjectively minded people of today would say, go!

The Irish-language poet Nuala Ní Dhomnaill described in a television documentary how her mother, working as a doctor in the north of England in the 1960s, unquestioningly followed her low-paid husband when he announced that he was taking her and the children back to Ireland where he had got a better job— that is, a better job for himself, not for her. And the same mother, later seeing Nuala declare her right to emotional independence by falling in love with a Turkish man, summoned her brothers to beat him up. The independent survivor Nuala is of the type of a modern hero. In the view of her mother's generation, she was a thankless slut who might be judged insane and locked up for being so out of touch with the norms of decent society. Two views of life confront each other in almost total incomprehension. And this describes the transition we have gone through in Ireland, from one to the other.

This was the divide that Edna O'Brien crossed, the journey represented through the characters of *The Country Girls*, towards deciding for themselves what was right for them. This is a rejection of a social order rather than of God, but God gets carried off in the blast because God was the shield and banner of those who insisted on social conformity and responsibility before intuition—on meeting the expectations of your parents before finding your own way. God appears able, however, to creep back into people's lives once the subjective right is secured.

Within the Christian tradition there are some orders and sects which teach precisely this subjective way of living. Some define the inner voice as the holy spirit or voice of God. Some, of course, expect that voice to pull us back to authority. They say that if it doesn't, the fault is in our hearing. The evangelical culture seems ostensibly to be a culture that encourages people to attend to the voice within and experience God subjectively and be born again. But once you are born again, they expect you to obey. The subjective journey stops with that one big insight. But some, even in the traditional churches, find that it is only the language of psychotherapy and self-discovery that makes them relevant. Orders of nuns find that many sisters want to break out of communal living and live alone. They keep those women in the order by letting them do that.

There are strong indications that Ireland still values the congregational, authority-focused attitude and praises people for how well they fill their social role rather than for how rich their subjective lives are. On the *Late Late Show*, Pat Kenny's core theme is achievement, and the markers of achievement are always wealth and recognition, particularly recognition in the USA or 'stateside'. The popularity of this approach must surely reflect an essentially rural and congregationalist mindset which asks how well our own people are doing in their working lives rather than whether they are happy or have arrived at insights into the meaning of life.

Senator Maurice Hayes, in *Sweet Killough, Let Go Your Anchor* (Blackstaff 1994), recalls a time when this rural culture valued people for their role and position rather than for their personal qualities.

> In previous generations the romantic dream was of descent from noble blood, or great wealth fallen on hard times, leaving a latent residue of decency and pride or good breeding ready to be discovered by the appropriate fortunate circumstance or fairy prince. Then there was rags to riches, log cabin to White House and greater merit in having made it on your own than through inherited wealth or privilege.

A common fantasy among people of low status was that they would be elevated by recognition. Someone would turn up and tell them that they had been misplaced in society and that they were really the children of the rich or the royal. That fantasy disappeared in a society in which people began to dream of personal freedom and happiness, which is discovered within, rather than inherited. A variant of the old fantasy remains, pathetically, among people who imagine that they can be discovered as celebrities without actually having to acquire any skills or develop any talent.

What precipitated this change from a sense of personal value as of right, from breeding and class, to a sense of value developed in the forge of the soul? Well, the space within which you can contentedly obey your betters and elders, or expect to be obeyed by those below you, has shrunk. We have to be subjective because we have to make decisions individually. The collapse of the vertical family is part of it. In a previous generation, even a man of 40 would consult his father before his wife.

The lateral family is different from the vertical family in that it obliges partners in a marriage to be happy together if they are to survive. Our parents and grandparents didn't reflect over and over again on whether they were still in love with each other. If they weren't, they had little choice but to stay together despite that, and they had other company anyway. When your wife or husband is the only other adult you live with, then you have to get to know each other better and understand yourself better in order to be able to consider how the other sees you. That means you have to learn to think subjectively, about the state of your heart rather than about your position within a group.

In the vertical family, parental approval still counts for as much as the love of a spouse, perhaps more, and estrangement from the spouse is cushioned with the consolation of belonging. In that structure, it is easier to endure the church's instruction to stay with the marriage whether it works or not. In the lateral family, the church's injunction is recognised as often plainly untenable.

————

We are subjective by orientation and necessity now, but we are perhaps not very competently or astutely subjective. Prosaic expressions of feeling are at the limit of what most people are capable of, and are enough for most media purposes. Even when champions of introspection are questioned by those of a congregational perspective, they are asked not to share their insights but simply to accept applause. When John Banville won the Man Booker prize, he was asked on the BBC, 'How did you feel?' But this was not a query about the state of his soul. It was simply an invitation to say the same sort of thing a footballer might say: 'I was chuffed.' Or 'I was gutted.'

And the New Age religions, which are said to be more concerned with the subjective inner life, are often not much better. Anyone who thinks that they can sort out life's difficulties by hanging a dream-catcher above their bed has not yet grasped how difficult life is. The first generation of New Ageism has been giddy and trite. Those who are picking up spiritual vibes from crystals haven't probed their own subjectivity deeply enough to find out how suggestion works and how strong it can be. But it is not the quality or depth of subjectivity that counts here—just the orientation towards it. People want love; they know the stress of self-contradiction; they want to find where they fit, not to have to shape themselves to fit.

In a past generation, a young man who became a plumber's apprentice would watch other plumbers to know how to speak, dress and comport himself, even how he might talk to his girlfriend. He would shape himself into a plumber. In a subjectively orientated generation, he will not be able to bear the strain of this and will simply plumb differently, in his own way, or walk away and become a teacher. And if he sees that teachers wear tweed jackets with leather elbow patches, he might be tempted to get one of those, too, but he'll adapt to doing what is genuinely compatible with himself, or at least to dressing as his wife prescribes, rather than like the blokes at work.

This is the revolution we have undergone and there was little prospect of a religion that teaches conformity surviving it. The revolution against the church was led by teenagers and young adults, the first rebels, perhaps anticipating the trap. They were the growing tip of the new subjective culture. How had they intuited that their subjective lives would be more important than their social roles? How often did a younger person urge an older friend to make a radical change in life only to hear the familiar answer: 'It's all right for you; you're young. I'm too old to change'?

It is tempting to read the secular revolution in Ireland as a mature and reasoned response to a culture that had become untenable. But it wasn't the older people who led that revolution. It was led by teenagers who, when they left home, were able to shrug off all the conditioning that had bound generations before them and to live differently. Not that many of them lived fresh, subjective, spiritual lives. With the first taste of freedom, the priority was to spend your own money and get drunk. The casting off of the patrician congregationalist ways did not lead to a spiritual revival for most, to a deepening of subjective experience, but to the loss of all moral concern. This is what worries John Waters and Cardinal Seán Brady and practically every observer of the decline of the Irish congregation; it seems we are not very good at subjectivity. We look into ourselves and are disconsolate and urgently need to look away. The value judgement of the young, when left to form a value judgement of their own, is coolness. Who would have thought that they would have picked a word that was in vogue in the 1950s? And it can apply to anything. The visitors' book at Donegal Castle has at least one comment entry on every page pronouncing the place 'cool'.

Cardinal Brady challenged those who celebrate the decline of religion in Ireland to say now how the cultural malaise that has followed from it is to be relieved. Speaking at the Knock Novena in 2007, he said:

> The truth is that many of those who claim to set Ireland free from the shackles of religious faith in recent years are now silent in the face of the real captivities of the 'new' Ireland: the increase in alcohol and drug abuse; the pressure to work and consume; the pressure to look good and have the right image; the increase in suicide and violence; the constant worry about finance and future security. It is not religious faith which is leading people to stress and despair; it is those elements of the 'new' Ireland which are increasingly empty of meaning.

Anomalously, in the same week that Brady dwelt on the spiritual malaise of 'new' Ireland, a report on the health of schoolchildren showed that they were both drinking more than they should and getting happier. The NUI Galway report for the Department of Health and Children reported that children were happier than they had been four years previously, 92 per cent of boys and 89 per cent of girls being happy or very happy. Perhaps for some people happiness does not necessarily equate with spiritual well-being but perhaps for most of us it does. Then again, maybe a lot of miserable children think it would be un-cool to own up to not being happy, or maybe they'd be afraid the interviewer would call a social worker. More young people were using seatbelts and fewer were smoking; there had been a drop in the numbers drinking but a third of 15- to 17-year-olds said that they had been 'really drunk' at least once in the previous month. And in the 10–17 age group, 16 per cent said that they had used cannabis at least once, though there was a decrease in the proportion of older teenagers who were using it. Whatever else that says about the moral health of Irish youth, it suggests that it is not in rapid decline.

Twelve per cent, mostly girls, said that they were on a diet, and 17 per cent said that they often went to bed hungry because there was no food in the house. This demonstrates that some problems are material rather than spiritual.

But when Seán Brady turned to reflect on the malaise of modern Ireland, the primary evil he identified in that speech was fortune telling! For him, the distinctive weakness of the non-Christian is a concern for the future, expressed in a fascination with fortune telling and divination. Surely he doesn't think that these are new to Ireland or that the fatalism with which our agricultural forebears faced the future was grounded in Catholic theology. Does he?

————

The congregation is a model of the obedient society. The people gather to apologise before God and commit themselves to better behaviour, before a minister or priest. They renew and restore their society and their individual belonging to it. They affirm tradition and its stability. The model of a modern responsible adult sweeps this away and tells a person to find love and direction, not to be told by others where you fit in or what the duties of your role are. Life is not a role any more; it is not a performance of one's place in a group; it is a journey of discovery and unfolding. People seem to understand that instinctively now and to suffer anxiety when they have failed in those terms.

Nuala Ní Dhomnaill, had she chosen her family before the man she loved, would have been enveloped in a society, back then, which affirmed that choice. All the consolations of love and security would have been available to her, and, though those things would once have been enough, they are not enough now. You can trace the changed attitude in our folksongs. Nuala Ní Dhomnaill's dilemma was expressed in the song of the 'Gipsy Rover'. A woman runs away after a charming gypsy and her father pursues her. But all is well in the end, not as it was well for Nuala but as her father would have hoped: 'He is no gypsy, father dear, but lord of this land all over.'

The story ends happily because the man turns out to be socially worthy of the woman—as she, no doubt, had sensed all along. Society's order is restored. The song understands that the lady would not have loved the gypsy if he had been a real gypsy. Today we think she either loves him for his inner qualities or not at all, and her heroism could only be in doing this despite what society or her parents wanted. But that's not how it was only a generation ago. The song indeed grasps that there is a need for a little anarchy and mischief in life—for the man!

In the later Planxty version, the man really is a gypsy and it is the lord's wife who runs to him, choosing love before wealth, a perfectly modern choice.

In *Romeo and Juliet* the only conceivable ending is that both die or that the entire social order, by which families are divided, should change—and that wasn't going to happen.

Even the 'Wild Rover' of the other famous song meets his social responsibilities in the end: 'But now I am returning with gold in great store, never to play the wild rover no more.' Today, he would still jet about the world and probably own a couple of hotels in Dublin.

———

Those who live by the morality of the congregation follow rules. In their perspective, those who do not follow rules have no morality at all. Those who live life with regard to subjective feelings intuit their morality, learn it from experience or, indeed, do not have a morality to live by. Those who live by rules, from a congregational attitude, do not value subjective feeling. A clergyman says: 'If I lived by my feelings, I would not get out of bed in the morning.' Such people are as disgusted by the expression of feeling as they are by the expression of bodily fluids. They see a new television culture in Britain in which people are expected and encouraged to cry, and they find that excessive. They have a point.

The subjective life is untenable if it is just a response to the feelings of the day. But the clergyman who says he would not get out of bed cannot conceive of having educated feelings. And the feckless, and the drinkers, and the people who live by no rules and flounder perhaps can't either. Which challenges society either to restore spiritual authority, so that people will live by rules, or to educate us on how to understand our feelings and not to be overwhelmed by the strong but transient ones.

The deputy governor of a Belfast prison explains the difference between young offenders and adult offenders. If a young offender trashes his cell and you ask him why, he doesn't know. He has no sense of action and reaction. He looks on it as something that just happened. If an adult offender trashes his cell and you ask him why, he will tell you what it is you have done to annoy him. He can see his own mental processes. Many of the younger ones just can't.

A product of the congregational, rule-centred approach is the inability of clergy to express feeling. And this is obvious everywhere they speak. For a profession that practises communication, it is embarrassingly inept. It isn't that they have no experience or training; it is that their orientation is away from the subjective, inner person and towards a world of rules and order in which life is expressed through biblical stories rather than with reference to life as lived and reflected on. The effect is a detachment from reality, especially obvious on occasions when human feeling is the most appropriate response.

Take the sermon of Fr Michael Porter in Donegal, speaking at the funeral of a mother and two children, of Ciara Dunne and her girls, Leanne and Shania, who died with their father in a shocking suicide pact in Wexford in April 2007. Fr Michael had known Ciara and spoke fondly of her childlike ways, but in trying to get to the heart of the tragedy he was almost helpless. 'Why did death have to happen in this way?' he asked, expressing the bewilderment of the whole country, but few would have made much of his answer.

> Even Our Lord cried out on the cross, 'Oh God, why have you abandoned me?' These crosses come to us as they did to His own Son. God does not explain why these crosses come to us, and even if He did, we would not be able to understand.

Well, right enough, we probably wouldn't.

Fr Michael said that the only explanation would come at the end of time when 'the graves yield up their dead, and there will be no more suffering, and God will wipe away our tears'. He is saying, in effect, that God wills these things, and we don't know why but we have to learn to live with it. This is a classic evasion of the subjective. There is no point in even trying to understand what goes on in the mind, though that was the vital question: how had parents come to kill their children and themselves? The answer had to be one expressed in terms of human psychology, not in the actions of a detached, incomprehensible God. But, of course, if you are to comprehend how a parent might kill a child, you have to dwell on the possibility that you might do the same yourself. It isn't the job of congregationalist religion to guide you into that darkness but to reassure you that you don't need to go near it. And it's not hard to work out why the new subjectivist religions would prefer dream-weavers and crystals to embarking on such a journey.

In sermons, radio talks and books and lectures, there's hardly any category of people who sound more inept at communication and more out of touch with the mood of the country than the clergy. This derives from more than a lack of training in public speaking; it is about their whole grounding in the sense that the subjective life is not central. They are cut off from it themselves and cannot help others to connect to it.

And the contrast with the mourners in Donegal was clear in the way they dressed, in the fashionable, extroverted care, in clothes they had bought for partying, their hair coiffed finely. Everything in their manner said, 'We are not made for this.'

Chapter 12

The Catholic Primate of Ireland, Seán Brady, ordained ten priests in a single ceremony in June of 2006. It was a rare type of occasion for him. Vocations to the priesthood in Ireland have been tailing off to single figures. The men prostrate before him, committing themselves to God and a life of service, were men who had been inspired by the heroic tradition of the Catholic church in Ireland. But they were not Irish. Dr Brady had gone to Nigeria to participate in a vigorous and growing church. This must have been, for him, an occasion to reflect on what the church in Ireland had lost.

Fr Hyacinth Egbebo, the Superior General of the Missionary Society of St Paul in Gwagwalada, had invited then Archbishop Brady to perform the ordinations. Irish Catholicism had been the driving spirit behind the Missionary Society's work to build a seminary in Nigeria. The Irish Catholic culture that had moved its founder, Cardinal Ekandem, however, was now on the wane. Nigeria, on the way up, was meeting Ireland coming down.

Cardinal Ekandem had got the very idea of building a national missionary seminary when visiting the seminary of Maynooth in 1950. In his memoirs he describes an Ireland that has gone, though the memory of it was a living inspiration for him:

I was really impressed to witness the large numbers of priests ordained. I was hoping that someday in Nigeria we might succeed in establishing a similar institution. I also concluded from the constitution of Maynooth that it gave the Irish priesthood a wonderful unity. This gave the Irish Church the strength that facilitated the work of evangelisation throughout Ireland and even beyond ...

What the church in Nigeria needed, he reasoned, was a similar coherence to the training of priests:

If Nigerian priests are trained together, some dioceses that had not enough vocations for the priesthood could be helped by priests from other dioceses within the country ... Through a national seminary, the unity of our nation would be very much enhanced. The experience of Maynooth, Ireland, so much impressed me that on my return home, I continually dreamt of such a possibility for Nigeria.

The beauty of having central national training of priests is that networks are formed. The men of each graduating year may stay in touch for decades, supporting each other when morale is low. Every priest, theoretically, is part of a 'year'. When Maynooth was turning out hundreds per year, a lonely priest in a rural parish would still have many of those hundreds to turn to when he was in doubt about his vocation or needed practical help. That's what you need to sustain a vibrant living church, reasoned Ekandem—a community of priests similarly inspired and homogeneously trained.

Pope Paul VI approved the idea for a Nigerian Maynooth in 1975, on the condition that it would provide missionaries for work abroad. It does. Today, the MSP has missions in Nigeria, Cameroon, Liberia, the Gambia, Malawi, Botswana, South Africa, Grenada, Chad, Sweden, England, Ireland and the USA. Its present Superior General, Fr Hyacinth Egbebo, studied in Ireland in the late 1990s. Since that time, several priests in succession from the Missionary Society have assisted in the parish of Ardee, County Louth, while studying in Dublin. Other members of the Society have worked short-term, in various parishes throughout the Archdiocese of Armagh.

Speaking before leaving for Nigeria, Dr Brady said that the links between Ireland and Nigeria were growing closer:

> Since 2000 several thousand Nigerians have made their home in Ireland, making a valuable contribution to the Irish Church, society and economy. Both Ireland and Nigeria have much in common, including a strong commitment to family values, and we look forward to a greater sharing of each country's talents and gifts now and in the future.

The Catholic church in Ireland will need these new Nigerian priests. Dr Brady ordained more priests in that one ceremony in Nigeria than he did in the whole of Ireland that year, which means that there are now more old priests than young ones.

A good place to see a gathering of them, and sense the average character type, was at the National Conference of Priests of Ireland which met every year in Dublin, though in recent years there was a marked reduction in the number of events at the conference that the public or press were allowed access to. This cut down on embarrassments like the occasion on which a woman stood up and berated the priests, during a talk on St Paul by Jerome Murphy O'Connor, for not having stopped to say the Angelus at noon. Most of the priests seemed to bristle at her intervention. She didn't get her way.

Entering a hall full of priests is a bit like entering an all-male old people's home, or a bowling club. There does seem to be a consistency in style among them; a lot of woollen cardigans and checked open-neck shirts; more of the fragrance of the doused pipe than of Old Spice. They are grey and balding, naturally enough, but few have taken measures to restrain the advance of ageing. Nor are they animated. These are quiet, thoughtful men, and quiet, thoughtful people rarely look happy.

Priests have been demoralised by the sex-abuse scandals and by the general decline in reverence for them. A priest of 60 will remember a time when he had many more colleagues than he has now, a time when he was saluted when he walked the streets, even a time when his car was the best in the parish. These men are jaded realists. If a total fundamentalist like, say, Vincent Twomey or John Paul II joined them, many would perhaps shift away from him to the other side of the room, to seek more congenial company. Their whole mission is to find a working accommodation with a world that doesn't look to them for leadership any more, so that they may not fade into total irrelevance. They are not going to thrive in that mission by continuing to insist that they know best the rules by which we should be living our lives.

————

There is probably no way to live the life of a priest without sinning sexually. Celibacy made hypocrites of all priests, or at least venial sinners of those who had the decency not to tell others that masturbation was a sin. The rest of the world might not think of it as sin, but the priest does or ought to; otherwise the theological contortions made in *Humanae Vitae*, demanding chastity in marriage for the purpose of preserving the sinfulness of masturbation and sodomy, were wasted effort. In recognition of the sin of masturbation, priests and religious brothers in the past hectored young men about the awfulness of self-abuse. Were they really confident themselves that they could contain their temptations without manually assisted release? If so, they had a power of which to be proud. The reality is more likely that they lectured against it fervently in the hope of rebutting suspicion that it was their own main crutch through life. So they inflicted their own guilt on young men who were in no danger of anything worse than muscle strain or light bruising.

Many priests take lovers. Some occasionally have sex with a woman. Others have sex with men or boys or little girls.

Some, perhaps most, manage to observe their vows. No one is counting.

A nun says that her friends understand that about half of priests have lovers. She believes the figure is much lower among sisters in her order.

> It's because women give all of themselves in a relationship or a commitment. So nuns who fall in love leave. Men can divide themselves between relationships and work, so they can do both, even when they contradict each other.

She believes that many priests rationalise the law on celibacy as an injunction not to marry rather than as an injunction not to have sex with anyone. Still, even if their sexual relations are not breaches of the celibacy law—in the letter—they are breaches of the law on sex outside marriage. But then, we've all broken that one, so who are we to point the finger? Except that we don't and they do.

Priests appear to be carrying the stress of the contradictions by which they live and the sexual deprivation, which they can't even joke about as other men do. They are fraught and stiff. They seem to sweat a lot, have red faces. Few are relaxed and happy. The cause of this stress seems obvious to an outsider, to a man who would not contemplate living without sex, who would not trust himself not to be conspicuous in his unhappiness if he had to.

'And men', the nun argues, 'do not form community as well as women do, and therefore do not find the consolations of friendship and warmth in companionship.'

Some priests assertively defend their commitment to celibacy. One says: 'You would not sneer at a gay man for his sexual choices, so you should not sneer at me for mine.' It is a trick response. A choice of celibacy can hardly be described as a sexual orientation; it is not a functioning means of sexual expression, after all. Or perhaps, for a few, it is.

But the Catholic church cannot be blamed for inventing the idea of celibacy. It runs through the Hindu and Buddhist monastic traditions too. The difference there is that it is part of a discipline aimed at attaining spiritual growth in hothouse conditions. There may be some sense in celibacy within lives governed by strict contemplative exercises. If not, the damage afflicts the anchorite alone. Imposing a discipline on someone who must work among others in a world full of relationships and opportunity seems reckless, dangerous.

Celibacy can be a really fulfilling lifestyle, and priests need to get that message across, according to Dr Brendan Leahy, a professor of moral theology at St Patrick's College Maynooth. Dr Leahy says that the big challenge for all Christians, whether they are married or celibate, is to love other people. Well, yes: the married man must restrain himself in relation to all other women, to preserve his love for his wife and hers for him, but he knows that this is easier if he is receiving his comforts at home.

Dr Leahy was rejecting calls for a change in the rule on celibacy following press revelations that a County Clare priest, Fr Michael Hogan, had advertised on gay websites and sent photographs of himself in his underpants to a journalist entrapping him. The awful thing about disclosure of sexual weakness is how embarrassing it always is.

Dr Leahy says that marriages run into difficulties, but we don't overthrow the institution of marriage because of that. Neither, therefore, should the church change the celibacy law, just because some priests have difficulty with it. You can, he said, be terribly happy living a celibate life, just as you can be terribly happy living a married life.

Really? Surely celibacy suppresses urges, which then come out in 'warped' sexuality? No, says Dr Leahy, celibacy does not warp people if it is lived properly.

> Very often priests can live too much as loners. That is not the idea Jesus had in his mind at all. What did he do? He formed around him a community of people. Priests are called to form a community with the people from their parishes, but also a community among priests.

Priests should give moral support to each other, not least to face the challenges to celibacy.

> The one thing we all have to do in life is to love people. To love people in a way that is right and true, whether you are married or celibate. The important thing is not to live your sexuality in a warped way, but to live it in a way that is a gift of yourself. As priests, we are called not to express our love in a physical, sexual relationship. We are called to love with our hearts, our affections, our will and our minds.

Don't sexually active people also love with their hearts?

> Just as a married man enters a relationship with one woman and therefore can't flirt with every woman he meets, with a priest the relationship is with God, whom we experience as love, and with other people, and priests.

Indeed, and if a priest can have full affective gratification in his relationship with God, and other people and priests, and suffer no stress in the containment of his sexual inclinations, then there is no problem. If he can't, he is ill-equipped to lecture others on their sexual conduct.

A dilemma for the priest is that he represents an authority which is doctrinaire about meaning and morality and which expects him to convey that doctrine to the laity. Yet he lives among people who want his services—occasionally—but rarely take the doctrine literally. He must pass himself off to his bishop as one who cares that doctrine should be properly understood; and he must pass himself off to the laity as someone who will try not to make his service conditional upon their acceptance of doctrine, unless he has to.

What stresses must this tension create? Perhaps he rationalises that the laity, as good Christians, don't need to understand doctrine. It used to be his job to ensure that they obeyed doctrinal law. The country priest was known for beating the hedge at night with his blackthorn stick to flush out covert couples. Now he may be glad that they will at least come to him for a pre-marriage course or, failing that, to have their child baptised.

Some priests reconcile themselves to the tension by arguing that only the core of doctrine matters, that it is enough for people to accept that God loves them and to try to love God in return. Issues arise to refute that. The differences between churches do cause trouble and they are doctrinally based. A Scottish cardinal tells MPs who speak in favour of an abortion law that they needn't expect to be able to receive communion in church. Again, doctrine is more than trusting that God loves you and loving Him in return; it is a battleground on which some tell you what to believe and on which you must decide whose side you are on. The paradox is that the church continues to emphasise that message and the people continue to act as if they haven't heard it or don't need to take it seriously.

How does the priest cope? Some do it by shifting the moral responsibility onto the lay Catholic. In the kitchen of a Dublin priest in a working-class area, a group of women are discussing an absent friend. This other woman—say, Mary—is divorced and does not come to communion. But she would like to. Her friends are sounding out the priest on whether he would refuse her. They know that some priests would.

'Well, let's be strictly hypothetical about it,' he says to the journalist in the company. 'If you feel you're in good standing with God, then I am not going to tell you that you are not in good standing with the church.'

'So she can come to communion?' asks one of the women.

'I think that's what he just said,' says the journalist.

But some priests are more conservative. Fr Denis Faul was a prison visitor who said mass for paramilitary prisoners in the Maze. Would he refuse communion to a divorced person?

'No,' he said. 'Not to one who was living a chaste life.' But if the person was in a new relationship, which, by the law of God, cannot be regarded as a marriage? 'I would refuse them communion until they had ended that relationship and confessed their sin.'

Did he refuse communion to prisoners who had murdered people and not confessed to the sin of that because their paramilitary logic persuaded them that they had done right?

'No. I don't know what they have confessed or what state their soul is in,' said Fr Faul.

———

At the 2006 meeting of the National Conference of Priests of Ireland, the guest speaker was *Irish Times* columnist Breda O'Brien. Breda, it is relevant to say, has a beauty that is wholesome. She is a well-rounded mother with soft, creamy cheeks and a voice so fine that it probably tinkles like a little altar bell when she coughs. The men in tweeds regarded her, before she spoke, with evident adulation, with smiles brimming with love for her. Well might they love her, for she defends them better than they do themselves, and she seems the embodiment of a Catholic sweetness that most of them would be shy of claiming could possibly still exist, if she wasn't there in front of them. Breda is goodness and she shines. She is probably the woman that every one of those priests would want for a daughter, if they could have daughters; and since they can't, she is the nearest they will ever get to a devoted and lovely woman who shares their principles and calls them 'Father'. Does this sound cynical? It is probably the plain and simple truth.

Breda had been invited to speak on the theme 'Priesthood: A Greater Need Than Ever'. She let them know quickly that she knows how they have suffered:

> We live in a climate that is sometimes anti-Catholic but is more often anti-clerical. The day-to-day reality for many priests can be a difficult one. It involves loneliness, a sense of frustration, a sense of overwork, the feeling of not being appreciated and lots of different tensions and disappointments.

Yes, lots of them.

Yet she seemed also aware that there would be radical activists among the priests in front of her when she tentatively broached her first theme, that the era of the priest as social worker is gone:

> And before you say, O God, a right-wing attempt to go back to the days when the priests said their prayers and made no challenge to the social order, that's not what I'm talking about at all.

She said:

> A priest may be heavily involved in social issues, but if it is not clear that he is so involved because of his commitment to Christ, then I think he is probably in the wrong business. A ministry that is not founded on deep spirituality is in danger of becoming empty activism and that's a danger for anyone who considers themselves to be a committed Christian.

Empty activism? Is that what she thought they were all in danger of succumbing to? Was it empty activism that all those other busy people were engaged in who were running hospitals and radio stations without the benefit of a connection to Christ?

But priesthood, she said, had to be defined as including all believers, not just the ordained. So presumably that would include empty activists too. Or would it?

> The priesthood of all believers is not emphasised enough, and if we are talking about priesthood being needed more than ever, it's on that foundation that we need to build the common priesthood that we all share.

It would have been very easy to imagine Breda herself as a priest, and indeed as a much more inspirational priest than many of those she addressed. It seemed entirely proper that it should be she addressing them rather than any of them addressing her, given her natural charm and eloquence, though it's unlikely that she would concede that. But she told them some harsh truths.

> When people seek a balance in their lives or experience a search for spiritual meaning, the local presbytery or the local church is not likely to be their first port of call. And to be extremely blunt, if people do decide to try churchgoing, they may be very rapidly disenchanted, because they may not find a living community there and may drift away again.

Well, they could take this sort of criticism from her, since she wasn't one of the Dublin 4 media clique whom some in the church blame for all their ills.

> And I think many of us here in Ireland are asking ourselves, if the faith was as important to Irish people as we were always told that it was, how did it evaporate so easily? And where did all the faithful Catholics go in recent times and why do we not hear their voices?

If that line had appeared in a column by Vincent Browne, it would have triggered a flurry of protest against media pessimism about the future of God's work among us. Breda could deliver it and provoke knowing nods all round. She tried to paint a picture of the cultural change that Ireland was facing with the disappearance of the religious orders. Those orders had connected Ireland to the third world.

> There wasn't a child in Ireland that didn't have an aunt or an uncle—you'd be mortified if it was only your cousin— that was out on the missions. And those people came back and there was a very fruitful collaboration between schools and parishes. And then returned missionaries tended to be very radical and they were a good influence on Ireland.

They fought for radical and unpopular causes.

I don't get the worst letters when I write about the church; I get the worst letters when I write that prisoners should be treated as human beings; and what do I find? I find the religious and priests stuck in those ministries as well (doing the unpopular work).

But it is not just radical energy that is disappearing; it is the simple faith of the simple people.

'I am a great believer in the Guardian Angel,' she said. She was serious. 'I got through four labours with the help of my Guardian Angel. Children have no sense of there being a Guardian Angel.'

And she said that it isn't Catholics any more who are distinguished by calmness and an air of sanctity:

> I remember being at an interfaith meeting and being totally struck by the fact that the only Buddhist present radiated calmness and serenity and the Catholics were like headless chickens. If by their fruits ye shall know them ... Where is our joy? Where is our walking advertisement for the wonders of the Christian message? Where is the witness of our lives?
>
> I know you are going to say to me, you can't visit people now; they are never in and if you go and knock on the door they are getting the kids ready for bed and they resent you. But if you don't have a living community to which to invite the marginalised, you end up with more disaffected and marginalised. People in Ireland are very cynical about this and the preaching to the converted and the ones that are already listening to you. But, guys, you don't have the converted with you for much longer if you ignore them and if you don't nourish them. And it is very difficult for those of us who want to raise kids and Catholic kids. It is very, very difficult.

So, she said, the church was not only failing to reach out to new recruits among the alienated but was failing to service the community it already had and was therefore losing that community. So how might Catholic priests re-engage with their communities and fire them up with Catholic enthusiasm? Breda had laid out the problem. Now, what was the solution? What was her answer to the challenge of our times?

It was balloons.

> Where I go often to mass, on St Patrick's Day, they gave out green helium balloons to the kids after mass. It was fantastic. It was like being a member of a secret society, because everywhere you went and you saw a green balloon, you knew they'd been to mass. And I went into the Dundrum Shopping Centre.

Breda didn't want to go into all the details of why she was shopping on a holy day, but she assumed that there might be some alarm among the priests in the hall at the image of her going straight to the temple of mammon from the temple of God.

> God help me. There was a reason why I went in on a feast day—a sad reason which I won't go into here, but I wanted to get a gift for someone who was in grave difficulties.

That covered it.

> And I looked around and there were all the green balloons in Dundrum Shopping Centre.

Breda did not judge the people there by the standard by which she had judged herself, unless she thought they were all buying gifts for 'a friend in grave difficulties'.

> And it was fantastic having people stop us with our four kids and saying, 'Where did you get the balloons?'

Suddenly it didn't seem to be such a sin after all, to be shopping on a holy day, hardly worth the trouble she had taken to explain.

They were expecting to be told the third floor, and we'd say, 'We got them at mass.' It was just amazing. And you're going to say it was gimmicky, and it wasn't gimmicky; it was people who understood children and understood the way to a child's heart, you know. And there is stuff like that going on all over the place and it never makes the headlines. [—a fact which, to a working journalist, should hardly have been surprising. Would she have put it on the front page of *The Irish Times* if she had been editor?]

Sometimes it seemed that Breda herself was caught between two generations and their separate ideas of the good and holy life, one minute trying to justify being in a shop and the next declaring herself delighted to see all the other Catholics there. But the priests in this audience would be gentle with her, as she was gentle with them.

I think the standard of preaching has improved in Ireland. As someone who visits the four corners of Ireland in the summer, I was horrified when I heard someone had said his idea of hell would be to look up and see me in the congregation. God, am I that ferocious?

She's not.

Actually I am the easiest person to please in a congregation.

We'd worked that out already.

If you make some reference to the gospel and link it in some way to my life I'll think you are the best preacher I ever heard. I'm actually down there in the pew rooting for you if you are making any attempt at all.

———

Not all of the priests were entirely impressed with Breda. One of the radical priests who wasn't quite with her was Fr Vincent McDevitt, a Holy Ghost Father based in Dublin. He said:

> I expected that Breda would look more at some of the challenges in the church and present a broader version of Christianity and a Christianity in touch with some of the broader issues in the world today. And when she said that the priest shouldn't be involved in social work I'm not sure precisely what she meant. Would she call working with immigrants and Aids victims social work? I didn't quite get her on that. She didn't seem quite relevant to the issues of today, the selfishness that's growing, the materialism. She didn't quite address those in the manner in which I would have liked her to raise them.

To be fair to her, she had said that priests were involved in heroic work among prisoners. She had been a bit clumsy in her argument that the priest was different from the social worker and came across as sounding as if there was something to be disdained in the 'empty activism' of those who help their fellow human being without a connection to Christ while they are doing it. Then again, in referring to a 'priesthood of all believers', she left open the possibility that the professional social worker or lay volunteer was also motivated by Christ. Fr McDevitt said:

> I understand our religion basically as love of God and love of neighbour. So that love of neighbour has to be translated into very practical things, has to be loving and creative, whatever the great suffering and great needs, to be there.

And how did he assess the morale of the modern Irish priests?

> A lot of tiredness. We need to be more sharing and supportive of each other. Morale is somewhat low, yes. I think if we talked more together, in friendship as well as in

planning and faith sharing, we would get over that. But priests are coming out now and sharing and looking for something and seeing the need for doing that, so morale is rising.

Fr Michael Sweeney has retired to Ballyliffin in County Donegal after forty-two years spent working in the north of England. He appears to be an optimist.

> The lay people see it as risky for us because they see what has happened. And they don't want their sons associated with that. But if they only knew the privilege that it is to stand up there on a Sunday morning and to be able to serve people …

He said:

> I agree that it is years since I have heard a mother say that she would love her son to become a priest. I have known a family that had a son at Maynooth and the sister said to me that she was praying that he would get out of it. And that was twenty years ago.

And was there a happy outcome? Did he get out? 'Oh he did, surely to God.' Fr Michael admitted to having been tempted himself to leave.

> It hits everybody. After about fifteen years you ask yourself, am I in the right job? There are tough times when you are young for there is everything to contend with: your sexuality and that. I took a sabbatical and I came back and it was the best thing I ever did and I worked harder than I had ever done and enjoyed every single minute of it. People ask me if I would have liked to get married. I would have loved to have been married but I couldn't have done the work I was doing if I was married. There is no woman that would have put up with that.

But there are many people who would not put up with the demands of the priest's job now either. Fr Michael Murphy of Ballyphehane in Cork city had been thirty-eight years a priest when he attended the 2005 meeting of the Conference of Priests of Ireland. He could look back then at a time when ordination was for life, pretty much as marriage was too. He said:

> When I was in the seminary there was only one priest I had ever heard of who left the priesthood at that stage and then *Humanae Vitae* came in 1968, and my memory of '68 and '69 is that a lot of guys were leaving. At that time we didn't have room in our churches in Cork for those that were coming and now it's the other way round; we are going out and looking for people to come into our churches.

Paradoxically, he thinks it was easier for men to leave the priesthood then, though it is still often difficult today for families to understand a man wanting out.

> The guys who left, in my early days, were well qualified, by the standard of the day. They had a degree; they could get a job. The problem for priests today is that if you leave, your qualifications aren't special in the world, so in one sense I think it is harder for the guy who leaves the priesthood today than it was in the early days.

Are some staying on simply because they wouldn't trust themselves to find a decent job on the outside? No, that's not what he's saying. The man leaving the priesthood today is doing what is expected of him. He creates no major scandal in his family or community. In the past, some of the men were ostracised.

> I can remember one guy, a friend of mine, and he was disinherited by his family and he spent some of the time sleeping in his car because that's all he had. But, thank God, the guy did work out fine and he has been very much

integrated into the church, and in the parish he is living in now he is very much part of the church.

One thing the priest of today misses is the consolation that he is respected.

> In my early priesthood, people always believed that they could trust the priest. That trust has been broken and that can spread to us all being tarred with the same brush. I know some priests say you couldn't walk Dublin dressed as a priest. Now I have done it repeatedly and only twice have I come across anything that bordered on an attack and then only verbal.

Only twice has someone scowled at him in the street for being a priest, and he regards that as a hopeful sign!

Fr Seán McCartan from Armagh diocese is one of the few younger priests. He says that he enjoys the life for the 'great sense of solidarity and support, of friendship and sharing'. Nor does the flight from the priesthood alarm him.

> We are in a changing climate in all sorts of ways in Ireland. I don't think there is too much to worry about. I think we are moving forward rather than regressing.

But he gives stark figures for the scale of the change.

> There was eighteen of us started out together in 1984 to study for the priesthood. In the seminary that I went to, we had to share a room for the first two years because it was filled to capacity. That seminary is now closed, twenty years on, as are five others. So it is very different. And a few men dropped out as students and a few have left since they were ordained as well.

To others, that might read like a calamity within the priesthood, but not to Fr Seán.

I don't think it needs to be explained. I think it is probably something quite positive. Priests, like other people, are finding their own lives now and don't feel that same necessity to remain when they discover that the Lord has another path for them.

In short, it is all God's doing and for God's reasons.

I think the change has been too rapid for us to grasp but we have to be optimistic and hopeful and trusting that the spirit, in spite of everything, is working away. And I think there are signs of that.

One way to recover would be to ordain women to the priesthood. As far as the hierarchy is concerned, that isn't even up for discussion. Fr Seán replied:

Well, officially I don't think we are allowed to talk about it but at a personal level I would certainly be an advocate of the ordination of women. I think that any role that can be shared by both men and women is at its best when it is shared, and I don't see any reason—and I don't understand the reason—why the church is opposed to the ordination of women.

And if the church is running low on priests, that doesn't mean that people are not spiritual.

When you just scratch the surface, you almost always find deep faith. So while there is rejection of the model and the structures I don't think there is any rejection of faith. I think people's faith is still very strong. It is maybe not as easily defined as it once was but they all still have great faith in God.

The big question, though, is whether that residual faith in Irish Catholics is enough to sustain an institutional church. And how will that residual faith respond to a church that wants its followers to adhere to strict doctrine?

Fr Ciary Quirke is a Jesuit priest at a retreat house in Dollymount, Dublin. Like virtually every priest you ask, he admits to having been tempted to leave.

> Many times I have wondered if I should have gone, and how am I still here. That too is part of the providence of God in my life. I am very conscious that I am not called to be a Jesuit for anything great on my part but that this is what God wants. It was very clear to me when I left home at 17 that this was something I was being asked to do. It wasn't my idea. I didn't want it—in one way I didn't want it; in another way I did and was very happy to do it.

The Jesuit charism, or gift, is for retreat and spiritual help, for which people are still going to them.

> One of the basic premises of my faith is that it is God's world and that God is present when we know Him and don't know Him. And God is at work, even in the mess that I make, and he is offering me a gift of some kind, even in my very sinfulness. I know this. I have seen it in my own life. A lot of my work is one to one, helping people to work with their own experiences and recognising how God is offering them new life and new hope and new ways of being who they are.

But Fr Ciary is also angry at times at the failure of the Catholic hierarchy to listen to the concerns of priests. At the 2006 meeting of the Conference of Priests of Ireland, the bishops were invited to meet the priests and hear their problems. Four bishops accepted the invitation. They were Gerry Clifford, Auxiliary of Armagh; John Kirby of Clonfert, Philip Boyce of Raphoe and Larry Forristall of Ossory.

'These are people who have no sense of there being a problem,' said one angry priest who was there. 'Some people should acknowledge that they might be in particular danger, by virtue of their vocation, of being Pharisees,' he said.

One of the problems the priests raised with the bishops, behind closed doors, was the readiness of the bishops to suspend priests when complaints of abuse were made against them. Does the priest have any rights? This was a concern for many of those present. One priest said that the meeting was 'a first step'. It turned out to be the last step.

In 2006, the NCPI tried to elect a president to replace Fr John Lyttleton. No one was nominated. The conference then actively went out looking for a new president and couldn't find one. Lyttleton stood down in 2007 and, under normal circumstances, would have had a successor shadowing him through his last year.

There are two rival explanations offered by priests for the demise of their national conference. Some say that the priests needed a strong representation of their concerns to the bishops and that the conference had failed to provide this. Others say that, though this was a strongly expressed anxiety, there was no basis for it. The NCPI was not a trade union, nor could there be a trade union for a vocation governed by the principle of obedience. Unless the priests were going to assert some independence of the bishops, there was no job of that kind for the NCPI to do.

The outgoing secretary of the NCPI was the Vincentian missionary Fr Paschal Scallon. He said that he didn't think that anyone really wanted a clash with the bishops: 'The four bishops who came along: it was good to see them there. There was some exchange. And it was hoped that that might continue this year.'

But weren't priests angry with the bishops and the 'B team' that had been sent to speak to them?

> Actually there was very little anger. There is enough solidarity among priests to understand that there is no point in getting up in the middle of a meeting and lashing out wildly or in an ill-considered manner because, though it may vent someone's spleen, it is a wee bit self-indulgent.

But that doesn't rule out the possibility, surely, of disaffected priests making a strong and assertive statement, if it is in them to do so.

> What we are looking for is to promote dialogue between bishops and priests and laity. What we are really hoping for is to create a forum where all would meet in a national assembly of the Catholic church in Ireland … There is absolutely nothing to be gained by setting up a forum so that we can have a war. It is just not feasible or helpful or even Christian. The task is to promote dialogue. There is an aching need for a wide and wide-ranging conversation among Catholics in Ireland because we have this rich heritage that we really need to oversee more widely and more responsibly.

The other explanation offered for the demise of the National Conference of Priests of Ireland is that priests had simply lost interest and their morale was so low that they could not even rouse themselves to save the conference from extinction. There is perhaps a connection between the two theories; morale was low in the face of the blunt reality that bishops did not have to listen to priests and priests had already accepted this when they willingly entered the lowest stratum of the hierarchical pyramid. Once there had been an even lower stratum, the laity. Now many of them had gone and the rest of them had ceased to regard the priest as their superior. According to Fr Scallon:

> I think there is an immense amount of frustration and disenchantment among priests. We are very conscious of our vocation and very keen that we fulfil that vocation in the Catholic community at the service of the people to whom we've been sent, but there is, as well, a deep sense of frustration, disappointment, disillusionment, and even depression on a wide scale, perhaps low level but it's definitely there. People just don't feel enthusiastic.

He had had an indication of how difficult it would be to rouse priests to action when the NCPI sent him on an outreach to dioceses.

> I remember one very stark experience I had, where I stood in front of a coterie of priests, having given my input, and asking them for feedback. Not a dickie bird. And I am talking about a group of fifty to sixty priests all fanned out in front of me. Not a word came back. I found that extraordinary. I just got the impression, going away, that this exists to some extent all round the country and it is weighing us all down. These men are grossly demoralised.

———

One witness to the beginnings of the decline of the NCPI was the extraordinary Soline Humbert who used to attend it because she believes that she has a vocation to the priesthood. That ageing, dull, male clique of subservient and dispirited men was not going to re-energise a dying church, she said, but maybe the spirit acting against all their expectations would. The Pope had declared that women could not be priests, but as far as Soline could tell, this stricture had not bound God, and God had called her. And there were some ordained male priests who accepted that. Her former chaplain at Trinity, Eamonn McCarthy, had turned down a parish because he would not assent to the principle that only men could be priests. He had been brought to that position by his belief in Soline's vocation. Enda MacDonagh, president of the NCPI in the late 1990s, had invited Soline Humbert as a representative of Brothers And Sisters In Christ (BASIC), an organisation she had helped to form to campaign for the church's recognition of the vocations of women.

> The last few times I was there, it had a very sombre and depressed mood. I was almost relieved to get out into the Dublin traffic because at least there was a sense of moving

and life. Sometimes when I came out of it, it was like having been in a tomb. There was a sense of something actually dying or dead. It was actually very painful. The priests were going through a very painful time and it was very, very dark.

Priests then were coping with the humiliation of the paedophile scandals.

That was really rocking them. Of course, that was only one aspect and underneath there was the whole sense of the breach of trust at the heart of ministry. And then there was also the fall in vocations—that is, vocations in the narrow sense of the male celibate clerical vocations, and at the same time a lot of them had issues with the whole teaching of the church and the hierarchical structure.

She says, 'It was a questioning, dark mood. They were not men who were confident, happy or secure or hopeful. I felt for them. You couldn't but feel for what those people were going through.'

But it wasn't just the dispirited mood of the priests that made her position among them pointless; it was Pope John Paul's ruling that the ordination of men only was a matter that was settled and beyond all discussion.

Unless they open to the married priests who have been pushed out, and many of them still have a sense of vocation; unless all the women, religious and lay, who have that sense of vocation; unless they are part of the process, I don't see any future for the priesthood. There is also a need to recognise what the spirit is doing in the church. Are we surprised or unhappy that as usual the spirit does not confine Herself, Himself, Itself to our narrow little expectations? Perhaps it is very good news that the conference has died because then there can be something new, more alive.

The closure of the National Conference may be a symptom of a deeper malaise in the church. It's not just that there aren't enough priests emerging to sustain a conference; there aren't enough priests for anything. Priests are dying out.

Fr Gerard Moloney, editor of the Redemptorist magazine *Reality*, laid out the scale of the crisis facing the Irish priesthood in November 2006. Since 1 November 2000, 1,173 Irish priests had died but only 101 new Irish priests had been ordained. That meant that only one diocesan priest in five was being replaced. In the religious and missionary orders the figure was one in 30. On average, the deaths of Irish priests continued to outnumber ordinations more than tenfold. In 2005, 199 Irish priests died, whereas only eight priests were ordained. On top of that, many others had simply left.

'These statistics', said Fr Moloney, 'are catastrophic.' He wrote, in an article in *The Irish Times*:

> This is good news for the Catholic church's enemies and for those who want to eliminate religion from society but it is a tragedy for those who love the church. And the other tragedy for the church is that there is no short- or medium-term solution to this crisis.
>
> The number of seminarians in training is tiny and, unless something entirely unexpected happens, will not increase any time soon. However, the biggest tragedy of all is that the Catholic church does not appear to have even a Plan A as to how to face up to the shortage of clergy, not to mind a Plan B. Possible radical solutions, such as redefining what we mean by priesthood, are not being discussed. Even the possibility of ordaining worthy married men or of extending the ordained ministry to women are not options. And all the while the church continues on its merry way, closing churches here, twinning parishes there, and asking overstretched priests to take on more and more.

The optimists like Fr Seán McCartan must drive Fr Moloney to distraction.

At the same time, the new president of Maynooth, Fr Hugh Connolly, is saying that there is a need now to provide a foundation course for new entrants because most of them are coming from professional backgrounds and the trades and don't have the same 'faith basis'. Recruitment efforts will now be directed at older men, rather than boys coming out of Catholic schools, with the sort of familiarity with the religious environment that schoolboys would once have had.

He said that the foundation year might focus on prayer, the Church's teaching and tradition, liturgy, being able to read and pray with scripture, and perhaps developing leadership roles in prayer, so that a man would learn to feel comfortable sitting with someone else and leading prayer. The sort of boys who would have come out of Catholic secondary schools and into the seminaries in past generations would already have been at ease in a context in which other people were praying.

Fr Louis Hughes, a Dominican priest in Drogheda, thinks that the worries about the survival of the church are overstated:

> There is an age bulge but there are priests in every decade. There are young ones. That bulge represents a hangover from a period when we had an excessive number of people in the priesthood.

One had to decide whether to view this as a crisis or an opportunity. 'It's interesting to note that the number of vocations in Maynooth this year is up by a third,' said Fr Hughes.

In fact, in 2007, twenty-four new seminarians entered training for the priesthood at Maynooth. This represents a doubling of the numbers coming from some dioceses, from one to two in Down and Connor, for instance. But it is two fewer than the twenty-six who enrolled in 2006, not an increase at all.

'The church is not about to disappear in Ireland', says Fr Hughes. 'Its death has been prematurely foretold. I see greater openness, greater lay involvement, greater involvement of women, greater creativity.' This sounds more like the church that Soline Humbert envisions than the one that the current leadership governs.

Doesn't the admission of more people into the church also require a relaxation of the sort of doctrinal rigour that has distinguished this pope and his predecessor? According to Fr Hughes:

> The core doctrine is the reality of the person of Jesus as God and Man. If we agree on that, we can debate a lot of other things. I don't relax that doctrine for myself one bit. I believe that doctrine. I teach that doctrine.

But that is elementary Christianity and has nothing distinctively Catholic about it. He may think that everything but the reality of Jesus as God and man is open to question, but the Pope doesn't. Nothing in what Fr Hughes says distinguishes a Catholic from any other type of Christian. Well, maybe the way to be inclusive, and therefore to involve more people, *is* to speak less of the distinctive theologies.

In April 2007, the newly appointed Church of Ireland bishop of Connor announced that before taking up his post he would be going on retreat with the Benedictines. Canon Alan Abernethy said:

> They are such open people. There are no labels. There is no denominationalism. Unfortunately we don't have retreat houses in the Church of Ireland.

It's as if the Reformation had never happened. And Alan Abernethy was no theological lightweight. He was Central Director of Ordinands for the Church of Ireland, essentially a Director of Vocations, with responsibility for supervising students as they progressed through their training to the ministry. He was also a member of the church's Theological Inspection Team, which assessed the quality of training.

Doctrinal differences were no bar to him because no one cared to confront him with them. Much of a tired priesthood doesn't want to confront anyone with them. But it is in the job description that they must.

Chapter 13

Few now want to be priests. Fr Kenneth Brady says that applications to join the Passionists are almost nil:

> About thirteen have been meeting on and off, three or four times a year, considering if they wanted to apply. Four said they did. When it came to the crunch only two made a formal application. One postponed it and one decided it wasn't for him. So we interviewed two and one was deferred and the other was accepted. Then they met a psychologist.

Because no one in their right mind would want to be a priest? All applicants are assessed now, Fr Brady explains. They have to be mature adults. He's not exactly saying that there is something immediately suspect about anyone who wants to be a priest, but he's getting there.

> They are going to meet the same kind of humanity as anywhere else and more pressure because of diminishing numbers. Older communities. We had a province in Holland who decided they weren't taking any more and two or three years afterwards four guys turned up and said,

we know you have taken that decision, but we want to join. One of them is a psychologist.

Disillusionment is inevitable now for any idealist with a vocation. Fr Brady remembers his own and thinks that it is better now if men are confronted with the difficulties early and then back off before they have committed themselves.

> I remember coming here as a young fellow and playing football with the students and going back to my father and mother in Belfast and saying, 'I've just been with the happiest people in the world today and I want to join them.'
>
> Then I come here after the novitiate and some of the old boys in the community are annoying me, and I hear people saying, 'Father so and so is wonderful', and I remember saying to myself that four horses and a chariot wouldn't drag me to go near him.
>
> And I was kind of disillusioned. I was expecting more of them. My idealistic phase. And then I discovered that, almost unknown to myself, relationships were built; there were some days I would have killed them and there were some days I would have died for them. And I suppose that was me becoming a bit more realistic.

He survived that disillusionment but so few do now, and so few can conceive of the priesthood as a rewarding life that the church really needs to redefine the job. On that, both Breda O'Brien and Soline Humbert are agreed. Soline wants to be a priest herself, properly ordained within the church; Breda wants recognition of the 'priesthood of all believers'.

Soline first felt that she had a vocation when she was 17 and a student at Trinity, studying History and Politics. It seemed a mad idea from a mad young woman who should have known better. She was recognised by her chaplain as profoundly religious. One day, when she was studying in her room at Trinity, during the September exams, a man walked in. She was immediately terrified because there had been reports of rapes and robberies on the campus and she realised that she had left herself reck-lessly exposed to danger. The man asked for food and she sat him down in her sitting room and gave him hot chocolate and bread and jam. She went to her bedroom and fetched a little rosary ring that she had had since cub scouts and gave it to him. As she remembers it, he was enormously grateful for the gift.

The sense of vocation came back when she was 33 and she experienced it as a stripping away of her personality. She was married now and had two small children. One morning, she went to mass, and a man whom she knew approached her and showed her a rosary ring and asked her if it was hers. In her sensitised mental state, she read this as a divinely intended, symbolic connection back to the rosary ring that she had given to the stranger in Trinity. She decided that she must show the rosary ring to the Trinity chaplain who had remained a friend in the years since. He was then taking a retreat for priests at Milltown.

> The secretary said they were just going to celebrate mass. I went there and my friend was there and they just had a few minutes before mass. There were sixteen priests, diocesan priests. A Jesuit priest was to say the mass. And I said, 'I need to come in,' and the Jesuit said, 'No, it is a retreat.' But my friend said, 'Let her in.'
>
> So I sat in the upper room in Tabor House and we sat there and it was midday. We were on cushions on the floor and the priest, the Jesuit, was at one end and he presided. And he started the Eucharist and I am sure he was wondering, 'Where has that woman come from?' And he read the gospel and he read the scripture and then he said, 'Has anybody got anything to say?'—as you would.
>
> And lo and behold, I opened my Bible—don't ask me why I had my Bible—and I read: 'The spirit of the Lord is upon me. The spirit of the Lord has sent me to proclaim good news.' Jesus in the synagogue in Nazareth.
>
> So I read it and it was good. It just happened. I had not planned to read anything. And then I sat down and nobody else said anything.

And then came the next part of the mass, the con-
secration. And all the priests stand and they put their hand
out, and that was the day I put my hand out with them.
And that was the moment I knew that my vocation was
alive, and after that I knew that I could never undo it.

And afterwards, shaking hands with the priests, this one
time, I felt in my hands, it was as if my heart was in my
hands, pulsating. And after that they said, 'Well, you can
stay for lunch,' and that was that.

Then she went home and told her husband that she was now a
priest and reported to the bishop to offer her services, which he
declined. She went on to be outrageous like many religious
women before her, once putting up a sketch of a naked woman,
nailed to the cross, on the notice board at the Milltown Institute,
where she studied theology. It didn't stay up for long.

Soline Humbert's journey is an extreme one. Any priest could
have told her that she was not going to be accepted by the
bishops, that if she announced publicly that she was saying mass,
she risked being excommunicated. But her position was
emblematic of the position of most priests, which is why many
did not shun her. They were humiliating themselves too. It was
part of the package.

Most priests live and work in an uneasy middle ground
between the laity and the bishops. They know this is not how it was
supposed to be after Vatican II. They serve a laity who expect—and
want—no doctrinal rigour from them. To work alongside the few
in the laity who care, priests adapt themselves to laity needs, to
ordinary people's needs. They know that the strict letter of the law
of the church says that to be gay is to be 'intrinsically disordered'.
Few Irish priests today would risk using that kind of language
with the mother of a gay man or woman.

The thousands of women who have been to Liverpool and
London for abortions are understood in Canon Law to have
excommunicated themselves. Most of them don't know that
because few priests, even if they got the opportunity, would dare
to tell them.

The doctrinal relaxation of the priests in their humane dealings with the laity has somehow to be reconciled with subservience to the bishops, on the understanding that the bishops are appointed by God over them. This is the grace of Christ flowing down to them through an apostolic succession to the Pope and from him, like champagne down a pyramid of glasses. This grace—and the doctrinal exactitude of the Pope—is supposed to reach the laity at the bottom. It doesn't. Some say it never did, since most Catholics didn't read theology. The difference is that most people baptised as Catholic now have very definite contrary ideas to those of the church. That is new. Since *Humanae Vitae*, the laity has decided to exercise an informed conscience of its own.

The doctrinal discipline doesn't even reach the priests, since they have liberalised to secure what is left of their relationship with the laity. It stops with the bishops, who are now the lowest tier of the hierarchical pyramid actually to take doctrine seriously.

'I hope I am at least a good Christian,' says Fr Brian D'Arcy. It's what many of them say. It doesn't amount to being an apostle for the world view of Pope Benedict XIV. But if a reformation has occurred within the Catholic priesthood, why does it not express itself as an honest revolt against the bishops?

There was some anger expressed in the death throes of the National Conference of Priests of Ireland. It was anger at how out of touch with the needs of priests the bishops were. If the tweedy priests in their conference looked dour and musty, the bishops look like a sleepy bunch of old eccentrics. The priests were angry with them, primarily, for their handling of sexual abuse complaints. The priest who is complained about is always named and always suspended. This implies that, to the bishop, the credibility of an accuser is always greater than the credibility of that priest. But there is more. Priests are shifted at short notice from comfortable houses and familiar postings. They are heard but not heeded. The bishops are the last dictatorship in Christendom. Like other dictatorships, they won't feel the need to adapt until revolution is at their door. And it isn't.

The power politics of this says that priests should just decide to ignore the bishops. Occasionally one, like Pat Buckley in Larne, does that. But even Soline Humbert's campaign for the ordination of women seeks to preserve the church intact. When Buckley, now a bishop on elevation by another dissident, ordained a woman, Soline sent her blessing but declined to attend.

The priests do not revolt against the bishops because they do not have the intellectual focus to see that their own doctrinal liberalism entitles them to do this and because they don't have the energy. Beyond that is a whole Catholic laity that allows the bishops to dictate how their schools are run. What is a Catholic school these days? Even the bishops now talk of the need to integrate and to allow other cultures and faiths to benefit by a Catholic education. But why would the other cultures submit to Episcopalian rule? Well, because the standard of education is higher in Catholic schools. Do you need a bishop at the top to determine that?

Surely moments will come which make plain the irrelevance of the bishops. If most pupils in such schools are not mass-going Catholics; if most teachers are not mass-going Catholics either, and are women on the Pill, some of them already self-excommunicated by having used the morning-after pill; if the bishop has no actual authority over the decisions they take in their own lives, on what basis do they acknowledge that he is the boss and can tell them, for instance, to shut down Amnesty International groups in the school, without discussion, as Bishop Donal McKeown did in Belfast?

Well, that issue doesn't express the contradiction sufficiently strongly to make the authority of bishops untenable, but something may someday, as *Humanae Vitae* did in the relationship between the priest and the laity. And then the teacher will simply ask the bishop to leave the room. It can't be presumed that the church won't in the future clash with science again and ban the teaching of a scientific theory. John Paul II foresaw a clash arising from likely scientific determinations about the evolution of consciousness.

In Northern Ireland, in 2006, when the bishops asked schools to arrange a special day of reflection on the Catholic ethos, the teachers' trade union simply told them that teachers were too busy and had more important things to do. Tony Carlin of the Irish National Teachers' Organisation said that the union had not even been consulted, but that he had heard of it through angry teachers contacting him. Bishop Donal McKeown said that his understanding was that he didn't have to contact unions about such things.

The people have only once to ask what bishops are for and the game is up. If the priests were to lead them in this, there might be some chance of there still being a priesthood that people would listen to in twenty years from now. And a bit of creative theology might solve some of these problems—a few more 'Irish solutions'. But no one has the imagination or energy to try.

The clampdown on Amnesty International in schools followed a policy change by Amnesty to promote a woman's right to choose to have an abortion. Dublin Amnesty said that it would not campaign on that issue. That appears to have secured it the freedom to continue to organise in Catholic schools. In Northern Ireland, one bishop ordered a group to close in a school of which he was a board member, and all other Catholic schools shut down their groups when they heard of it.

Couldn't the bishops have accepted, if the argument was put to them, that not every sin needs to be classed as a crime, that to suppose a sin is a crime is to promote Catholic imperialism? Can't Amnesty ask for the decriminalisation of abortion without being understood to have pronounced on the Catholic principle that human life begins at conception? There are all sorts of compassionate and practical reasons why a woman who has an abortion should not be hounded by the police. Can't it be a matter between herself and God without the police getting involved? Doesn't the church wanting the police involved reflect a lack of confidence in its own moral authority?

As with Soline Humbert: surely it is possible to allow her to break bread and share wine in the name of Jesus without

181181

treating her like a heretic. Couldn't the church argue that the priest's sacrament is simply something different, and even allow her the right to disagree? Why argue with every dissenter? Cardinal Daly wrote to her to ask her to 'desist'. Why bother? She was more offended still by the Papal Nuncio's and Cardinal Brady's not answering her letters, but they might have taken the more diplomatic approach.

Fr Eamonn McCarthy suggests another theological resolution. The church baptised and confirmed this woman and told her that the spirit was now moving in her: might it not now at least have the courtesy to hear what the spirit has said to her? Logical, of course, but letting everyone listen to the spirit within would put the bishops out of business.

Couldn't the bishops have said that the difference between an ordained man's Eucharist and Soline's is that in one transubstantiation occurs—a phenomenon which no one can claim to understand or define anyway—and that in the other, Christ is present in the sense that He is always everywhere anyway, or in the sense that he is always among those who gather in his name? Of course, that would have brought them into trouble with their theology of communion which forbids Catholics to receive communion in Protestant churches and forbids those not baptised Catholic to receive it in Catholic churches.

Fr McCarthy argued that, by giving communion to ordinary lay people, when Jesus himself had given it only to the apostles, the church was already elevating the laity into a priesthood. There is no suggestion in the Last Supper that some are entitled to share the bread and others only to receive it.

———

The future of the church is the collapse of ordained priesthood. It is going to be lay Eucharistic ministers alone who will be serving communion in the future, and most of them are women. And in preparation for that day there are already more women than men studying theology in Ireland. It is mostly women who will be teaching religion in Irish Catholic schools.

But another element in the mix is the suspicion that many of the new priests are conservative. There are two good reasons why they should be. Many have had late vocations. Anyone in Ireland who reaches his thirties or forties now, and still wants to be a priest, must have a very thick ecclesiastical skin. He must take the role very seriously. He will probably have worked in other institutions and he will be ambitious to rise within the church and not stay in the lower tier. In that case, he will know how to play the system. He will know that new bishops aren't recruited from among liberal priests. And if he wants to be a bishop himself, he will know what game to play, even if it ultimately leaves him in charge of a vastly reduced church.

Chapter 14

The collapse of interest in religion in Ireland might have evolved into an easy secular indifference, such as prevailed in, say, England or Australia ten years ago, but the global climate has changed. A new idea has entered public discourse on religion: it is that you no longer have to be sensitive to the feelings of believers. Until recently it was acceptable to disagree with believers—huge numbers did—but it was considered a mark of normal civilised behaviour not to accuse them of being superstitious and silly but to show some respect for that for which they show reverence. That principle took a knock from militant Jihadism. A willingness on the part of some religions to attack others licensed those of no religion to attack all. And those who wished to attack all religions were freed to argue that their brash language was as nothing compared to the actual physical violence that some believers used. The bar had been raised on the vehemence of public discussion of whether or not there is a God.

It was now okay to say plainly not only that there is no God but that those who think there is one insult the intelligence of the rest of us and demean themselves. The main champions of this argument have come to be known as the New Atheists. Chiefly they are Richard Dawkins, Christopher Hitchens, Daniel Dennett and Sam Harris. There are also A.C. Grayling, John Gray and Polly Toynbee.

Suddenly atheism is loud and strident again. You would think from the tone of writers like Dawkins, author of *The God Delusion*, that atheism was breaking free from centuries of shamed silence within a prevailing religious culture, but that more accurately describes its experience in the nineteenth century than in the twenty-first. Today religion is an easy target. What has worked atheism up into a temper is the sudden re-emergence of religion as a force in global politics. Jihadism reached a new level of violent militancy in confrontation with western leaders, Tony Blair and George Bush, who also defined their missions in religious terms. Suddenly the kind of war that had made our own Northern Ireland, from the 1970s, appear backward and ridiculous was being imagined as our global future. Several writers then saw it as their responsibility to try to deflate the ardour of the religious militants by proving that belief in God was a delusion.

In the 1960s, we had thought that religion was no longer a force in the conflicts that would characterise the age. We had class war. The stand-off between western capitalism and the Soviet Union stood in for all the minor class tensions around the world, including the clash between trade unionists and bosses at home. What we didn't realise until the Cold War was over, was that the global stand-off had been dampening down ethnic tensions. It was replaced not by diverse wars over class and capital, as might have been predicted, but by wars over ethnic rights to nationhood, in which religion was nearly always a definer of ethnic allegiance. Suddenly there were Northern Irelands all over the place and that type of war seemed standard rather than eccentric.

What exasperates the New Atheists is that the nineteenth-century discoveries, which scientifically invalidated belief in a benign creator god who had made the human soul in his likeness, have not been taken seriously by everybody. So, they say, it is time to restate the simple facts of science in a bolder, more populist way. One hundred and fifty years ago, Darwin showed that we are not made in God's image, but that we evolved slowly alongside our primate cousins, adapting to random circumstance. Nothing at the start of evolution determined that we would emerge in the form we did. Still, most people in the world prefer the god version.

Behind their ardent attack on religion, for some of the New Atheists, is an assumption that human society can be changed by argument, that reason can filter down from these astute thinkers to the rest of society, and that it can ultimately abolish the superstitions by which we have lived for aeons and which emblazon the banners under which we march to war. But how true is that?

Certainly the new scientific culture must be having some effect. There was a time when everyone you met was a believer. The decisions of politicians and pedagogues were taken with reference to the understood will of God. Wars were fought in the belief that God required them. And if you started work in a factory the day after you left school, you did not enter a world of cynical atheists but you moved again among people whose world view—whose god-view—was the same as your own, and the same as your own had been at the age of 10 or even five. The erosion of religion must have something to do with the collapse of the ideas that underpinned it, even if only a few understood those ideas.

Perhaps the famous vehemence of Professor Richard Dawkins is grounded on a frustration at the failure of mere humans to be impressed by science. What an obtuse bunch we appear to be. Yet if reason alone does not erode religion, the evidence is plain that something does. Societies do change their religious cultures and change them very quickly. In fact, it seems to be the rule that when they change, they change quickly, as in the revolutionary upheavals that introduced Christianity to the Roman Empire, Buddhism to India and Islam to the Mediterranean. Religions come quickly and now we are learning that they die quickly. But religions followed armies in the past and secularism didn't arrive in Ireland on the point of a sword. We have secularised later than most of the rest of Europe but we have secularised faster. When we got around to facing life without religion, we embraced it with an unprecedented enthusiasm. For those who want to know what turns people off a dependency on the idea of God, there can surely be no better place to look than here.

And if you are concerned that Islamic countries show themselves to be obsessed and inflexible, well, look to Ireland for reassurance that a country that is steeped in religion today can be more concerned with cable television and chick-lit tomorrow. Whatever expectations Richard Dawkins might have for the transformative effects of reason and a scientific education, secularisation in Ireland and elsewhere is no proof of it. We are still irrational and emotional. We might think that our secularism is a more reasoned approach to life, but you cannot argue that we are, broadly speaking, reasonable people. An ordinary Saturday night in our cities is a bacchanalian extravaganza.

So, what did change us? Well, that is the question that Dawkins and Hitchens should be asking. If you really want to sweep religion from the face of the earth, find out what changed Ireland, and spread that everywhere.

The shocking thing about the writings of the New Atheists is that there is nothing new in them. It is not a revolutionary idea that there is no God ruling over us. All people ask themselves in youth if they believe in God, and the swing against belief, though rapid, has no particular novelty to it, in European countries anyway. When New Atheists attack belief in God, they write as if they have had a fresh insight into the question, but they haven't. None of them mentions Durkheim, who explained the phenomenon of religious belief over a hundred years ago in entirely human, sociological terms.

Why are they so angry in pursuit of an old, familiar cause and why are their books selling so well in Ireland when what they say is so familiar? Alexander Chancellor offers a suggestion in *The Guardian* (29 June 2007). 'The explanation may lie in the fact that nonbelievers feel guilty about their non-belief and cannot get enough reassurance that it is okay to be an atheist.'

But why should they feel guilty in a society that will not ostracise them for their atheism? The New Atheism, by this view, is fascinating because it is still naughty. People thrill to the idea of atheism the way teenagers thrill to the thought of sex, because it is ahead of them still. We Irish are not as atheistic as we think we are and the thought that we might complete the journey excites and slightly unnerves us. Maybe even Richard Dawkins, in the quiet of the night, still feels that there is something there that his daylight arguments betray.

And maybe our atheism thrills us because our motive for promoting it is a secret, slightly shameful one; it is not an engagement with ideas for ideas' sake but an effort to annoy others, the believers. In a world in which religious fanatics take to the streets in protest against a play or a cartoon, it is mischievously tempting to provoke that.

Of course, there is plenty to mock. The modern person might step back and reflect something like this: Imagine that there had never been religion and that it was an entirely new idea. Imagine that for the first time in human history we are confronted by a prophet who tells us that we are the creation of an omnipotent and omniscient God. Imagine that this is an idea that has never occurred to us before and that there is no trace in human culture of such a suggestion. The prophet, of course, offers no proof but he makes his case impressively and persuades us to consider it.

Well, we would not have the culture of atheism either. Without a tradition of believing in God, we would not have had the reactive tradition of insistence that there is no God. There would be no pope but neither would there be a Richard Dawkins. We would be starting afresh with the entirely novel and, perhaps, intriguing idea that we are a creation and not an accident. And from that idea we might extrapolate the further idea that a God who had created us had some plan for us, even some rules for us to live by. And we would start asking ourselves what those rules might be.

Is it plausible that we might come to an early conclusion that one of those rules is: don't masturbate? Or: don't eat pork? Is it not also possible that we would come up with better answers today than we did five thousand years ago?

Of course, without the tradition of religion behind us, we could regard this new prophet sceptically and feel no emotional hurdle in the way of our rejecting the message. But we do have a tradition and maybe the atheists are lumbered with its familiarity as much as the believers are lumbered with its oddities.

Richard Dawkins has made several trips to Ireland to promote *The God Delusion* and has given high-profile media interviews in Dublin and Belfast. The New Atheists have been star turns in Ireland. Irish religious champions have not fared well against them. This is largely down to the simplicity of their message. There are few things more embarrassing than listening to Catholic writer David Quinn or the columnist John Waters trying to challenge these thinkers on their own ground.

Quinn faced Dawkins on Ryan Tubridy's radio show and argued with him about the origins of the universe. Dawkins' answer is simple: however implausible it is that the universe emerged from nothing, it is less impossible than that an infinite, all-comprehending God emerged from nothing first and then made it.

Religion still offers itself as a rival explanation of the origins of the universe, yet its history since Galileo is of its having had to cede every piece of ground it tried to defend against science.

Dawkins wiped the floor with Quinn because he tried to make theologically grounded claims about the origin of matter. He tried to insist that it was the prerogative of religion or philosophy to determine what had preceded the Big Bang.

Previous generations took it for granted that their religious tradition could tell them how the world had come about, could give them a reliable history of humankind and a clear set of moral rules by which to live. That can't be the job of religion any more. And if we were now inventing religion for the first time, we would have more sense than to give it that job.

David Quinn conceded early to Dawkins that many practising Catholics accept evolution and have come to an accommodation between the scriptures and the science that contradicts them. That's true. And it describes a very different Catholicism from that of fifty years or a century ago, when most Christians accepted church teaching. Religious people have been inching back, giving up ground, all the way through their encounter with the challenge of science. They have lost the centrality of the earth; they have lost the historical Jesus; they have lost the benign creator. And they should by now have got accustomed to being defeated on the ground of science every time they stake a claim to any of it.

Have they no ground of their own? Richard Dawkins has evolution and the Big Bang on his side. He may know nothing of what preceded the Big Bang, but he has a better chance of finding out, through scientific researches, than David Quinn has through reading the Bible. Who knows? Maybe a sentient being in another dimension did light the touch paper and stand back. Maybe that sentient being has no idea of the outcome of that experiment; maybe it was killed by the blast. This is all science fiction but, as speculation, it is as meaningful as theology or philosophy on that same question.

Intelligent religious people should give up all claims to knowing that God made the world. There are other religious traditions that leave creation out of the God story. Christian thinkers will have to drop it, too.

But religious people have inherited the need to defend God as a creator and guardian of the universe. The first question in the penny catechism is: Who made the world? Answer: God made the world. That has left us with the habit of thinking that creation is the starting point for all discussion about God and the fear that the whole game is lost when creation is disproved.

But what is religion for? If it is an alternative account of the origins of the cosmos—that is, if it still competes with science— then science wins. If it is something else, what is it?

The philosopher John Gray regards religious faith as ubiquitous and enduring. 'Human beings', he writes, 'will no more cease to be religious than they will stop being sexual, playful or violent.' Coming from Gray, author of *Black Mass* (2007), this can sound very strange, for he is a pessimist who blames the Christian tradition for producing the political faith in utopia which inspired both Communism and Nazism in the last century. But Gray says that religion is humankind's way of coping with mystery, and not, as Dawkins sees it, an alternative account of the origins of the universe. Gray goes so far as to accuse Dawkins of being innately religious, too, in his faith that humankind can buck the forces of evolution. What is this if not an essentially utopian religious idea? Nothing in the science of evolution tells us that any such freedom is remotely attainable.

Another great celebrant of the new religion of evolution is also wrestling with these ideas. Steven Pinker, a Harvard professor, is an evolutionary psychologist. Within Gray's pessimistic view, there is no improvement in humanity which does not come from the adaptive forces of evolution responding to chance and circumstance. Pinker asks if morality has an existence outside humanity and is in the nature of something that we are learning about rather than producing out of ourselves adaptively. How else do we explain the fact that we are better, more decent people than we were a few hundred years ago when we tortured heretics with hot tongs?

Gray would say that we aren't better and that we may well go back to hot tongs in the future. Gray says that we are better owning up to our religious tendency, for faith suppressed, like sexuality suppressed, has ways of bouncing back and wreaking havoc.

At least what Pinker and Gray have concluded is that there are far more interesting things to conclude from a century of reflecting on Darwin than that there is no God.

———

The ancients gave us a story of creation. It is an intriguing myth, when read as one. We discovered our nakedness when we sought a shortcut to the truth about good and evil. What's that all about? It appears to be an attempt to say more about our psychology than about our material origins. But the story of a solitary intelligence, creating the universe to toy with, is not only devoid of inspiring value today, but it actually describes a God who is responsible for a flawed creation, a God who is easy to fear and despise.

When the magazine *Granta* invited modern writers to imagine God, many said that they thought of him as malign and manipulative. And is it any wonder that people are embarrassed by religion when it clings to the redundant job of explaining matter, and still manages to find no more to say about it than it could 3,000 years ago?

A spiritual person looks at the night sky and is silenced. The response is not to ask how that got there. It is for science to measure and religion to marvel. Other religious traditions do not depend on the idea of God as a creator. Vedanta and Buddhism don't. What David Quinn could have said to Dawkins is this: I am entirely indifferent to whether God or a stray spark produced the evolving, unfolding universe, and I defer entirely to your greater knowledge of these things. But my challenge is my personal existence. I pray to a God I can hardly conceive of, whose mysteries I cannot unravel, and I always feel better for it afterwards.

He might also have argued that reflection on evolution itself prompts, in thinking people, a numinous vertigo, not unlike the sense of wonder that is at the heart of religious or aesthetic sentiment. But there is no space for such reflections within the religious traditions we are currently discarding.

——

John Waters declares himself impressed by the 'Goldilocks enigma', by which this universe is just right for us, a fact that suggests creation and forethought. But it is also just right for everything else that is in it, and given that we are so small and so recent, we can hardly conclude lightly that it was all for us. If there is a creator who made this world to a purpose, there is no way of proving that we are that purpose. This is an old universe and we are late arrivals in it. Who knows? Its creator's purposes may have been fulfilled a billion years ago.

Perhaps Evolution is God. The discovery in late 2007 that humans have continued to evolve at speed since the Palaeolithic age prompts awesome reflections surely and challenges moral philosophies that until recently seemed rock certain—such as that we do not improve and are as barbarous as cavemen underneath all our civilities, a point apparently proven by the Holocaust and now in doubt again.

When Waters took on one of the New Atheists, Christopher Hitchens, he made a more coherent effort to stick to his point and defend safe ground than Quinn did, though all that the audience saw was a mauling, because Hitchens was bullish and irreverent and funny. The New Atheists are doubly difficult to confront because, aside from having the better logic on their side, they are aggressive. Christopher Hitchens, like Dawkins, is quick to attack the intelligence of those who argue with him and to interpret their opinions as insult.

In June 2007, he was the star guest at Dublin Writers' Week, in town to promote his book, *God is Not Great*. He debated that question with John Waters at the Gate Theatre. It seemed easier to fill a theatre in Dublin for a debate about God on a Sunday night than it would have been to fill a church. Every seat was taken and there were dozens left standing on the stairs by the box office, hoping for a spare ticket, even when it was clear that there would be none.

Hitchens travelled to the theatre with Bob Geldof's sister, Lyn, and was received like a great celebrity by the crowds at the door. But there was something sixth-formish about it all, down to Hitchens' bawdy jokes on stage. Asked by Brenda Power if he would like to take the podium or speak from his seat, Hitchens said: 'Well, if I can't be erect, I can at least be upright.'

Ireland is still new to atheism and relishes the novelty of it, and there was something akin to giggling over sex in the audience's enthusiasm for sporting its contempt for anyone who believes in God. Hitchens was acting like someone who had read that in their manner. Or perhaps he was just carrying on as he would have done in many parts of the United States, where you can still find atheists who are chuffed at their own daring.

In his preliminary speech, Hitchens made three points. Religion infantilises us and insults us with the assumption that we could not make moral choices ourselves if not directed by a 'celestial dictator'. Here he had Yahweh in mind.

I don't believe that my Jewish ancestors got all the way to Sinai—not that I think that journey was ever made, but let's accept the metaphor—under the impression that murder and theft and perjury were all right, only to be told, perhaps to their shock, this is not kosher after all. They wouldn't have made it that far, ladies and gentlemen, brothers and sisters, it must be obvious, if they had been under that impression.

The problem with this argument, of course, is that it takes the revelations reported in the Bible for the whole of religious history. It doesn't disprove the possibility, indeed the known history, that says that before Moses, the Jews and others were under other religious influences. Hitchens hadn't refuted religion, only the idea that the Jews had needed the vision of Moses to put manners on them.

Religion begins by attacking us in our deepest and most important integrity. It says of us, makes us think of ourselves, that we wouldn't know right from wrong, that we'd have no sense of solidarity with each other, no ethics, no morals, if we were not afraid of a permanent, unalterable celestial dictatorship that was in charge of our thoughts, that could convict us of thought crime while we're asleep, that if not for the fear of punishment from this or reward for that, we wouldn't be able to act rightly or justly. I believe that is an insult, even to us in our imperfection.

Well, he is right. He has nailed the fallacy promoted by several clerics quoted above, that the alternative to belief is moral dereliction. Kevin Myers answered this in his *Irish Independent* column that week. He argued that religion is indeed a restraint on human barbarity and that even if it is untrue, we are better off with it than without it.

Religion, Hitchens said, 'pisses in the well' of morality, adding genital mutilation and other absurdities to human laws which would be better without these additions. Religion, he said, was man-made, in both senses, masculine made.

Show me a religion that doesn't demonstrate some kind of revulsion or disgust for female sexuality, for the female anatomy, some terror of menstrual blood. Name me a single god or prophet of any importance who wasn't born of a virgin, right down to Buddha emerging from a slit in his mother's side. Anything but the contemplation of the fact of our mothers that makes them human. That is real poison injected into the very heart of the human personality, a disgust for women and a disgust for sexuality. Religion is guilty of this and for the maiming and ruining of millions and millions of lives up to this moment, and making a mystery and a nastiness where none need exist.

Well, all that aversion to menstrual blood is plain in the *Book of Leviticus*, and sexual coyness is normal to most modern congregations, but is it really fair to assume that the modern male believer in the pews of a Catholic church in Galway or a Presbyterian assembly hall in West Cork is shuddering with disgust at the proximity of women? Many of Hitchens' arguments covered their shallowness with grandiosity. He finished with a challenge to the audience: name one ethical act or statement made for a religious motive that could not have been made for ordinary human motives. No one would be able to think of one, he confidently predicted, and he would thereby have won the debate. Later he said:

But ask if you can think of an unbelievably wicked thing that was done by somebody because they believed God wanted them to do it. You have no difficulty there.

What morally normal parent would mutilate the genitals of their children if they didn't think that God wished and required it? Who would blow themselves up, wishing to take others with them, if it wasn't a divine instruction? Lecturing to children that they will go to Hell for the tiniest infraction, a thoroughly wicked thing to do. No one has any difficulty in seeing how religion can make you behave worse. Well, I win again, don't I?

John Waters approached the podium with rather less bluster. Hitchens was game to play on pugilistic terms. Waters was not. So he started by praising Hitchens' 'fine book'. He said that he agreed with most of it and that, twenty years earlier, when he had given up Catholicism, he would probably have agreed with all of it. But he read the book as an attack on institutional religion rather than as a polemic that successfully undermined religious faith.

> Religion fundamentally is a question with which we are all imbued, whether we know it or not, whether we call ourselves Christians, believers, agnostics, atheists. We are imbued with this question. That question is: What is the meaning of everything? What does the world mean? Where did the world come from? What is the meaning of my life? So, fundamentally religion is a personal thing. It's not necessarily to be found in books. I am born with a question and the question presumes an answer.

Hitchens, he said, asserts the importance of reason, but we live by more than reason. We don't formulate our responses to the world from a list of facts. We use intuition. We attend to the world with heart and with spirit.

> My reason is not just my mind. My reason doesn't deal just with what is demonstrable. My reason is many things besides. It is intuition, it is feeling, it is spirit, it is heart. I apprehend the world in many, many ways, not just by listing facts and deciding between them.

He said: 'You can get rooted in a book like this. It is impressive in a three-dimensional reality and, for me, I need more than three.'

Waters was at his weakest when he was challenged about statements he had made about God. 'How do you know that?' 'I believe,' he said. And the audience laughed.

Waters had been arguing that there are viable questions about the meaning of life. Hitchens argued that those questions are unreal. Why had the Indian Ocean tsunami killed good people? Because these things happen.

Waters quoted a book to which he had referred previously in his *Irish Times* column, *When Bad Things Happen to Good People* by Rabbi Harold Kushner. Bad things happen either because God is not good or because he is not all-powerful. Waters clearly likes the idea that God is not all-powerful and that creation continues and that we have a contribution to make to it.

One of the things that exasperated Hitchens was that Waters would not present himself in the debate as a Catholic believer. He said that this was a routine experience for him now, to find that the champions of religious belief wilted before him and refused to defend the whole package and give him a proper argument. He accused John Waters of wearing the medals of his own defeat. Who had won for him the right to be an à la carte Catholic but the secular humanists? No priesthood would have permitted him to pick selectively from Catholic teaching. The fact that he could do so now weighed on Hitchens' side of the argument, not on Waters' own. He forced John Waters to be candid about his spiritual travail.

> JW: It's a struggle. It's a struggle with rules; it's a struggle with belief every day. Of course everybody is different, and each person is imperfect in that relationship with faith. There are days when I doubt; there are days when I believe strongly.
>
> CH: Can I just ask you what religion it is that you don't belong to?
>
> JW: I was born a Catholic.
>
> CH: I know that, but where are we now?
>
> JW: I go to mass, I go to church.
>
> CH: You're back in the bosom.
>
> JW: Yes.

Waters argued that there is a critical mass of hope in a society of believers that enables atheists to saw at the very branch upon which they sit. But the near parity of the strength of the arguments of the two men was lost on an audience that was appalled at Waters' hesitant and meek presentation.

No one had met Hitchens' challenges to cite one ethical act or statement by a religious person that might not be made by an atheist. The weakness in this challenge as an attack on religion is that it supposes that it is ethical conduct which is the distinctive marker of religious behaviour. There is little reason to suppose that it is. Some religions have very little ethical content. But there is something that all people do and which is essentially religious and makes no sense in rationalistic terms. It is the act of putting flowers on a grave. We all do that; we have no rational reason for doing it; and we have been doing it for 40,000 years.

In the week after this debate, there was outrage in Omagh in County Tyrone because the hospital trust there planned to dig up the graves of 140 unnamed mental health patients from a past generation, to use for a hospital extension the land in which they had been buried. Rationally the protest was absurd because the hospital was for the good of the living. Only a religious perception, a regard for the sacred, could put any value on the remains of the unknown dead, yet it appears that an innate sense of the sacred was outraged by the decision.

After the debate, John Waters reflected on the claim by Christopher Hitchens that the very dilution of religious conviction among believers was a credit to his side of the argument, that the à la carte Catholic was evidence of the damage done to religion by secular humanism. He said:

It is most inconvenient for them that they have written these books about fanatics and then they come out and they can't find any. Their books are a total distortion of reality. They are a total immersion in the negativity of religion and the bad history and the awfulness of the Inquisition and abuse and so on but they don't acknowledge in any way the 99 per cent of faith-based activity that has been beneficial to humanity. They deny that.

And he said he believes that religion is coming back to Ireland, that people are already thinking the thoughts that will revive it, though it is not yet visible in the public square.

> We saw that with the retreat from Catholicism, with the reaction against the Catholic church which really didn't happen in the 1990s with the Bishop Casey affair and so on. Really that was happening twenty years before in the hearts of people. And I believe that there is a change happening right now in the hearts of people and it won't materialise for perhaps a decade or more.

He says that he agrees with David Quinn that Ireland may lighten up about Catholicism in the way that it lightened up about Britain. But why would it be Catholicism that would provide us with answers to spiritual questions? Why not a more diffuse Christian tradition from which Catholicism would risk excluding itself by being too specific? In the meantime, he concedes that he will appear eccentric in a media milieu that sneers at religion.

> The only thing that distinguishes me from everybody else is that it is my job to say what I feel, what I believe, to speak from my heart, so I have to find some form of courage to transcend the resistance that is still in the public arena at any given moment and say something which I feel to be coming true, which I detect in other people, because this isn't just purely me. I feel this from elsewhere. I'm not saying that I'm a prophet or something but I am saying that the feelings that I have are not unique.

Perhaps he is a prophet; he certainly martyred himself to Hitchens in front of an audience that was not impressed by him. That's the sort of thing prophets do.

———

In Catholicism, the à la carte approach, though widespread, is regarded as dilute and inadequate, not quite the real thing. In Judaism, it is at the heart of the genius of the whole culture, according to Rabbi Julia Neuberger. She explained this in a debate at Westminster on 27 March 2007, on the motion that society would be better off without religion. She was facing some of the big guns of the New Atheism, too: Richard Dawkins, Christopher Hitchens and A.C. Grayling.

Rabbi Neuberger contested the view that religious people were made ridiculous by the untenability of their beliefs. She said that Jews did not define themselves by belief but by the practice of ritual and service within a community. Belief in God was fluid. It came and went. It made no sense to attack a Jew for holding creationist beliefs because he or she might not, and certainly did not feel obliged to. Faith was not subscription to a set of fixed ideas which contradicted reason but a sense that life had a purpose and meaning, best expressed in love and service, in attachment to family and community. This resonates with another concept, expressed disparagingly as 'the simple faith of the simple people'.

Rabbi Neuberger enjoys the old joke, 'two Jews, three opinions'. Her Jewish culture is argumentative. A Jew at a family gathering or in the synagogue is perfectly free to express doubts about the existence of God or the merits of prophecy, or the literal account of the exodus, and will still not be at risk of being presumed to be less a Jew. In Catholicism, by contrast, there is the awkward reality of a papacy and a hierarchy that see their job as one of directing people back to the true set of teachings. And the current pope, Benedict XVI, has form as an enforcer of doctrinal conformity. He is also old fashioned. He wants us to worry about Hell and Purgatory.

A.C. Grayling, in this debate, referred to the Pope's affirmation of the existence of Hell. He joked that Benedict XVI was clearly trying to influence the outcome of their debate, though it wasn't clear which side he was on. He might be supporting the anti-religion motion by making religion absurd.

Benedict went on to make it even more absurd in December 2007 by announcing that pilgrims to Lourdes would receive plenary indulgences, which would spare them the need to purge guilt of past forgiven sins, were they to die straight away. The man has a mediaeval mind. Many Catholics simply don't believe in Hell and won't be told that, by virtue of this unbelief, they are not really Catholics at all. This is partly because, no matter what the Pope says, they will always be able to find a sympathetic priest to agree with them. Their Catholicism is like Rabbi Neuberger's Judaism: it is belonging, not believing. And faith for them is a sense of comfort that comes from belonging and the enjoyment of ritual and prayer, not an intellectual assent to a set of propositions like: God created the world, or Mary did not die but rose into Heaven.

Still, there are many Catholics who do subscribe to the simple faith and, paradoxically, they are often serviced in this faith by educated theologians. At the Clonard Novena in Belfast, people gather to pray to the Virgin Mary for help. The priest from the altar reads out the petitions of the faithful, and many are simple letters from one mother to another, asking her to talk to her son to procure a favour, much as a mother on a housing estate might approach the mother of a local politician or gang boss.

The debate at Westminster was interesting because it produced no defender of this kind of religion; no one who would stand over its elemental terms. No one said, there is a God and, that being the case, we should live in conscious awareness of Him, turn to Him for help and give Him the credit for having created us. No one. Julia Neuberger's case came closest to this when she said that the one 'given' among Jews was a sense that life had meaning and purpose. She did not even try to present the argument that Jews were God's chosen people and that religion was an expression of their compact—covenant—with Him. But surely that is a Jewish fundamental? Apparently not.

The philosopher Roger Scruton drew an analogy between love and religion. He said that love clearly produced disastrous outcomes—broken families, jealous rages—but that this was no reason to argue that we would be better off without love, nor would he expect anyone to propose such a thing. Similarly, yes, religion produces wars and cults, but this does not mean that there is not a possible proper use of the religious urge available to us. He went further to argue that the aspiration expressed in art and music had meaning only within a religious understanding of life.

Dawkins mocks these liberal, à la carte believers, as people too embarrassed by the nonsense they endorse to be able to defend it. He doesn't consider that they might be able to regard themselves legitimately as true devotees, might go through the verbiage of liturgy without taking it literally and yet not regard themselves as hypocrites.

In fact, none of the speakers in this debate defined religion, not even those attacking it. Hitchens classed communism as a religion; Grayling merely demonstrated that those who call themselves Christian don't adhere to the ascetic values of Jesus Christ. Dawkins saw religions as dependent on non-existent supernatural forces. These New Atheists are having an easy time of it. Their trick is to treat religion as the inadequately reasoned response of stupid people to the mystery of life. There are far more interesting discussions to be had out of the material they bandy about than those they offer or confront.

———

Richard Dawkins has wasted his breath on naïve creationists who are easy targets. Then he has turned on modern, à la carte religionists and been exasperated by their refusal to be fundamentalists. There was a far more worthy and appropriate opponent available to him whom he appears not to have taken under his notice. That was Pope John Paul II, who had a concern that was as strong as his own, with the boundaries between science and religion. Where Dawkins wanted those boundaries to be strong and clear, John Paul wanted them to melt away.

In a period of religious transition in which it was normal for even religious people to stand aside from their faith and critique its applicability to real life, Pope John Paul II understood himself unreservedly to be the custodian of God's revelation to man. He revered as exemplars the very thinkers at whom Dawkins scoffed, Anselm and Aquinas. Where Dawkins argued that logic dismissed the idea of God and that faith and logic could not work side by side, John Paul argued that logic, philosophy and science could not reach the ultimate truth without incorporating the truths of revelation which were in the custody of the Magisterium. He longed for a return to the mediaeval way in which philosophy and theology were one.

If the real world seemed to contradict revelation, then—sure enough—the Magisterium might have to reconsider the meaning of revelation, as it had eventually done in the face of Galileo's discovery that the earth was not the centre of the universe. But science would also have to accept at times that it was wrong, when revelation plainly contradicted its findings. There could not be two separate bodies of knowledge contradicting each other and we should be working together to bring faith and science back together as a single corpus of understanding of the world and our place in it. The fissure between science and religion after the tragic mismanagement of poor Galileo would have to be mended. And John Paul loved to lecture scientists on the need to consider revelation—as understood by the Magisterium— if they were not to reach false conclusions in contradiction of it. He blithely explained to evolutionary biologists where they were in danger of going wrong. The church accepted the reality of evolution and accepted also that man was made in God's image. When evolutionary theory sought to explain life and spirit as products of adaptation, it would be in error.

Evolutionary theory is now attempting to explain the emergence of consciousness, and evolutionary psychology is trying to explain the adaptation of the brain to biological needs. It would appear that science is in the precise territory now that John Paul warned it off, and that another great clash between theology and science is imminent.

Dawkins could have fought on a global stage against a religious leader with a massive following and annoyed hundred of millions of Catholics worldwide. Would he not have enjoyed that?

And there is the potential for a more exciting debate than we have heard so far.

Evolutionists, for instance, inevitably mock the Biblical literalists when they say that the world is only 6,000 years old. They know the real age of rocks and our progression from simple-cell pond life. But how old are we? We humans? We left Africa about 80,000 years ago. We could paint and carve about 40,000 years ago. We survived the Northern ice just 12,000 years, or 400 generations, ago. We invented agriculture 6,000 years ago. The Biblical literalists are right about the time of the first garden!

Modern philosophers indulge the sense that they have just discovered from the horrors of the twentieth century that we do not progress. Well, maybe within the span of one century, or five centuries, we don't, but in 6,000 years we have progressed from the hoe to the Internet, from savagery to law.

The sense of how recent we are, when you dwell on it, is almost overwhelming. That was not us coming out of Africa. We changed. It is since then that we found beauty and morality and framed ideas of how to manage a civilisation—brutally still of course. And dwelling on how recent we are leads to reflecting on how little time we have left. The doomsayers of nuclear war and climate change give us hardly a century. Certainly 1,000 years would be painfully little, for a new arrival like us. And 50,000 years, as much as we have had since we first thought of putting flowers on a grave, takes us to another ice age. We are ephemeral and we are amazing. Nothing in nature has been like us.

Dwell on the pain of human existence and you may be pessimistic; you may conclude that God is either not omnipotent or not good, and worry over that, but look at the alternative; the alternative is that we are still just another monkey. What force or circumstance determined our rapid brain growth and our removal from that? How could we ever have imagined that it has not been amazingly beneficial, no matter how much pain the gift was set against? How can we be what we are and not notice that nothing else in nature is like us? The Psalmist in the Old Testament noticed and wrote: 'What is man that you should note him, and the human creature that You pay him heed?' (trans. Robert Alter, 2007)

Individually we are splashes of wave on shingle, cast up to die. Collectively we are the wave itself, smashing to our deaths, expendably, while waves follow behind us. But viewed in time, in a small span of geological or evolutionary time, say as viewed from space by a consciousness that could comprehend the whole life of the planet, we are an astonishing and brief event.

None of that proves the existence of God. It may suggest an extra-planetary experiment. How else could nature have produced a monkey that needed years of nurture before it could feed itself? Yes, science fiction, of course, but fodder for spiritual reflection and query that is far more interesting than speculation on the Big Bang and the creation of the planet. For nearly 100 per cent of the span of this planet we were not here. It is not the creation of the planet that is the intriguing spiritual question; it is the emergence of humanity, just a few hundred generations ago.

Part Three

The Future

Chapter 15

Another argument confronts the New Atheists. It says not that they are wrong—who really knows that there is or isn't a God?—but that they are wasting their time. And Ireland is the proof of it! The case was made by Mary Eberstadt in the magazine *Policy Review* in the June/July 2007 issue. The article was called 'How the West Really Lost God'. Her case looks at the connection between family life and religious faith. Go back for a moment and consider the case made by Eric Kaufmann in his *Prospect* article, 'Breeding for God'. He says that since religious people form more stable families, religious communities grow. The religious will not defeat the New Atheists through argument but will simply outbreed them. Religion will always bounce back.

Interestingly, this was the fear of Northern Ireland Protestants, that Catholics would demographically overwhelm them and vote them into a United Ireland. Demography was the big shift in the North and, if Kaufmann is right, that might be evidence that the Catholic community was the more religious community.

Eberstadt's argument is slightly different. It is not that religion makes people more likely to have families but that families are more likely to make people religious. She concedes that the traffic moves both ways but argues that the power of the family to nurture religion is overlooked. Look at the basic model of secularisation, she says. By this model, a new scientific age has discovered that the old religious truths are rationally unsustainable and rejects them. This rejection is slow but progressive and inevitable. From the first few pioneers of reason, the word spreads to the masses, and eventually everyone just sort of shrugs and says, 'My, what were we thinking?'

This is a model into which the New Atheists fit. They are calling us back to the insights of the nineteenth century and chiding us for not having assimilated them yet. We are frustratingly slow learners.

Eberstadt argues that maybe the model is wrong; maybe we don't just learn from the wise pioneering rationalists. Maybe their heroic leadership into the uplands of reason does not explain why so many people have let go of religion in the West. Maybe something else explains it. And maybe when we know what that something else is, we will know how to predict whether religion is dying out or is likely to return as a predominant social force.

She looks at demography. One of the big changes accompanying secularisation has indeed been the decline of the 'natural' family. The assumption of many writers on secularisation is that this decline has followed the collapse of religious belief. Eberstadt says that it preceded the collapse and actually explains it; because family life makes people turn to God and the decline of the family removes the great source and inspiration of religious feeling. To make her point, Eberstadt looks at demographic shifts in that early seculariser, France, and the late seculariser, Ireland. She writes:

> Not only has Irish religiosity been anomalous in the speed of its collapse; so too was Irish fertility. Essentially, the Irish stopped having babies and families and shortly afterward stopped going to church. Ireland's twentieth-century baby boom came markedly late—the 1970s, during which births were roughly double replacement level. This boom was followed by a dramatically steep decline of fertility such that by 2000, the total fertility rate was 1.89. As one analyst

put it, 'The biggest difference [between Ireland's demographic trends in fertility and those of the rest of the continent] is that while most of Europe experienced these changes over a period of two generations, Ireland went through them in one.' Once again, as in the case of France where the chronology is equally clear albeit more spread out, why is it not easier—i.e., more fitting with the facts—to suppose that the dramatic collapse of fertility has been helping to drive the collapse in religiosity rather than just vice versa?

Eberstadt says that we didn't stop having babies because we had lost our faith but that we lost our faith because we stopped having babies, though—like the typical academic who doesn't want to make a plain statement—she qualifies the argument by saying that it's a bit of both.

She also looks at the big exception to Western secularisation, the USA, and finds that the spread of religious faith matches the demographic pattern there too. Where families are strong, religion is strong. Of course, we knew that, but we had always assumed that religion was the cement of the family rather than that the family was the engine of religious conviction. That was the sense of the motto: the family that prays together stays together. Then she asks: What is it about family life that promotes religion? What makes families want to pray?

Well, it is love and wonder. It is the mystery of childbirth and acquaintance with the death of loved ones. This is romantic stuff, but her argument gets more specific:

> All men and women fear death; but only mothers and fathers, and perhaps some husbands and wives, can generally be counted upon to fear another's death more than their own. To put the point another way, if 9/11 drove to church for weeks on end millions of Americans who had not darkened that doorstep in years—as it did—imagine the even deeper impact on ordinary mothers and fathers of a sick child or the similarly powerful desire of a devoted spouse on the brink of losing the other. Just as there are no

atheists in a foxhole, so too would there appear to be few in the nursery or critical care unit, at least most of the time.

One can also, of course, explain the family's promotion of religion more prosaically, more sociologically. Maybe the family is just the best medium for conveying tradition. Eberstadt concludes that if families generate religion, you cannot write off religion, because you cannot write off the family.

Secularisation sees the spread of reason as progress and change for the better. It is part of our growing up. No one sees the decline of family life in these terms or makes confident predictions that it won't wax and wane as radically in the future as in the past, driven perhaps even by mere economic changes. The revival of family life will lead to a revival of religion.

The weakness in Eberstadt's case seems to be the argument that families, by the concentration of love and wonder within them, generate religious belief. But would they try to promote churchgoing in a society that had lost the habit? They might inspire wholly new ways of thinking religiously. Her conclusions, however, affirm the good sense of successive popes in trying to preserve religion by opposing contraception and encouraging marriage. It is the single and the childless who are the enemy.

Intriguingly, Christopher Hitchens, who was one of Eberstadt's targets for his presumption that reason could erase religion, denied shortly after this article was published that he believed any such thing. This was in an interview for the BBC's Radio Ulster programme *Sunday Sequence*, when he visited Dublin for the debate with John Waters. Hitchens' public address tone suggests that those who believe in religion are unreasonable and stupid. When he is not playing to an audience, he takes a more moderate view on this. He said:

> It isn't possible to defeat the forces of religion because they are lodged deep inside our mammalian, poorly evolved nature. It is not a thing that can be eradicated. I don't think, in the meantime, that anyone should despise reason as the only faculty which distinguishes us from the other mammals.

And does he think that only atheists are reasonable? He doesn't even argue that.

> No, because there have been great religious dialecticians, men and women who have been able to argue from premises to conclusions, and even including sometimes a respect for evidence, though they always say that faith will trump evidence. No, the objectionable thing for me about the religious is their feeling that the universe is preoccupied with their own souls, the essential solipsism and selfishness that's involved in that.

The mother with a sick child, pleading with God for help, makes the same mistake as the man who immerses himself in a pool for baptism, trusting that the maker of the universe has noticed. Hitchens does not foresee a time when even western civilisation will eschew religion and live by reason.

And there is another sideline critique of atheistic rationalism in Eberstadt's argument. It is essentially a feminist one, though no feminist has stepped forward to champion it. Most religious people in the world are women. They are the ones who still go to church. What's that about, then? If you take the Dawkins criticism, that clinging to faith is a lapse of reason, then it follows that women are more unreasonable than men. The feminist has reason to challenge him on this or must concede that there are more women than men acting irrationally. Hitchens explains it in much the same way as Eberstadt does, though at the time of the interview he had not yet read Eberstadt's article.

> It is a question with which I have often had to wrestle because it's very true of the Catholic faith, I have noticed, and also of the Muslim faith, that those who are most despised by it or relegated by it, or who are considered second class by it, whose very genitalia and monthly effusions are revolted by it, should nonetheless prostrate themselves before it. But I believe I understand in this way: for women, the production of children and the rearing of

children—I hope I don't reduce them by saying this—is perhaps the main thing. The possibility that a child might die or become ill is, to them, a change in the universe, unthinkable, an unbearable thought. If anything will make you superstitious, that will.

And though the 'natural' family may have been a strong unit of the church, there are reasons to suppose that other types of family could be, too. Take the single mother. As a woman, she is already more predisposed to religious belief. And as a vulnerable and lonely person, she would likely welcome the practical support and fellowship that a church could offer. But the church tells her that her children were conceived in sin, so she's hardly likely to listen to the rest of what it has to say.

Chapter 16

The religious Ireland of our past was different from the Ireland of today, but not every change tends toward secularisation; some tend against it. Once we were predominantly rural and conservative. We communicated more inside our families than outside them. Our lives met the expectations of our parents, as theirs had too. And we didn't want to offend Mother. We thought that she needed us to be religious for her to be happy, because we thought that she was religious. And we also needed to think of her—because we loved her—as bound for Heaven and not for the cold grave. Today we mix more outside the family than in it, live far from our parents, doing work, often, that they do not understand, and frankly Mum isn't as attached to God at all as she let on when we were little.

We live in an Ireland of extensive and rapid communication. We are less often alone with the sort of thoughts that dwell on the inner being and reach for God. We even have less to wonder at in the natural world. We are more likely to be stimulated to reflections on the mystery of life by something on television than by something happening in a field. Most of us have seen more lion cubs on nature programmes than calves on Irish farms. In the cities, we can no longer see the starry firmament. Most of us probably wouldn't recognise whether tonight's moon is waxing or waning.

Of course, it is easy to exaggerate how moved by natural wonder the ordinary Irish country people of the past were. City people, who saw sunsets rarely, were always more likely to be moved by them than were country folk, who studied them for signs of the weather to come.

———

The restoration of the 'natural' family will bring back religious values. That is the theory of Mary Eberstadt, with the unexpected endorsement of Christopher Hitchens. And it fits with the emphasis of all religious traditions on what they call 'family values'. It is as if they understand instinctively that it is the heterosexual and vertical family that they depend on. Knit the generations together and you have a tradition that can thrive.

However, there are other forces at work and they are social. Ireland is changing. We have huge numbers of new migrants among us now and that is good news for the churches. It gives them campaigns to be involved in, in defence of people threatened with deportation, for instance, and it swells congregations because, by a fluke of history, most of those migrants are believers. Pews are filling up again. The clergy have new faces in front of them. There is a prospect in the air that the secularisation of Ireland will be reversed by the newcomers. In November 2007, after a horrific house fire in Omagh, neighbours flocked to the local church, to the evening mass, to pray for the dead. That mass was said in Polish.

The arrival of the Polish raises the most intriguing questions about Ireland's Catholic future. The Polish are Catholic in a way that we were before. Indeed, their nation was defined as a Catholic nation at the same time that Ireland was, during the Counter Reformation at the start of the seventeenth century. We did it in Ireland as part of a strategy to align ourselves with Spain in the hope that Spain would join with the exiled Gaelic chiefs to invade and kick out the English. At the very inception of the idea of a Catholic Irish nation, the motivation was practical rather than spiritual. Poland similarly felt that it had to define itself against neighbours and secure allegiances—take sides, in other words.

In modern times, Polish Catholicism has been inspired by the native pope, Karol Wojtyla. We were charmed by him, too, in 1979, but the Polish had more invested in him. He was theirs and he played a huge role in the defeat of Communism. He was also a conservative pope but that fitted with a conservative religious and sexual culture in Poland, much like our own of previous decades.

The Polish abroad are keeping their faith—so far—and missionary priests from the homeland are serving them wherever they go. And there are enough of them to do that. Poland has about 30,000 priests and 23,000 nuns, and vocations are rising. Ten years ago, there were just over 4,000 vocations a year to the priesthood. That has nearly doubled since then. This means that Poland has enough priests not just for the diaspora but for the ordinary parishes in Ireland and other European countries which have no Irish-trained priests left to serve them.

Pope Benedict XVI gave his blessing to that project when he told Polish priests on a visit to their country: 'Do not be afraid to leave your secure and familiar world to go and serve in places where priests are lacking and where your generosity can bear abundant fruit.' But if it is up to Poland to save an Irish church that can't produce enough priests to serve its own needs, what difference will those priests make? Poland has priests because the Catholic culture there is where ours was forty years ago. But if we left it behind with good reason, we are hardly likely to appreciate Polish priests trying to revive it.

Justyna is in her twenties. She works in the health service in Northern Ireland, as a translator for Polish families. She left Poland in 2003, first to live in London with her Irish boyfriend, and she now lives in Belfast, having broken up with him and met someone else. Her sister is an artist in Belfast and she has another sister at home in Poland who visits often and is thinking of moving across too. Justyna was a devout and serious Catholic when she lived in Poland. It has to be said, whatever the risk of stereotyping, that she has that look—a wholesome loveliness that could pass for grace. But she has moved gradually away from Catholicism while living in Northern Ireland.

> I had my ups and downs in Poland as well, but when you are in Poland you have that urge, because everybody goes to church on Sunday. You grow up with that sense that you have to go.

It's a habit, and a deeply ingrained one. She says:

> When I detached myself from my own culture it took me a few years before I started to think in my own way about what I believed. It was very difficult. I was fighting with myself and my culture.

This experience will be familiar to many Irish Catholics of an older generation in whom Catholic attitudes were so deeply embedded that they could not be lightly set aside. Young people who believed in the teachings of the church had to rationalise their way out of that belief. It was part of our experience, too, that a younger generation started that journey by rejecting Catholicism's conservative attitudes and impractical teachings on sex.

'Catholicism is associated with narrow-mindedness in Poland. It is very controversial,' says Justyna. 'You have many prominent and controversial Catholic figures on TV and people are actually turning against the church now.'

Independence has a price, often a simple monetary price. It isn't easy to be free if you can't afford to move out from under the influence of the generation over you, and for many in Poland the first opportunity to do this comes when they move to Ireland. The freedoms available to them here were difficult to access at home. 'Young people use contraception but many people cannot afford it and don't use contraceptive methods. They are very expensive,' says Justyna. Life can be hard for a young woman who gets pregnant before she is married:

In Poland we are still taught that you are not supposed to have sexual intercourse until you are married. There would be no one to help you if you got pregnant and you would not get benefits. It is a shame to the family because Catholic culture is so much about waiting to be married.

There is something intriguing about her use of the specific term, 'sexual intercourse', that perhaps derives from a moral code which makes a distinction between penetration and general physical intimacy, or technical virginity: that's familiar too.

However, although she thinks that many Polish will give up routine Catholic practice and Catholic attitudes when they settle in Ireland, Justyna says that, for many of them, going to mass is a way of staying in touch with other Poles and not being lonely or alienated:

> For many, Catholicism gets stronger because it is the only thing that connects them back to Poland but a lot I have spoken to say they don't care, they are more open minded now.

That suggests that they will assimilate into the secularising trend in Ireland and will not work hard to reverse it. This fits with the theories of University of Aberdeen sociologist Professor John Brewer:

> It is noticeable in earlier waves of migration, the role of religion in managing the identity tensions, moderated after the second or third generation. It is really a first-generation phenomenon for religion to be used to resolve ambiguity and identity concerns.

The Poles and others use religion, as did the Irish in London, to secure a sense of identity for themselves in a strange country. When they start to blend into that country and feel at home there, they no longer need religion for that purpose. He says:

It will be interesting to observe how long east European migrants stay. If they stay, one imagines that the next generation will find a diminishing level of observance. Religion will have less importance in resolving their identity concerns and that would put them alongside the Irish in Britain.

It doesn't always work out that way. Sometimes the 'identity tensions' don't go away. Sometimes they get worse, and then the newcomer becomes more assertively religious:

> There is one clear example of this and that is Muslims. It is noticeable that the first generation of Muslims tended to be more western, and it is their children who are being radicalised and tend to be more religious than their parents. They are turning to religion as a way of managing the ambiguity of being Muslim and British. The Irish in Britain provide one example and the Muslims an entirely different one.

He expects the Polish in Ireland to follow the Irish pattern and says that he would regard it as an indicator that they had failed to assimilate if they were still as religious in the next generation as they are now:

> If the Polish retain their religious practices, that will be an indication that they are not assimilating well, as second- and third-generation Muslims are not assimilating well.

Not that they will give up believing in God—few anywhere do that—but they will stop going to church in significant numbers. A Polish student called Kaçpar agrees:

> Actually, I would say that even the Poles who felt secular at home, liberal, who detested all this conservative Catholic atmosphere at home—I would say that they look for easy bonds with Poland. Some of them become more religious, visiting church on a regular basis, even despite the fact that

they weren't visiting church on a regular basis in Poland. That's what happened to me up to a point as well, and I know that many of my friends do that. It's like looking for a bond with home; and the church, the religion, the tradition makes the Polish people feel more comfortable here. You tend to go back to the tradition, even to things that you weren't that comfortable with at home. You end up hanging a picture of the Pope in a small flat. Things that say, 'This is us, I am Polish—these are the obvious Polish things.'

Maybe it is like Irish people in London going out to Kilburn pubs and discovering Irish folk music over there, having taken little or no interest in it before they left, but it seems to express a bit more commitment than that. Kaçpar says:

With some people it is an aggressive thing; with others it is a way of saying, 'This is what I cherish.' Already this is changing as the community gets more organised. Now people know how to get satellite TV services from Poland.

This helps them feel more at home and reduces the need to go to church to meet other Polish people. As in Ireland at the start of its secularisation trend, it is television that is the threat!

It is one thing to go to church to meet other Polish people, but for some the religious engagement is stronger than mere attendance, and devotional organisations report new members coming in from among the migrants. The Legion of Mary reports that its own numbers are swelling because of immigration. The Legion's outreach programme on Moore Street, Dublin, is recruiting Polish, Nigerians and Filipinos. Immigrants 'are always pleased to be welcomed to Ireland', a spokesperson for the Legion told the *Irish Catholic*. Some of the Filipinos, Polish and Nigerians have been members of the Legion in their countries of origin. The Legion of Mary claims to have more than 3 million active members, with a presence in almost every country of the world.

Kaçpar says that many Polish people will assimilate here because they have the same basic values as the Irish. They are not cut off by an alien culture the way Pakistani Muslims are. The journey to the heart of local Irish culture is not a long one for them. So, some will intermarry? His answer is shocking:

> The Polish guys will say the Irish girls are just not attractive. Put it this way, they are not on a healthy diet. That sums it up. A rude Polish man would say they are fat, they are ugly and they dress like shit. That would be it. The more common thing is Polish girls marrying Irish guys. That also contributes to the fact that Polish men hate … [He corrects himself] It's not a macho culture but they think these Polish women are being cheap in hanging out with foreigners.

He says:

> There is a kind of silly pride in being Polish and I took stick for defending Ireland and saying, why do we mock them? They are where they are and we are where we are. It stems from a feeling that Poland was a great country and then 300 years ago things started to go really wrong. There is a sense of hurt pride. You cannot be better than the Irish in terms of money but you can laugh at 'those idiots', you know.

The Irish might think that by admitting Polish immigrants they are showing how a wealthy, modern country extends its generosity to a poor and backward one, but that is not how some Polish see it; they confidently regard Poland as the superior country of the two. 'But it is us going to the Irish, not the Irish coming to us, I say, so we can laugh at the Irish in Poland if we want and stay in Poland. That would have more integrity,' says Kaçpar.

———

There are two basic types of migrant. One is like the Irish who went out to the oil fields of Libya and Saudi Arabia, in recent decades, or before that to England and Scotland as navvies on the railways. Their intention was to save money and come home, and they formed no attachment to the countries in which they worked. The other type is like the Irish who settled in Australia and Canada in the 1960s, many on assisted passage. They had no plans to return. Many didn't think that they would ever be able to afford to return. They made the new country their home, though they formed Irish communities in those countries.

There are Polish migrants of these two types in Ireland, with this difference, that travel between Ireland and Poland is now cheap. Those who have no interest in Ireland can take frequent holidays in Poland, even retain just a minimal sense of having left. And the others, who will settle here, need never assimilate to the degree that our cousins in Canada and Australia have done, for they will always be free to go home. Nor will they need Polish enclaves here while a flight home is no more expensive or inconvenient than a train ride. Kaçpar says that most of the Polish he sees on the flights between Dublin and Krakow are forming no attachment to Ireland.

> I mean, I travel home almost every month. You should see the guys on that plane from Dublin. It's not like these are guys with degrees, intellectuals, who perhaps didn't find their place in Poland like I didn't, but these are working-class, tough guys who don't give a flying eff about the Irish, their culture, their problems, their Catholicism, whatever. They are here just to get a few quid, as quick as possible, and spend it in Poland. My parents would sometimes pick me up at the airport and they would say, 'Who are these people? You are flying with these people?' I would say, 'This is the Polish community in Ireland.'

He says that the Polish in Ireland know the rules: you work and you get paid, so you keep your head down and you do the job. Their motivation is money so they are good workers.

And they are very conservative; they are of this upbringing where you go to church every Sunday and once in a while you go to confession and things like that. So I think, you will find all grades of people in the church, the small group of intellectuals, people with degrees, languages, but you will also find this bigger community—let's say, the working-class community. Some of them will find it so comfortable here that they will stay but it is going to take ages before they will turn into proper citizens of Ireland, to the extent that they would vote or think about politics. But I would say that the majority of them will go back.

Kaçpar is amused by how Polish indifference to Ireland is interpreted benignly here, though he argues against that indifference:

For example, Poland established diplomatic relations with Dublin in the early 1990s. I mean, the first Polish ambassador ever to Ireland wasn't a political figure or anything; he was a poet. I met low-level Irish diplomats who thought this was great. This guy would have poetic evenings and parties and stuff. And he would sit in the garden and write poems. So, you see the scale of importance that Poland attaches to Ireland.

Our people mock these sheep-eating idiots, but actually Ireland is a great case for us to study, how Ireland lifted itself up.

We thought that receiving a poet ambassador united us with Poland as another country that valued culture and the arts.

Poland's thriving Catholicism is the great hope of the Vatican. Poland will provide the priests for the depleted parishes of Ireland and the rest of Europe. But don't bank on it, says Kaçpar. The Catholic church was a place where you could feel safe during the Communist era, but 'if you don't need to feel safe, you don't need the church.'

Political parties which associated themselves with the church, he says, have not been rewarded for this by the electorate. Some of the debates around religious issues echo those that were held in Ireland in recent decades, but there are differences. Kaçpar says that under Communism there was no debate on contraception, because there was no problem with it. There has been some debate about the morning-after pill, because it expels the fertilised embryo. Young couples were not able to live together, however, because they could not get a flat unless they were legally married. Abortion was legal, though the laws were tightened up after the fall of Communism, so there are, he says, some underground abortions now. There had been an effort by 'ardent right-wingers' to enshrine in the Polish constitution the right to life from conception, but this had failed. The speaker of the Polish parliament resigned over it. Kaçpar says, 'There is a saying in Poland that if you want trouble, you just have to touch this abortion issue. It provokes too many emotions.'

He says that homosexuality is still very seriously frowned upon:

> I can't imagine people like my neighbours would tolerate somebody like that. Obviously there were problems with gay parades; they were banned and confronted with Nazi groups. The older generation would regard it as an illness.

He sees the future of Poland as being secular but with a 'Catholic blend' retained as a means of asserting the distinctive Polish identity.

> It is in the memory, mostly because of the novels and films. People like to go back to the old days when we kicked the asses of the Turkish and the Swedish and the Russians. That is part of the Polish character.

While Polish and Irish Catholics—and ex-Catholics—might recognise and understand each other, greater difficulty arises when religious cultures that are strange to us settle here. Many Nigerians in Ireland are members of the Redeemed Christian Church of God (RCCG). This is happy-clappy, and how! A huge evangelical church, it spread out from Nigeria and has established congregations in Ireland and Britain. The website sets a high standard for members, including the prospect of public retribution for backsliding.

In some ways, the RCCG seems much more radical than the Irish evangelical churches, for instance in relation to sex education. The RCCG advises, 'Remember, if you don't teach your children about sex education, someone else will.' Its objective in sex education is to promote abstinence until marriage. Where the Catholic church used to obsess about 'continence', the RCCG is cheerfully blithe about it in advice to boys:

> As boy, your voice suddenly breaks, start growing hair under your armpit, groin and chin. Suddenly wake up one day and find your pant wet and penis erect (wet dreams) congratulations! You are becoming a man.

But what is the impact of this enormous church likely to be? It appears not to cross cultural boundaries. Irish evangelicals have their own thriving small churches and are unlikely to be drawn to the RCCG. But might the RCCG grow so big that it would have a political impact in Ireland? If so, it would be likely to campaign on issues that are of concern to the other evangelical churches, opposing gay marriage, for instance. It will be conservative. In some ways, it is much more conservative than Irish evangelical churches. For instance, it bans it members from getting into debt. Then again, if we were to take all churches literally and judge their members by the letter of their doctrine, we would get them completely wrong. That's the Irish lesson.

The RCCG was involved in the huge Festival of Life at Gort, County Galway, in June 2007, with many white Irish participants in the singing there. However, when a video of them singing U2's

'I Still Haven't Found What I'm Looking For' was posted on You Tube, more conventionally minded evangelicals protested that this was an inappropriate song for Christians who should have found what they were looking for, Christ.

———

Ireland has many religious minorities and cannot really plead ignorance of religious cultures. We should be familiar now with Judaism, Islam and Hinduism. These have been here for decades, but they do tend to concentrate their worship within their own communities. It is when the people of minority religious cultures feel ready to join the wider population that the contrasts between different ways of thinking appear. Given that we have had a Jewish community for years, you would not have expected a public debate on the morality of circumcision of boy babies, but that was one of the biggest inter-cultural complications to hit us.

Jews do not rely on the state to provide this service. They have their own trained blade-wielders who do not make mistakes and therefore do not attract the curiosity of the law. Less well-organised communities have greater problems. When a Nigerian baby died after having been circumcised on a kitchen table, in Waterford in 2002, we had a media debate on where the state's responsibility lay—with many writers taking the liberal view that the state must guarantee the safety of the child by providing clean and competent circumcision to all families who ask for it. One doctor, at least, made plain his own belief that there can never be any justification other than medical for cutting bits off babies.

The death of little Callis Osaghae was followed by the arrest and acquittal of one man. Callis was 29 days old when he died and a man was charged with, and acquitted of, reckless endangerment. No one knows how many non-medically-managed circumcisions are carried out in Ireland each year, though a report in 2004 by the then North-Eastern Health Board counted forty-four of them. Following the death of Callis, the government set up an expert committee to assess whether there was a need to provide culturally required male circumcision in Ireland. No one, of course, was even going to raise a question about female circumcision.

The committee reported that cultural circumcision is one of the most contentious issues in medicine today. Doctors plainly don't see it as their job to conduct bloodletting religious rituals. They don't want to cut babies who don't need to be cut, but the danger is that, if the state does not provide the service, others less able will. And more boys will die. The report recommended that the state should, indeed, provide the service. It said that male circumcision is generally assumed to be lawful, provided that it is performed competently, is believed to be in the child's best interest and that there is valid consent, whatever that is.

The child's 'best interest' and 'valid consent' here sound like unspecific clauses that a lawyer could easily demolish. How can there be valid consent from a baby? What are the limits to a parent's right to consent on behalf of a baby to a medically unnecessary surgical intervention? Could a mother validly ask for a child's earlobes to be removed? Or hands? How can circumcision be in the best interests of a boy? The only interest served by it is integration into a religious or cultural community. And, of course, you don't miss what you never had, so most men who grow up without a foreskin suffer no sense of loss or deprivation. Put plainly, if no tradition of circumcision already existed, it is inconceivable that the state would permit it, to cater for the needs of a new religion.

In Finland, in August 2006, a court ruled that a Muslim woman had broken the law by having her son circumcised. The complaint had been brought by her husband, the child's father. The court ruled that even a long religious tradition could not justify a distinction between the legal treatment of boys and girls. 'There is a perception in Finland that only girls' circumcisions are banned by law,' said Jouko Nurminen, a local prosecutor. 'There is no specific legislation about them; both types are illegal under the same criminal law. After all, in both procedures, part of healthy genitalia is removed without medical foundation, or competent consent.'

Who knows what complex future legal challenges await an Irish society that imagines it has successfully shuffled this issue aside? The liberal take on this is that the circumcision of boys has to be facilitated for cultures which define masculinity by it or require it on the instructions of God. Nuala Haughey, writing in *The Irish Times*, after the death of Callis, quoted a Nigerian man's explanation of the cultural need for boys to have the foreskins cut off. 'It's like bringing the boy into manhood immediately, initiating him into society. It's our tradition and there is no way you can skip that.'

Irishwomen who would never tolerate male chauvinism from an Irish man surely patronise foreigners who make such arguments, when they let them off without contradiction. Yet many respond reflexively with sympathy to words from a Nigerian which they would laugh at coming from an Irish man. Is that generosity or condescension? Is it not almost racist to assume that the outsider cannot share the strain of the cultural difference between us? Shouldn't we have more confidence in the rightness of the journey that we have taken away from primitive sexual notions and put as much commitment into trying to lead Nigerian men in the same direction as Irish women have put into changing Irish men?

From the 1960s, Irish feminists, confronted with men who had been inducted into a native Irish chauvinistic culture, refused to accept the male-centred perspective of those men and fought hard to correct it.

> They would look at you as an inferior person for not being circumcised. The girls would run away from you.

Faced with an argument like that, the Irish journalist does not know how to assess it, whether to see it in the context of her own understanding of male chauvinism and patriarchy or to exempt an alien culture from that scrutiny, even when the question is whether a man should be allowed to take a knife to the penis of his son, to shape it to look more like the penis of a man. Who are these girls who are going to run away from a black boy in Waterford when they discover that he has a foreskin?

In Ireland, the answer to trite chauvinistic nonsense from men was protest, argument and education. And that is still the answer to the cutting of the genitals of girls. Somehow, cultural sensitivity trumps feminism, though only up to a point, that point being the point of a blade directed at a vagina. And maybe that is the right place to draw the line between the acceptable and the unacceptable. The circumcision of a girl *is* worse than the circumcision of a boy.

Certainly it is inconceivable that circumcision could be declared illegal, given that it is so widespread. And it is impractical that it be declared illegal, given that that would only drive it underground and further endanger babies. But let that be the argument in defence of it rather than that we, who have learnt so much from decades of women asserting their rights, should act as if we have learnt nothing when confronted with a Nigerian or a Muslim whose immature sexual attitudes are now familiar and intelligible from our own past experience.

Another controversy arose over the question of whether a Sikh member of the Garda Síochána should be allowed to wear a turban. This appears to be an easier concession to refuse. In August 2007, Garda Commissioner Noel Conroy said, 'No.' Many in the media endorsed his decision. The argument was that a uniform is a device for removing the cultural differences between people so that they can be seen to serve the state impartially. To allow an exception to that is to make it not a uniform at all— that is, not a uniform expression of the prior commitment of all gardaí to the service of the state. Superintendent Kevin Donohoe, head of Garda press and public relations, said:

> It is now accepted by many that a more modern, energetic approach is required to integrate diverse populations into a common liberal culture. An Garda Síochána believes that the inter-cultural approach can achieve this through reasonable and common-sense measures.

There was no talk of a common liberal culture when the question was the right of people of religious minorities to circumcise their baby boys, even though the medical profession was adamantly against it. The model for consideration then was multi-cultural: accepting that people do things differently and that the mores of one culture, though shocking to another, should be accommodated, within limits. But what limits?

Superintendent Donohoe said that the effective achievement of integration of many cultures into a single organisation would require a very fluid approach. Policies and practices would have to be altered and adjusted where it was appropriate. But not apparently in this instance, even though other police forces allow the turban. Indeed, many police forces are keen on having Sikh members because they are mostly big Punjabis who appear to have a native genius for policing, a bit like the Irish themselves.

The Garda Commissioner was satisfied that the 'inter-cultural approach and the decisions made within that frame-work, to date, is the right approach at this time for An Garda Síochána and the communities it is sworn to serve'. But there is 'no doubt that the Garda uniform and dress standards present unique issues in accommodating cultural diversity'.

The media debate on this bordered on vitriolic; expressive, it seemed, of a new intolerance. The Sikh who wanted to join the Garda was perhaps taking the rap for a whole run of cultural clashes in Britain, from plays being closed through intimi-dation, to public protests over cartoons depicting the Prophet Mohammed, to actual suicide bombings on the London under-ground. There is a new mood in the air permitting cultural retaliation. It probably would not have been a good time for a botched circumcision either.

The Irish Sikh Council president, Harpreet Singh, stressed that integration 'is a two-way process'. It could 'never be brought about by asking the migrant communities to give up their basic beliefs.' But he is wrong. Ireland does demand that some basic beliefs be given up. It will not tolerate honour killings by some Kurdish Muslims who believe that a father or a brother has an obligation to kill a woman who 'disgraces' them by her interactions with men not to their liking. When a Nigerian woman defended herself against deportation on the grounds that her daughters would be circumcised, the court agreed that she had a case.

But Ireland does not demand the surrender of all cultural and religious obligations understood by Muslims, Hindus and others. It just doesn't have a very clear sense yet of how to balance its own principles with those of other cultures. That is, it doesn't know how secular it wants to be.

Fintan O'Toole, in an *Irish Times* column, following the rejection of the Sikh who wanted to wear a turban in the Garda, listed the ways in which the Irish state still affirms its religious character:

> Christianity—and often a specific Catholicism—frames the functioning of the Irish State. The preamble to the Constitution invokes the 'Most Holy Trinity'. Article 44 commits the State to hold the name of Almighty God 'in reverence'. Juries and voters are sworn on the Bible, unless they specifically request another form of affirmation, so that a religious declaration, implicit or explicit, is central to the way a citizen performs the actions that define citizenship.
>
> Public hospitals are heavily adorned with Catholic symbols. Religious schools are, for most people, the only schools their children can attend. It is impossible to be trained as a primary teacher outside a college owned and run by a Christian church. RTÉ, the State broadcaster, starts its main news bulletin a minute late in order to allow it to mark a specific Catholic religious practice, the Angelus.

This seems to leave in tatters the case against a Sikh officer wearing a turban. O'Toole's conclusion was that the state had to decide to allow all forms of religious expression in public life, in equality with the Catholic forms that are there already, or it must allow none and remove the state's endorsement of Catholicism. But this is not a good time for the debate because tempers are high. Those who are enraged that British Airways workers have had to fight for their right to wear a cross around the neck and who feel that the pressure is constantly for our own adaptation to Muslims and Sikhs might rather enjoy the opportunity to refuse them something.

So where are we going? Ireland's limited secularisation is challenged by a strong inflow of believers. The religious culture of the country is diversifying. It was one thing for past Irish governments to bend to the will of Catholic bishops in an almost homogenous religious culture, but the future is multiple and some of the religious principles that migrants are bringing with them are strange and abhorrent and we don't know what to do about them.

Worse, we seem little inclined to consider the religious needs of people, even when they are not excessive and should not cause us any particular problems, because the public debate on religion is contaminated by fear and animosity. It is surely not beyond the imagination of the modern Irish to recall how important religious mores were to us in the past and to attribute that same importance to the religious mores of Sikhs and others. But we are embarrassed by our religious past and in no mood to concede that what we have ourselves shaken off may still be of value to our neighbours and new arrivals.

At a lecture in St Brigid's parish in Belfast for Lent 2008, the British ambassador to the Holy See, Francis Campbell, said that foreign service diplomats around the world had come to accept that they now had to understand religion in order to function. The old idea that religion disappeared with economic and educational progress had been discovered to apply only in Europe. He had the figures to support his point. In a 2005 gallup poll, two-thirds of the world's population claimed to be religious. The proportion who were adherents to the four great world religions—Christianity, Islam, Buddhism and Hinduism—was rising faster than population and could reach 80 per cent by 2050.

So, not only was faith spreading, but it was consolidating worldwide within four traditions that had all come out of the land between the Mediterranean and the Himalayas. In a sense these are just two traditions, since Islam derives from Abraham and Buddhism from Hinduism.

In 1900, Africa had 10 million Christians, representing 10 per cent of the continent's population. By 2000 that was up to 360 million or 46 per cent of the population. Campbell said: 'That is the largest quantitative change that has ever occurred in the history of religion.' Asked how he explained the unique secularisation of Europe, he traced it to the Enlightenment, which Europeans had interpreted as the right to freedom from religion while the Americans had interpreted it as freedom to exercise religion.

Another speaker in the St Brigid's Lenten talks series was the Appeal Court Judge Sir Paul Girvan. He had another, though complementary, explanation for the collapse of religious observance in Europe. Simply, Europe had had its fill of institutional power expressed through the churches. That fits the Irish story. Justice Girvan said: 'It was Europe which suffered much of the consequences of bad or twisted Christianity and legalistic Christianity, from a Christianity which turned Christ's teachings on their head and did the opposite of what Christ asked of his followers, the Christianity which failed to do or achieve justice.'

One person who defends religion as fundamentally good is the Dublin psychiatrist Patricia Casey. Dr Casey is a professor of psychiatry at UCD and a consultant psychiatrist at the Mater Hospital. She says:

> I think there are individuals within religious organisations and groups who give religion a bad name, the fanatics in Islam, the priests who abuse the vulnerable. But I think we mustn't lose sight of where religion comes from. Christianity comes from the message of Jesus. Islam and all the other faiths come from God, so all religions ultimately come from God and God isn't bad, God isn't evil; it is the people who interpret religion who sometimes are.

Dr Casey believes that the influx of other religious communities into Ireland is good and will ensure that Ireland will be a religious rather than a secular country in the future. But won't those diverse religious traditions bristle against each other?

I don't see an influx of streams that will clash with each other. There are some concerns. It depends on what form of Islam comes here, whether it will be a moderate form. A bigger worry for me will be the way in which the religions will clash with the native secular society and whether they will be pilloried and relegated to recesses like the cupboards in our homes.

The religions have more to fear from secular atheists, she says, than from each other.

A typical example: It's very difficult to talk on radio or television about God or about prayer—attempts were made at one point to get rid of the Angelus from television—so the fears of secularists that we will ultimately have a theocracy could lead to clashes, but I hope that with careful dialogue and explanations of what religion is all about, we will find secularists in Ireland having a new understanding of religion, rather than viewing it as a remnant from the past that's going to fade as we become more enlightened.

That new understanding would accept that religion is good—good for society and good for individual mental health.

I believe at two levels that religion is good for people. I believe that at a faith level religion is good for people and there is a huge literature on the benefits of personal faith in relation to physical health and emotional health. In the US now, something like thirty medical schools have modules on faith and religion, so I believe at a faith level belief in God is good for people.

But also at a pragmatic level, as a way of structuring society, religion is good for people, and that is the view of Francis Fukuyama, when he wrote his book *The End of History*; he believes that even if you don't believe in God, the benefits of religion are good for society.

Dr Casey has little fear that religious communities will challenge our human rights:

> There are different ideas of human rights. Many secular people would say that it is a human right to allow a woman to abort a baby at 24 weeks. Other people would say that that is totally against human rights. These are the things that we have to work out if we are to find a common language of human rights that transgresses the boundaries between secularism and religion, whether we will get to that stage or not—we probably won't—but we have certainly to get to the position where religion for itself is respected and its benefits are recognised. Secularism is a new religion, a religion without God, and as a religion it has its problems as well.

According to Casey:

> There will, of course, have to be lines drawn in the sand. We can't have people being stoned to death because they are unfaithful. It is where those lines are drawn that matters. In France, for instance, they ban girls from wearing the veil in school. Now one might say that in a secular society that should be respected. There will be challenges ahead but we have to get beyond the secular hegemony we have at present in which religious people are regarded as failures or rednecks.

A secular hegemony? And to think she was speaking in Donegal. She concludes:

> Around the world, there is an increase in religious belief, not a decrease. Europe is the exception to that, contrary to what we believe. So the trend in Europe at the moment towards increasing secularisation, increasing individualisation, I believe, will not continue.

Conclusion

R eligions arrive suddenly; they are delivered by prophets—usually celibate prophets. You have to wonder if that could happen again, too. The history of religion in Ireland includes periods of sudden revival, around Fr Mathew's anti-drink campaign, for instance, and various recorded surges around evangelical Christianity, particularly just after the First World War. Religion bounces back. Is it going to bounce back in modern Ireland?

Out of the Arabian Desert, Islam took Africa and Spain to the west and Mesopotamia and Persia to the east. Buddhism, with a similar energy in its sweep, took all of India and China in a historic blink. Christianity, a small cult around a preacher-healer in Palestine, took over the Roman Empire and, like the others, covers much of the world today. Within its story of growth there are dramatic episodes in which one prophet converts thousands of people, whole nations. Patrick took Ireland. Francis Xavier won thousands of Indian souls in a single day.

If entire civilisations can fall to the charm of a new religious message, is Ireland safe? Indeed, could it be that our secular revolution follows the model of past religious revolutions? It has certainly come with the speed of a religious conversion but it has not brought passion and commitment with it, unless a passion for shopping and television. A Polish woman new to Ireland says that we shop as if the shops were closing today and will never open again. That is what she finds distinctive about Ireland. Richard Dawkins is adamant that secular atheism is not a new religion because it is the rejection of dogma and the freeing of the mind to explore, untrammelled, but it evidently has brought considerable social conformity with it, and it was one of the big jobs of religion to do that. Today, the difference is that we pretend that our conformity is really diversity; we are all individuals following our own tastes and ideas and it is just a coincidence that we all want iPods.

Or maybe it makes more sense to rethink our religious past and question whether our conversion was as deep as we thought it was. Hasn't the spread of religion in the past really been borne on the spread of political power? The Emperor Ashoka spread Buddhism more effectively than Buddha himself had done. Muslim armies swept into Europe and Persia, establishing regimes around a religious message. Rome spread Christianity. People had been religious in other ways before these regimes arrived but religion was always linked to power, and religion was always either the expression of power or the means of revolt against it.

And another example is Northern Ireland where Catholicism survived longer as a mark of communal identity while it felt itself opposed by Protestantism. People there will say that they are Catholic to make the specific point that they are not Protestant, rather than to express any particular theological conviction.

We became a Catholic nation for political reasons in the seventeenth century, and we reaffirmed ourselves as such, to distinguish us from Britain again, in the nineteenth. Religion followed political necessity and waned when the political necessity passed. And there is currently no political necessity for Ireland to be religious. It is difficult to imagine that a religiously inspired revolution could reverse secularisation. It is perhaps likely that a Europe facing the challenge of Jihadist Islam will become more assertive of its Christian heritage. There have been signs of that already, with Christians demanding that their sensibilities be considered as valid as those of Muslims, sensing that Muslims are treated more delicately by the law and the media. But that doesn't translate into political power for the churches, yet.

If religion usually arrives in the form of a revolution and energises revolutions with extraordinary potency, maybe we are living deluded in the sense that religious ardour has passed from Irish society and are about to be overwhelmed by the sort of tsunami of faith that has hit the world so many times before.

But each of those past revolutions was against another religious tradition. Indeed, many of them were revolutions within their own tradition. Jesus and Buddha have much in common, but most of all that both were anti-clerical revolutionaries within their religious traditions, asserting the right of the ordinary peasant to participate in the religious life and not to be excluded from it by religious laws.

Buddha rejected the old caste laws of the Brahminical society that predominated in India. Jesus attacked the Pharisees and the temple. Had there not been religious structures in place, exercising power by excluding people from religious participation, it is conceivable that neither would have emerged with anything distinctive to say about God and how we should live our lives. Their primary concern had been to challenge temporal power.

Within the great institutional religious traditions there have often emerged rebels to say, 'You don't understand God, but I do.' There were the Sufi mystics in Islam, who would dance for Allah. There were the bhaktis and yogis in Hinduism, who said that caste meant nothing if you loved God. Some retreated to caves in defiance of religious imposition of traditions and family order. Often these rebels were later incorporated into the tradition and their rebellion nullified. Sometimes they were accepted as having established their own separate communities. That is what happened to Jesus and Buddha. It is what happened to George Fox and John Wesley. The Christian mystics of the fourteenth century formed orders that were assimilated into the institutional church.

Religious rebels from Buddha to George Fox have been saying, 'You don't need the institutions and the priesthood to tell you how to live your life; you need only find the spirit within yourself', but the institutionalising forces contained them. Where Jesus advised people that the Holy Spirit would enter their hearts and guide them, the Catholic tradition established that it was the Pope who listened for us and explained the rules.

The institutionalising trend in religion has always absorbed these people and made them symbols of its own requirements and then forgotten what they actually said. But would there have been such rebels anyway if there had been nothing against which to rebel? If the radicals and the institutions have existed by interaction with each other—the radical rebelling, the institution absorbing— then the death of the institution leaves the radical with nothing to protest against. The collapse of institutional religion, therefore, gives way, not to daring fresh new religious energies expressed by free minds, but to a culture in which, for most people, religion is not a consideration. And where religious activity continues, it has no power and no passion. No persecution fires the radical; no collusion with state power emboldens the institution.

In Ireland, we have a declining institution and a profusion of radicals. But if this theory is correct, the radicals have no future. An Irish Buddha or Christ would have to be a Catholic, would have to speak to the indigenous religious culture, as they did, and proclaim the need for change plausibly and impressively enough to win followers. And the indigenous religious culture would have to strike back. It would have to be someone like Soline Humbert, the woman who claims that she has been called by God to be a Catholic priest. If every pope had refused to listen to mad women who came and said that they had been given a mission by God, the church would be very different from how it is today. For one thing, the papacy would still be in Avignon. We would have no Lourdes or Fatima or many of the religious orders. St Teresa of Avila would be remembered, if at all, as an hysteric. Practically every significant religious revolution has been led by women, who appeared to be mad, confronting a sane and reasoned male world.

Catherine of Siena, Teresa of Avila, Julian of Norwich, Bernadette Soubiroux—all these women told popes that they had had personal communion with God or the divine, and the global church had to take heed of their visions. Soline Humbert seems to be entirely in line with this recurring phenomenon or tradition. She has told bishops and cardinals that she has been called by God to be a priest, even though she is a woman and married. She asked the Papal Nuncio to secure her an appointment with the Pope and was told that the Pope does not talk to women like her. But the evidence of history is entirely on her side of the argument—that popes have almost routinely been shaken to the roots by women like her.

And you could imagine that she would have a strong case to make for the ordination of women, but would there be enough people behind that cause? There is a desperate need for priests, but there is not a groundswell demand for women priests that would lend weight to her claim. Well, maybe there will be when there are no other Irish priests left. But Soline wants to be accepted by the church, not to overthrow it. The priests who might want to support her, because women could relieve them of their workload, are docile and obedient. At their ordination, the bishop asked each: 'Do you undertake to obey me and respect me and all my successors?' And they all said, 'Yes.'

Not much chance there, then. To have any impact Soline would have to be challenging a church that has the power to destroy her and the real need to oppose her, and she isn't. Cardinal Brady will ignore her. He will not have her burnt at the stake. There will be no prophet coming down from the hills to amaze and inspire us and revive religious faith in Ireland because the conditions that produce such prophets are not there. Those conditions are always a vibrant and powerful religious culture which the mass of people are motivated to demand reform of or to overthrow.

The other possibility is another kind of prophet, the one who represents the church and makes its case with new energy, a Jeremiah or Fr Mathew, to warn us that we are sliding into damnation, and to do it with such passion and charisma that we believe it. Many in the Protestant churches anticipate such a revival and believe that it has happened before. They had their showman preachers who filled mission tents and won thousands of conversions. Dennis Kennedy has written about them in his book *Climbing Slemish*.

Ian Paisley is of this type, as is Billy Graham in the US. It can't be ruled out that in the quest for an amenable type of indigenous Christianity, many would follow such a preacher. Notably, more of them have come out of the Protestant evangelical tradition than the Catholic. Maybe a firebrand Christian preacher, leading a reaction against Islam in Britain or Ireland, would attract an angry following or a rabble. That can't be ruled out in the new sectarian tensions. If a Paisley emerged in Belfast in 1966, why not a Paisley in Birmingham now?

Energetic parish priests don't lead crusades. They do things like building airports or organising local co-operatives. Their position within a hierarchy requires them to behave themselves, not to frame individualised messages. Paisley had no fretful bishop over him. He made himself the head of his own church but was careful to place that church securely within the Presbyterian tradition. Catholic priests who stand outside and free themselves from their bishops remove themselves from the hierarchical structure but don't inspire great numbers to follow them. Paisley can declare himself to be part of the authentic tradition of John Knox. The rebel priest, now bishop, Pat Buckley cannot declare himself to be in the apostolic succession that passes through Pope Benedict. That's for Pope Benedict to decide.

———

Religion in Ireland, as everywhere, was for the bonding of the community and the endorsement of agriculture. Here, as everywhere, it was eroded by urbanisation, which scattered the family and turned people towards their individual concerns. Ireland returned to the fundamentals in the nineteenth century, after the famine and consolidation. It might not have done so had industrialisation and the city been as developed here as in England.

Here, as elsewhere, religious observance was tied to expressions of national identity and was strengthened by its political relevance. But religion went into collapse in the 1960s and is unlikely to recover. As we have shown, the church accelerated that collapse by toying with the hopes of many for liberalisation and then seeking to entrench a conservative sexual theology. This theology was just nonsense to most Catholics and reads more nonsensically still with each passing decade.

We now have a hollow church in which large numbers still participate. It has a hugely depleted priesthood and is nominally governed by a hierarchy that retains little respect even from the remaining priests, let alone from the laity. This is a structure that might collapse on a nudge. No such nudge is likely, however. There is no energy or interest in those who want a revolution within the church. And the others have just walked away. They are no more interested in destroying the church than in joining it—they are simply indifferent.

It is conceivable that the church might yet make another wrong move as disastrous as *Humanae Vitae*. This might come in the form of a statement on the teaching of evolution or on AIDS. In fact, it has already made its silly statements but nobody has taken them sufficiently to heart even to muster a refutation.

From outside the church we have the attacks on religion by the New Atheists. Much of Ireland likes what it hears from them. But this has been a shallow debate. Much of it is driven by anxiety about religious fundamentalism, particularly within Islam. Much of the popular mood now endorses a kickback at religion, a sneer. But this is an ill-considered response. In Ireland, the church will fall in a heap one day, but religious faith may not fall with it. A political energy that sneers at belief will alienate many.

We should remember that we were nearly all religious once. We cannot understand or own forebears of a single generation back unless we can empathise to some extent with their religious feelings. Were we and they just deluded and manipulated? Did the church abuse us by weaving fantasies for us or did it abuse us by monopolising a religious impulse that would have been there in some form anyway? And shouldn't we enter the new debate about religion with a sense of being well formed by experience to know what religion is, what faith feels like and especially how people retain their humanity within closed religious cultures? We know—don't we?—that belief in God does not derive from the need to explain the origins of matter. We know that it is not an alternative to biology or physics, surely? After all, we were taught religion in schools that also taught us biology and physics. How can we have come out of that experience to marvel at the novelty and insight of a Dawkins?

And we know more. If a police officer turned up on our doorstep with a miraculous medal pinned to his lapel, we would recognise that as inappropriate and eccentric. We should be able to see that a policeman in a Sikh's turban is not being eccentric within his own culture in the same way. A Sikh in a turban isn't making a distinctive religious statement, because all Sikhs wear turbans. He is not advertising himself as especially devout. You cannot tell by the turban of one Sikh that he is more ardent or fundamentalist than another. So the turban has more cultural weight than religious weight. We should have had the sense to leave it alone and let Sikh Garda officers wear their turban.

The quality of debate on religious issues here is dreadful. We have leading churchmen making nonsensical statements such as that without belief in God there is no morality—as if they didn't notice that atheists love their children too. And we have energetic atheists sneering at the *Book of Genesis*, as if they believed that all Christians read it as literal history when their own acquaintance with ordinary believers should tell them that they don't. We should be well beyond both types of nonsense. But the churchman hears no one contradict him because those who would go to hear him would not do that. And the secular minded, who see through him, have little interest in even engaging him in an argument.

Into this stalled debate come the new migrants, many of them religious in the way that we used to be religious ourselves, some of them fundamentalist and plain daft but eager for converts. We don't know how this will change Ireland, only that there will be new debates on religious issues and that therefore we should be ready to speak sensibly about religion, informed by our own past. The simple fact that Ireland secularised as rapidly as it did tells us that Jihadist Muslims might secularise also.

And the other change of note is in the character of religion in the West, away from a sense of duty to church and God, towards a responsibility to find a true self. Religion is merging with psychology. The old idea that your happiness is of no consequence if you do your duty has given way to a belief that true happiness is always a symptom of spiritual well-being. That is the revolutionary religious idea of our time. The trouble for the church is that few of us are going to take guidance from lonely and depressed celibate men on how to be happy. The trouble for the rest of us is that we don't have the answer either.

The new prophet who would win interest would be a champion of the subjective life, would evoke truths about the human heart in language that we would recognise as authentic and natural. Such prophets are already among us. We call them singer-songwriters, poets and novelists. They don't summon us to church but into our bedrooms and down country lanes. There is no reason now why churches should take over that job from them. A community that really wants churches would not have empty pulpits. It would throw up enough clergy from itself to serve them. Ireland doesn't.

Bibliography

Alter, Robert (trs), *The Psalms* (2007)

Anscombe, Elizabeth, *Contraception and Chastity* (1977)

Armstrong, Karen, *Through the Narrow Gate* (1082)

Blanshard, Paul, *The Irish and Catholic Power* (1954)

Bolger, Dermot, *A Second Life* (1994)

Brown, Callum, *The Death of Christian Britain* (2001)

Bruce, Steve, *God is Dead* (2002)

Butler, Hubert, *Escape from the Anthill* (1985)

Collins, Paul, *From Inquisition to Freedom* (2001)

Connolly, Sean, *Priests and People in Pre-Famine Ireland* (1982)

D'Arcy, Brian, *A Different Journey* (2006)

Davie, Grace, *Religion in Britain since 1945* (1994)

Dawkins, Richard, *The God Delusion* (2006)

— *The Selfish Gene* (1976)

Durcan, Paul, *Paul Durcan's Diary* (2003)

— *Greetings to our Friends in Brazil* (1999)

Durkheim, Emile, *The Elementary Forms of Religious Life* (1912)

Eagleton, Terry, *The Gatekeeper* (2001)

Enright, Anne, *The Gathering* (2007)

Foster, Roy, *Luck and the Irish* (2007)

Grayling, A.C., *Against All Gods* (2007)

Hayes, Maurice, *Sweet Killough* (1994)

Heelas, Paul and Linda Woodhead, *The Spiritual Revolution* (2004)

Hitchens, Christopher, *God Is Not Great* (2007)

Holloway, Richard, *Godless Morality* (2004)

Hughes, Gerard, *God of Surprises* (1985)

Hussey, Gemma, *Ireland Today* (1993)

Inglis, Tom, *The Moral Monopoly* (1987)

Keegan, Clare, *Walk The Blue Fields* (2007)

Kennedy, Dennis, *Climbing Slemish* (2006)

Kenny, Mary, *Goodbye to Catholic Ireland* (2000)

McGahern, John, *A Memoir* (2006)

— *Amongst Women* (1990)

Norton, Graham, *So Me* (2004)

O'Brien, Edna, *The Country Girls* (1960)

O'Doherty, Malachi, *I Was A Teenage Catholic* (2003)
O'Donoghue, John, *Anam Cara* (1999)
O'Donovan, Gerald, *Father Ralph* (1913)
Pinker, Steven, *The Blank Slate* (2003)
Smith, Canon George D, *The Teaching of the Catholic Church* (1948)
Twomey, Vincent, *The End of Catholic Ireland?* (2003)
Waters, John, *Lapsed Agnostic* (2007)
Whyte, J.H., *Church and State in Modern Ireland* (1971)

Index